Curious Collectors, Collected Curiosities

Curious Collectors, Collected Curiosities: An Interdisciplinary Study

Edited by

Janelle A. Schwartz and Nhora Lucía Serrano

CAMBRIDGE SCHOLARS

PUBLISHING

Curious Collectors, Collected Curiosities: An Interdisciplinary Study ,
Edited by Janelle A. Schwartz and Nhora Lucía Serrano

This book first published 2010
The present binding published 2011

Cambridge Scholars Publishing

12 Back Chapman Street, Newcastle upon Tyne, NE6 2XX, UK

British Library Cataloguing in Publication Data
A catalogue record for this book is available from the British Library

ISBN (10): 1-4438-2958-7, ISBN (13): 978-1-4438-2958-8

TABLE OF CONTENTS

INTRODUCTION

ON THE VIRTUES OF CABINETS AND CURIOSITIES

AMY JOHNSON, JANELLE A. SCHWARTZ AND NHORA LUCÍA SERRANO

O bliss of the collector, bliss of the man of leisure!
—Walter Benjamin, "Unpacking My Library"

It is nowadays taken for granted that the organizing principle of places like museums, archives, and libraries is "the idea of accumulating everything," the desire "to enclose in one place all times, all epochs, all forms, all tastes."[1] Attempting to catalog the world is a foolhardy and, of course, hopeless enterprise. And yet, as the world becomes more and more crowded with data, the eighteenth-century impulse to catalog and classify becomes increasingly attractive—just as it is becoming less and less possible. Today's narrative impetus to construct a seeming sense of order and epistemology from the pandemic onslaught of new objects, peoples, and cultures into a single space is one that shares a kinship with the Renaissance *Wunderkammer*, the cabinet of curiosity.

As Neapolitan Ferrante Imperato's 1599 Renaissance engraving *Dell'Historia Naturale* can attest, the *Wunderkammer* was literally a private room that had bookshelves and *studiolos*, built-in cabinets with pull-down doors, to systematize the disarray that came with collecting novelties. Only accessible through the bedchamber, this intimate space contained a variety of curiosities from medieval volumes to taxidermied animals, samples of minerals, and other odd specimens from around the world. Anticipating the organizational strategies behind a Natural History Museum today, pre-modern collectors amassed diverse, seemingly unrelated objects for their collection that had caught their eye for one reason or another. Of interest to early collectors were the before-unseen oddities that would be equally as curious whether sitting next to a man-made object, New World artifact, or pre-historic fossil. Of further appeal were those myriad wonders that defied any systematic categorization, and thus drew attention to a cabinet's basic purpose: to arrange curios. Akin to Mesoamerican Maize that was introduced and harvested in Europe after contact with the Americas in the sixteenth century, these early curiosities (from the European perspective) had been uprooted from their natural locale, and so emphasized the cabinet's other basic purpose: to transport and replant.

Influenced by what Stephen Greenblatt describes as the Renaissance cabinet's marvelous objects,[2] contemporary curiosities have since been arranged with an eye to inspiring a sense of wonder and managing chaos. Ancestor of the modern museum, the cabinet of curiosity coincidently stands in contrast to modern systems of classification that deem cabinets too intimate in their reflection of their owner and too chaotic, too apparently random, in their reflection of the world's plenitude. Much like Walter Benjamin's anticipatory fervor in unpacking his crates of books, this serendipitous organization can illuminate the task of a collector's narrative, a task forgotten by many contemporary museum-goers: to celebrate the "chaos of memories"[3] and their epistemological renewals.

The bliss collectors have historically taken in their cabinets and collections has always been equally out of place in an institution for serious study. Such collectors became dilettantes, their passion for collecting, as Benjamin noted, "out of date." The cabinet of curiosity, however, is an interdisciplinary creature: "[T]he modern curiosity is what curiosities have always been: a mixture of the natural and the artifactual… the historical and the ahistorical."[4] A cabinet mystifies its audience through the oddity of its objects and their arrangement, an expression of its creator and his particular eccentricities.

Cabinets, in contrast to those institutions devoted to whole stories and full histories, are anecdotes that do not aim for a teleological presentation of the world. They are shortened, illusory episodes of a grander historical narrative that are by their very nature assemblages of design and rupture. Indeed, it is their individuality, incompleteness, and artifactual nature that point to the labor involved in their creation—at least for contemporary audiences, who must recreate the links between the objects in the attempt to make sense of the collection. Only with a gaze of wonder and the siphoning of chaos can appreciation commence, for it is the space *between* the objects that determines a collection. The wonder that cabinets inspire—through their unexpected curiosities, juxtapositions, and exhibitions—"continually remind us that our grasp of the world is incomplete," rather than presenting the illusion of an encyclopædic representation of the world.[5]

In the essay "Of Other Spaces,"[6] Foucault argued, "this whole idea" of the encyclopædic collection "belongs to our modernity."[7] "The present epoch," he claimed, "will perhaps be above all the epoch of space."

> We are in the epoch of simultaneity: we are in the epoch of juxtaposition, the epoch of the near and far, of the side-by-side, of the dispersed. [O]ur experience of the world is… that of a network that connects points and intersects with its own skein.[8]

This idea, nearly a quarter of a century old, of space as virtual, a versatile place where things near and far, both geographically and chronologically, can be side-by-side, now seems particularly prescient. The modern cabinet of curiosity has become a productive way of understanding many contemporary collections and the actual practice of collecting. The organization and experience of the cabinet offer an alternative vision to the rigidity of a museal gaze as well as the unyielding structure of linearly-organized museum collections, while accommodating a cultural moment that seems chaotic in its plenitude. This alternate vision exists in part because the cabinet can contain objects that now seem to belong nowhere (or everywhere) and juxtapositions of objects that do not ordinarily exist side by side. Thus cabinets suggest our experience of so much contemporary space as virtual—and unstable. In essence, the cabinet sanctions make possible an experience of synchronism, of chaos and renewal.

The modern mania for classification has tended to insist on the mutual exclusivity of different classes, particularly those of scientific scrutiny and aesthetic pleasure. As expressed by Greenblatt, René Descartes believed that "wonder has only knowledge as its object and thus occurs strictly in the brain," whereas Albertus Magnus considered wonder to be a "systole of the heart."[9] If we are to take Greenblatt's understanding to heart, we can then comprehend how the contested source of wonder suggests a likewise rupture of things that once seemed connected in the process of classifying them. In is in this light that the rupture appears as a particularly modern disease of the imagination. *Curiosity*, *marvel*, and *wonder*, those antiquated terms, are all, as Greenblatt noted, words that designate both the material object and our response to it, collapsing into one space an intellectual and a sensual response. The wonder of a collection of curiosities can be scientific, aesthetic, and emotional. One such contemporary museum whose organization, labels and objects encompass this idea of a cabinet and virtual space for the bewildering, sensory experience of wonder is the Museum of Jurassic Technology in Los Angeles, California, made famous by Lawrence Weschler's 1995 book,

Mr. Wilson's Cabinet of Wonder: Pronged Ants, Horned Humans, Mice on Toast, and Other Marvels of Jurassic Technology.

According to the Museum of Jurassic Technology's *Jubilee Catalogue* (2002), the Museum hopes that by exhibiting objects that "cause admiration and which are rarely seen… the people may be drawn and have their minds the more affected."[10] The *Catalogue* goes on to quote an unidentified individual named "Wittlin" in order to support the claim that collections can be "a means of emotional experience."[11] The return to a more holistic understanding of the world and its objects perhaps explains in part the new (or rediscovered) appeal of interdisciplinary approaches. The combining of disciplines or contexts is a trend visible in many recent museum exhibits, and even in the organization of museums like the Museum of Jurassic Technology. In fact, it is this very modern impulse that launches the cabinet as the praxis par excellence for the experience of wonder and the Museum of Jurassic Technology as an enterprise not so foolhardy as it may first appear to the contemporary spectator.

While the museal drive for completion means that we still require truthfulness and facts of museums, the Museum of Jurassic Technology inspires "a level of creative engagement that museums are perhaps no longer in the habit of demanding."[12] The Museum's founder, David Wilson, sees museums "as a place for the muses, a place of inspiration."[13] The Museum produces wonder in part through its refusal of certainty, a cataloguing that celebrates the chaotic. A cabinet's curiosities are "at once unbelievable and true."[14] Some sources seem to be entirely fabricated, while suspicious-looking references turn out to be thoroughly reliable. The Introduction to the *Catalogue* notes that "the text is extensively footnoted; this gives definiteness and avoids confusions with earlier publications"—publications which may or may not exist.[15] Those extensive footnotes, however, are the primrose path leading to the reader's surprise at discovering there is no Bibliography offering the full citation for any of the named sources. Readers are left to their own devices in determining what is true and what isn't, or whether for the purposes of the Museum such a distinction matters at all. The experiences of readers and the museum's visitors alike are individually rooted in a productive ambiguity, the wonder of creating one's own cabinet. By replacing the typical linear museal organization with an arrangement that is dictated by the experience of wonder, the Museum of Jurassic Technology productively disorients its visitors.

It is that uncertainty in questions of truth—that and the cabinet's cheerful failure of completion—that leads to our "sense of dispossession… a self-estrangement in the face of the strangeness, diversity, and opacity of the world."[16] The cabinet of curiosity thus makes possible James Clifford's desire to restore some otherness to objects:

> At a more intimate level… we can return to them… their lost status as fetishes… *our own* fetishes. This tactic, necessarily personal, would accord to things in collections the power to fixate rather than simply the capacity to edify or inform. [A]rtifacts could once again be *objets sauvages*, sources of fascination with the power to disconcert.[17]

Such objects can also provide pleasure and an alternative way of taking in the world. Although museum studies entered academic high fashion in the late 1980s-early 1990s,[18] Kenneth Hudson anticipated this trend in 1975 when he suggested that "there is nothing disreputable about…a love of museums for their own sake. … One can enjoy cathedrals without admiring bishops or cemeteries without being dead."[19]

"Walking through the Museum," the *Jubilee Catalogue* claims, "the visitor experiences, as it were, a walk back in time."[20] This step back is more than anything else a mischievous retreat to earlier concepts of collection and exhibition. Benjamin's "Unpacking My Library" has become a touchstone for thinking about the phenomenon of private collecting. In it he confesses, "the collector's deepest desire when he is driven to acquire new things" is "[t]o renew the old world."[21] It is this desire to renew the old world, to bring it back to life and to remake it, that allows cabinets of curiosity to help us make contemporary space habitable and, in some sense, our own. And if contemporary museum-goers are willing, they can accept the cabinet of curiosity's invitation to participate in this renewal of wonder and a return to the museum's mythological origins by making the spectator share in the task of the modern curiosity cabinet maker.

Like the conventional *Wunderkammer*, the Museum of Jurassic Technology extends an invitation to marvel at its collection of curiosities. So too does *Curious Collectors, Collected Curiosities: An Interdisciplinary Study* ask its readers to enter into an investigation of the nature of collecting as an aesthetic exercise. Spanning the sixteenth century through today, this book gathers together the work of current scholars to re-envision the task of collectors and their collections in broad strokes. Each chapter appropriates the idea of a cabinet of curiosity in order to expand its boundaries of meaning and to complicate our understanding of the acts of display and observation. These chapters also demonstrate that collecting is a universal trope which nevertheless depends on time and place for its particular expressions. Whether the collection is made up of literary texts and criticism, visual art, including mechanical reproductions, taxidermy and photography, historical travelogues, museum exhibitions, blockbuster films, or airline in-flight briefing cards, it conveys an urgent relevance to our consumer age, in which information is abundant and attention is a commodity.[22]

Chapter One, "'Very Rare, Fragile and Priceless': Transforming Leonardo da Vinci from Collector to Curiosity," opens the discussion by introducing Grande Exhibitions, an international company that designs and leases out autonomous touring exhibitions using current technology. Throughout this chapter, Grande Exhibitions is presented as a cabinetmaker that takes advantage of various multi-media projections and constructions to rearrange and reframe continuously the relationship between the objects and viewers. The primary focus is on the first of Grand Exhibitions' shows, "Da Vinci—A Genius," which incorporates 3D projections and large-size replicas of da Vinci's most famous machine inventions. A folio page from his sixteenth-century *Notebooks*, the exhibit today, and even Grande Exhibitions itself are all read through the lens of Walter Benjamin's notion of "aura," John Berger's idea of spectatorship, and Jacques Derrida's sense of frames, in order to present how the collector paradoxically transforms into the curio.

While scholars have long remarked the use of visual tropes of wonder in new world contact literature, their readings have largely focused on the European's gaze at—and display of—the native body as an exercise of colonial power. Chapter Two, "Cabinets in Reverse: Staging the European Body as Curiosity in the Literature of New World Encounter," offers a slightly different view by examining scenes in which the trajectory of the gaze is reversed. In a sampling of accounts taken from some of the most studied literature of contact, the European body is in fact staged as the object of curiosity and wonder for native audiences. These scenes depict natives looking at Europeans. Complicating the iconographic image we have of European purveyors of the gaze in the cabinet of curiosity, these scenes reveal Europeans looking at Natives looking at Europeans. Careful examination of such tripartite reversal scenes in Columbus's letters, Hariot's Brief Description, Behn's Oroonoko and Cavendish's Blazing World reveals key tensions between contradictory rhetorical justifications for new world colonization. This chapter suggests that close study of the conventions whereby these writers project their own appetite for wonder onto the native body lends a more complex view of the desires and fears attendant to the discourses of curiosity and collecting associated with the history of new world contact.

Whereas Chapter Two focuses on how literary representations, largely in the early modern period, reveal an appetite for wonder, Chapter Three, "The Ark of the Museum: Epistemological Change in John Tradescant's Cabinet of Curiosities," examines how changes in the perspective of art can be traced through the culture of collection in the same period. In the early modern period, art shifts from something that is simply the revelation of universal artistic principles to something constructed by artistic ability. At the same time as artistic taste is emerging in this period, subjective notions of external realities also emerge. Like art, physical reality increasingly becomes something that natural philosophers participate in constructing. How the physical space of collection coincides with this fundamental shift in natural philosophy is thus closely studied. As Tradescant's Ark moves from its private location in John Tradescant's home to an institutional location in Oxford, the perspective of collection and of external realities shifts from universal and eternal to subjective and contingent. The institutionalization of the collection indicates the shift away from understanding cabinets of curiosities as a microcosm of the macrocosm to an independent and provisional excerpt of physical reality.

Following up with an alternative interpretation of a cabinet's projection of physical reality, Chapter Four, "Botched Animals and Enigmatic Beasts," explores the aesthetics of natural specimens from sixteenth-century cabinets of wonder and seventeenth-century collections of natural history. While much critical analysis has been brought to considering the cultural, social, and intellectual histories of these spaces of wonder, no study has fully examined the physical appearance of their organic specimens. Early modern taxidermy was hardly a polished craft. Most creatures were only known through bits and pieces not susceptible to decay, rot, or insects: feathers, bones, claws, beaks, and horns. While such enigmatic shards fed the early appetite for wondrous nature, those same bits and pieces were increasingly difficult for later, more empirically minded collectors. How was objective knowledge (rather than wonder) to be extracted from desiccated parts of little known creatures? By investigating what such animal morsels looked like, this chapter explores the sort of information that could be extracted and suggests that bad taxidermy and botched animals made for truculently opaque objects. Materials count, particularly when it comes to organic materials and even more particularly for preserved nature. While always offering the anticipation of knowledge, some objects prove too obscure to decipher by purely empirical means.

Chapter Five, "A Curious Commodity: Antoine Galland's *Arabian Nights' Entertainment*," returns to literature as a topical curiosity by looking closely at the reception history of the *Arabian Nights' Entertainments*, the English translation of Antoine Galland's *Les Mille et une Nuits* (a text that Benjamin himself unpacked in his library). Given that the written record offers little evidence for how the text was read, the number of editions that appeared between ca. 1706 and 1799 and the references to the *Arabian Nights*' ubiquity in various sources suggests that it must have been quite popular. Those readers who recorded their responses also seem to have assumed that it offered a view, though of course of a questionable accuracy, of "Eastern" culture and society. Such a reading obscures the text's importance as literature, miring it in a debate about its origins and authenticity. In the written record, the *Arabian Nights* also serves as a useful frame of reference for any kind of fantastic image. Writers drew on its magical and marvelous descriptions of fabulous palaces and exotic cities, though only by vague allusion, when attempting to describe some other, unrelated object of curiosity. This chapter examines the text's fantastic nature, so useful for writers struggling with their own descriptions of curious objects; it considers why *Arabian Nights* attracted numerous critics, many of whom dismissed the text as unworthy and some of whom defended the value and importance of fancy. The critical reception of *Arabian Nights* demonstrates how this text projects a kind of infinite cabinet for the eighteenth century's collection of oriental places; it acts as a repository for curious tales. But it is also reduced to the status of a curious object itself.

Contemporary to such fantastic literature of the eighteenth century are the real travelogues of imperial explorers, most often collected in the form of personal journals published for public consumption. In Chapter Six, "Captain Cook's Cabinet: The Making of an Arctic Imaginary," the journals from the Third Voyage of James Cook are realized as the practical catalogue of a cabinet at sea. Defined as a floating cabinet, Cook's ship, the *Resolution*, is positioned as a charted nexus for natural and synthetic objects alike. As Cook's journals reveal, his ship was responsible for collecting specimens from the Arctic's indigenous peoples (oftentimes extending beyond tools and weapons, skins, timber, food, and water, to include the people themselves), as well as samples of arctic flora and fauna, and accurate charts of land- and seascapes. By extension, the *Resolution* was a kind of trading post, providing iron and other metals, buttons and livestock to the indigenous peoples in exchange for their goods (or as gifts, or as the result of outright thievery). But all such collections were secondary to the location of a Northwest Passage—itself a failed attempt to satisfy the practical curiosity of a more efficient trade route for the British Empire. As this chapter demonstrates, therefore,

Cook's ship becomes a staging ground to reveal the essential tension, or buoyancy, between the land and sea, and interior and exterior boundaries, in order to reconcile real and imaginary spaces. Based on Foucault's notion of a "heterotopia," the floating cabinet is proposed as a mixed space at once demonstrative of the actual challenges of an arctic expanse and representative of the aesthetic experiments deployed to capture it.

Trading in effect one moving cabinet for another, Chapter Seven, "Collective Animal Images: A Natural History of Cinema," investigates the motion picture, or cinema's contribution of life unfolding in time to human representation, by looking to the animals that populated the images of proto-cinematic apparatuses. Set against the backdrop of a nineteenth-century culture of collection in general and the emergence of the zoological space of animal observation in particular, this chapter argues that the works of Eadweard Muybridge and Etienne-Jules Marey seek to recuperate animals and reconstitute an animality that has been stripped from western culture and its practices of representation. Muybridge and Marey are integral in understanding the technological drive toward motion photography because of their shared singular focus to represent movement as such. Together, they overcame virtually all of the technological hurdles necessary for the cinematic apparatus to emerge. By comparing the emergence of the zoological space with the emergence of the cinematic space in their work, it becomes clear that the presence of animals foregrounds the pursuit of the representation of life at its fullest. Cinematic space allows humans not only to see animals in a new way, but also as a new type of representation grounded in the physical world. Central to this analysis is the question of whether or not we can understand cinema as the register of animality, and to the extent that we can or do, what does it mean to turn that back on ourselves. The chapter concludes then with an analysis of a series of self-portraits by Muybridge.

Chapter Eight, "An Incoherent Collection? André du Bouchet's *L'Incohérence*," studies French poet André du Bouchet's seemingly disparate collection of prose, *L'Incohérence*. The book collects prose poems, meta-poetic meditations, translations, reflections on translation, and texts on artists. On the surface, and despite the aforementioned grouping, *L'Incohérence* appears incoherent. Du Bouchet, when asked about the book's structure, claims that "there is in *Incoherence*, a contradiction found in the title itself. At bottom, it is a book that, in a certain fashion, appears very constructed all the while escaping the order of succession. The book is not paginated. A text leads to another, a page is read in regard to another, yet one could begin the book in the middle or read it backwards in all senses." How can a book be "very constructed all the while escaping the order of succession"? What does it mean to call such a book—or any book—*Incoherence*? What does such an appellation imply about reading? What does such a book, glimpsed as a collection, if not a *Wunderkammer* as described by Giorgio Agamben, say about textuality, about what happens to texts and to the subjects of those texts when they are apposed? These questions are addressed by closely reading selected passages from *L'Incohérence* with support from other du Bouchet texts, paying particular attention not just to what the poet says, but to how he arranges his words on the page.

Chapter Nine, "Anatomy of an Exhibition: W. G. Sebald's *The Rings of Saturn*" continues the discussion of twentieth-century literature-as-cabinet by exploring the "museum effect" of Sebald's novel. *The Rings of Saturn* depicts the troubled relationship between aesthetic pleasure and the ethical treatment of others. The museum effect, as this chapter argues, is one that describes the relationship between the object and the observer, rather than a transformation of the object, charting the different ways we find it useful or necessary to arrange objects and thus produce stories. While criticism of Sebald's novels has generally focused on their use of photographs or representations of trauma, this chapter analyzes the way in which his narrative is structured like a visual and a temporal experience, even as it critiques the value of various kinds of visual experiences. *The Rings of Saturn* presents narrative interruption as an opening to the otherness of history, its places and its people. The trope of the museum allows Sebald to make an ethical argument about representation, making "visible" people or moments that are gone, without suggesting that we can know them.

The epilogue to *Curious Collectors, Collected Curiosities* offers another twenty-first century vision of the curio cabinet to complement that of the Museum of Jurassic Technology with which this introduction opened. But rather than be a structured space, like that of a museum, the concluding cabinet of this collection is situated largely in the open and makes up part of the everyday of our popular culture; it draws the gaze back to humankind as the curious object itself—able to travel far and wide. "On Being Embedded: Some Notes on the Environmental Curiosities of Air Travel" explores conjunctions of "natural" imagery and commercial flight. Collected into this concluding vignette are a range of visual texts that unpack the environmental implications of how flight is depicted in these images, from official airline schematics and advertising schemes, to a Google image search and the Hollywood smash hit *Avatar*. It demonstrates how the contemporary air travel imaginary reflects a paradoxical arrangement: humans are both inescapably "embedded" in environmental existence, but also constantly defining themselves against and transporting themselves as if outside any environmental reach. To see the curio aesthetics of air travel is to gain an oblique perspective on this paradoxical arrangement, and to catch a glimpse of the vexed environmental awareness of being human.

This collection grew out of discussions from a three-day panel that we put together for the *American Comparative Literature Association*'s annual conference in 2006. The panel focused on cabinets of curiosity and their role in defining the human. Support for this project came largely from the innovative research and continued enthusiasm of its contributors, and from the editorial team at Cambridge Scholars Publishing. We would like to thank especially Carol Koulikourdi and Amanda Millar for their enduring patience and generous guidance, which helped to see this project through to completion.

CHAPTER ONE

"VERY RARE, FRAGILE, AND PRICELESS": TRANSFORMING LEONARDO DA VINCI FROM COLLECTOR TO CURIOSITY

NHORA LUCÍA SERRANO

One can have no smaller or greater mastery than mastery of oneself.
—Leonardo da Vinci, *Notebooks*

In 2006, when Australian-based Grande Exhibitions, an international company that creates and markets autonomous touring exhibitions, unveiled its very first traveling exhibit, it focused on Leonardo da Vinci, Renaissance artist, writer, and inventor, and a collector of curiosities in his own right. It is no surprise that they chose da Vinci as their focus since they already owned and operated two permanent museums dedicated to this collector of curiosities in his own right: "il Genio di Leonardo da Vinci Museo" in Florence and Venice, Italy. "Da Vinci—A Genius" (formerly known as "Da Vinci—An Exhibition of Genius, 1452-1519")[1] is an interactive exhibition, traveling to the National Geographic Museum in Washington, D. C. from June 18-September 12, 2010, and composed of da Vinci's drawings and paintings, anatomical studies, and the major scientific studies and inventions found in his *Notebooks*.[2] In short, Grande Exhibitions has created a modern cabinet, using current technology, in order to display the works of an iconic figure from the fifteenth century. From 3D projections of two of da Vinci's most famous works, *The Last Supper* and the *Vitruvian Man*, alongside a replication of his most ambitious sculpture project, the *Sforza Horse*, and large-size replicas of his most famous machine inventions, this is an exhibit that seeks to engage actively with its viewers as it looks back nostalgically to the earlier days of the *Wunderkammer*.

As the Grande Exhibitions' catalogue emphasizes, the comprehensive scope of "Da Vinci—A Genius" is presented "under one roof"; one of its kind, it is equal almost to the "rare, fragile and priceless" inventions themselves.[3] The catalogue goes on to stress the exhibit's commercial appeal because "all can *marvel* at the brilliance of this great mind."[4] Again according to their website, Grande Exhibitions advertizes "broad mass appeal"[5] as one of its profitable features so that prospective venues would be interested in renting their traveling exhibits. In the case of "Da Vinci—A Genius," the unparalleled focus on the artist is for the viewer's benefit, allowing the magnitude of da Vinci's stature as "genius" to remain undisputed just as the exhibition itself projects its own outstanding ability to craft da Vinci's innovative technologies, in some cases for the first time. The catalogue, like the traveling exhibit itself, thus privileges the spectator by re-presenting the past in a present moment. In doing so, this model ironically transforms da Vinci's inventions into not-so-rare or fragile or priceless artifacts, but into reproduced (and reproducible) technological novelties.

If a task of a cabinet of curiosity is to mesmerize the viewer with individual specimens within their paradigmatic arrangements, then Grande Exhibitions proffers a wondrous spectacle with most of da Vinci's inventions standing side-by-side in life-like proportions. What makes these models even more astonishing is that Grande Exhibitions employed Italian artisans, who for the most part used the very same materials and techniques available to da Vinci in fifteenth-century Italy. Grande Exhibitions' aim for da Vinci's inventions to be realistic and enticing to the viewer is made possible not only with the attention paid to the authenticity of materials and the location of their construction, but also to the machines' scale. Some of the reproductions are small in size, others are truly life-like as da Vinci envisioned them, and even others are larger-than-life for the viewer's appreciation and edification, all of which stress that the gaze and the display are crucial for the show's success as an interactive, educational tool. With the awesome reproductions, da Vinci's genius is paid homage. But more suggestively Grande Exhibitions emerges as the cabinetmaker of a unique collection as-yet-unseen. In other words, what Grande Exhibitions ultimately displays are not da Vinci's inventions alone, but Leonardo da Vinci himself; the persona surfaces as the true curiosity in this traveling cabinet.

However, it is impossible to access this persona without the context of his works. Da Vinci's *Notebooks* have long been esteemed by many scholars to be the treasure trove and key to his overall *oeuvre*. Robert Zwijnenberg claims in *The Writing and Drawings of Leonardo da Vinci*, that da Vinci's *Notebooks* are the "most important of his activities, perhaps even the foundation of the others."[6] The *Notebooks* have survived as loose fragments torn from the original notebooks and reassembled—literally cut and pasted in some circumstances—into ten very different codices located all over the world, from England, Italy, Spain, France, and the United States. While the folio pages are fragments in the sense that they are scattered around the world without knowledge of their original pagination and interconnectedness, Zwijnenberg disagrees that they should be considered disparate or chaotic in the modern pejorative meaning of the word. The purpose of the *Notebooks* was not about organization or categorization *per se*, and much less about following a linear narrative trajectory; rather, the *Notebooks* reveal one man's scientific and artistic curiosity for nature, the human, and the world. In sum, the fragmentary status of the *Notebooks* attests to their "collectedness" as well as their collective value for enthusiasts like Grande Exhibitions and da Vinci himself. Zwijnenberg further posits that the *Notebooks* need to be seen as a "useful and functional instrumen[t] with which to acquire knowledge of the world,"[7] like a stream-of-consciousness narrative. The *Notebooks* themselves were a verbal and visual cabinet of curiosity written onto the 2D, flat plane of a page in an effort to articulate 3D inventions and observations.

With so many drawings dedicated to anatomy and the general make-up of engineering, da Vinci clearly was an observer, dissector, and collector of curiosities. For example, one of the Windsor Folios drawings depicts a seemingly haphazard juxtaposition between a human leg in the lower right-hand corner and an early sketch of one of his mechanical inventions in the lower left-hand part of the page.[8] In jotting down these thoughts and observations together, da Vinci was potentially creating links between the inner workings of a machine's mobility and those of the man. With only a partial sketch of each object, da Vinci was seeing their interconnectedness. He was dissecting man alongside his mechanical inventions in order to grasp both: man was the paradigm for the mechanical inventions, while the machine served as the skeletal frame through which human anatomy was to be understood. This combined methodology of dissection using scientific and artistic lenses, resulting in a written paradigmatic comparison, suggests that da Vinci's genius lies truly in his being an early cabinetmaker of human and technological curiosities.

To organize and give life to these paradigmatic curiosities in the *Notebooks*, as Grande Exhibitions has done, is perhaps an impossible reading and curatorial task not unlike any attempt to reclaim the loss of "aura" that Walter Benjamin laments in his seminal essay, "The Work of Art in the Age of Mechanical Reproduction."[9] Like the Grande Exhibitions' traveling show on da Vinci, the cabinet of curiosity as a mode of (re)presentation permits us to understand better the appeal and need in this day and age for wide-ranging, technologically savvy museum exhibitions of older canonical works, collections, and masters.

In what follows, I propose that the cabinet of curiosity and its praxis could be vital critical tools for understanding the tasks and implications of displaying curiosities from the past (like Grande Exhibitions has done with da Vinci's mechanical inventions and two additional exhibits, "Planet Shark" and "Van Gogh-Alive"). Modern theorists like Walter Benjamin, John Berger, and Jacques Derrida will help to elucidate how Grande Exhibitions successfully demonstrates that mechanical reproductions do indeed cause a decay of aura, allowing in turn for a shift in framing to expose the eponymous curio of the exhibit. Benjamin's notion of the displaced object's eroded then refurbished aura, combined with Berger's idea of spectatorship in *Ways of Seeing* and Derrida's sense of the frame in *Truth in Painting*, illuminate further how historical curiosities reproduced within a modern cabinet derive their multifarious meaning from displacement and reframing (i.e. in a technologically rendered cabinet).

In "The Work of Art in the Age of Mechanical Reproduction," Benjamin introduces the concept of aura as an explication of how modern day re-presentations of past and current works of art can unveil newer understandings toward the public's consumption and experience of these "sacred" objects. Defined as the art object's special power, a relevant and unique quality that asserted its original historicity, the aura, according to Benjamin, is eroded when mass-produced, i.e. when taken from its original cultural milieu and reconfigured through mechanical reproduction. The sacred object, whether relocated, reframed, photocopied, filmed, or photographed, inhabits an essentially new historical and cultural space once it is moved *as if* it were indeed a *curious* object. For Benjamin, the newly displaced object marked a change of value not only for itself, but for the important epistemological practices of observation and reception. Hence, while Benjamin's particular focus was on photography and cinematography—the new means of mechanical reproduction in his day—this pivotal essay drew and continues to draw attention to how a new context, frame, or border for the work of art could challenge the viewer's critical perception of it. For example, with a penchant to challenge the viewer's critical understanding of an artist and their works of art through an emphasis on traveling, spectatorship, and the creation of new frames "under one roof," Grande Exhibitions and their innovative exhibits fit the Benjaminian bill for displaced objects.

Grande Exhibitions acts like a hidden museum or clearinghouse that one cannot physically visit but whose attic nevertheless boasts of sheltering rare works of art and collections. Because it markets its pieces out to other museums and venues, it functions much like a specially curated show. As of 2010, Grande Exhibitions has marketed five stock exhibits, each of which travel world-wide, moving from venue to venue with the potential to change with each move. Following the success of "Da Vinci—The Genius," the company constructed "Planet Shark," "Secrets of Mona Lisa," "Van Gogh-Alive," and "Game On." Each one of these exhibitions demonstrates both a cabinet of curiosity's theoretical approach to display, reception, and collection, and the company's own role as collector of disparate phenomena. "Planet Shark," for example, an eco-educational, interactive display, juxtaposes the shark as both predator and prey. Advertised as traveling for no more than three months at a time, the viewer is educated through interactive modules about the animal and about humankind's fascination with it. Amongst the videos and displays, there are also collections of diving cages, hunting and commercial fishing equipment, and fossils not unlike the curiosities found in a traditional cabinet. Besides marvel and fear of the shark, another overarching frame that emerges from this exhibit is a very contemporary, socially and politically charged message: the exhibition works to promote an understanding of how the shark is important for our ecosystem. Clearly treating distinct subject matter, the da Vinci and shark exhibits, as manufactured by a single company, reflect the seemingly unsystematic composition of a traditional cabinet's contents.

Since their focus is on "broad mass appeal," it is not strange that Grande Exhibitions runs the gamut of museums, from Natural History exhibitions to Fine Art exhibitions. For example, another recent exhibit is "Van Gogh-Alive," a multimedia projection of twentieth-century painter Vincent Van Gogh and his works. This is another show that travels for no more than three months at a time, during which the viewers experience Van Gogh's images in a specially created space that permits them "to be immersed in the artist's work rather than observe it."[10] With accompanied sound and larger-than-life projections on walls and floors, Grande Exhibitions examines up close Van Gogh's brushstrokes and color by zooming in on artistry as a curiosity. It allows the viewer to walk literally through the reproduced paintings of Van Gogh. Here technology and high-definition optics are the frames through which artistry, as well as art criticism, are transformed into objects for study and wonder.

The very fact that Grande Exhibitions delights in having "its own in-house design,... [which manages] every visual aspect of [a] traveling exhibition,"[11] secures their role as cabinetmaker, as *the* manufacturer of what Berger defines as a spectatorship. And yet, as Derrida's analysis of truth and frames in painting illuminates, a cabinetmaker who employs technology as a framing mechanism cannot control this spectatorship, or "mass appeal," much less what viewers will consider to be the real curiosity. The cabinet therefore takes on a life of its own. Together with Benjamin, all three of these theorists demonstrate that the cabinet of curiosity is a significant system of organization relevant not only for Grande Exhibitions and the manner in which they display their objects, but perhaps for all modern renderings of a cabinet of curiosity and their audiences.

Given the primacy of aura for a work of art, Berger argues that Benjamin extolled the virtues of the age of mechanical reproduction because the essay privileged (for Berger) spectatorship—i.e. a new dynamic use of the gaze that favored the viewer—over cult veneration—i.e. the static experience of an art object's aura that favored the object—as the critical *modus operandi* in the twentieth century.[12] Similar to Grande Exhibitions' marketing strategy of mass consumption, Berger himself privileges the museum-goer and their relationship with an object's aura. For Berger, the decay of aura is vital, because without it new forms of art or innovative, critical methods that challenge the viewer—like the cabinet of curiosity—would not be possible. Moreover, without a decay of aura and the nostalgic gesture to recreate the art object's historicity, assorted museum exhibitions about the very same objects or artists would not be possible, and perhaps much less appealing for the curator or museum-goer.

Berger's emphasis on spectatorship as a mode of consumption complements Derrida's idea of overlooked frames, or the context and truth-value of a work of art, when considering Grande Exhibitions' traveling cabinets. Derrida argues that a truth in painting is an impossibility not unlike a truth in language. There are inherent contradictions and oppositions—e.g. inside and outside, the framer and the framed—that make any so-called truth unstable, complex, and impossible.[13] Like an object relocated to a cabinet—seen as curious because of its dislocation from a natural setting to an artificial one—any understanding (i.e. placement on a shelf or in a drawer) or description of it (i.e. in museum guidebook or an exhibition catalogue) inevitably reverts to a discussion *around* its curiosity without necessarily being an explanation of it. Stuck vacillating between the framer and framed, a displaced object moves back and forth between cabinets and the epistemological understanding of its curiosity; its meaning is overhauled continuously wherein meaning is only relayed through a passage of difference. Derrida's idea of frames thus suggests that what resides outside the frame is as important as what is depicted within the frame and even the frame itself. Cultural context, therefore, is as important as the work of art within this context, the cabinet that frames it, and the act of collecting itself. "Da Vinci—The Genius," as an exemplum of this idea, derives meaning from its contemporary placement, its mechanical reproductions, its existence in varied venues, and its curatorial procedures.

In the context of this Derridian-like cabinet of curiosity, the museum-goer who sees one of Grande Exhibitions' traveling cabinets is overwhelmed with everything simultaneously: the curiosities, the collection as a whole, and the cabinet itself, whether literally a shelf, box, an interactive module, a projection, or furniture piece. Separately and all at once, the viewer quickly realizes that the experience of approaching a Grande Exhibitions' cabinet is at once elusive and enticing, furthering the decay of aura, yet closing in on its new contextual meaning: a Derridean wonder. By suggesting that the meaning that a work of art conveys is as varied as its effect on a person, and from person to person, Derrida echoes Benjamin's essay in that the frame points out that there is already a loss of aura that is not completely lost. This loss of aura is vital to project meaning for a work of art. For instance, a museum-goer who visits "Da Vinci—The Genius" will leave with a sense of wonder because they feel as if they have seen a real artifact, even if it is an enlarged facsimile of a folio page from his *Notebooks* or a reproduced, 3D model suggested by one of his sketches.

All in all, Grande Exhibitions' traveling exhibitions emphasize the technologically savvy, relatively mobile cabinet of curiosity, which grants previously seen and unseen objects a new meaning, contextual frames, and experiences no matter where it is displayed in the world. As their website claims, Grande Exhibitions prides itself on the "highest quality" show,[14] a performative frame through which the multiplicity of meaning is filtered and strained. Since the exhibitions are traveling shows, however, each exhibit cannot help but emphasize in its own unique way the shifting aura and cultural context of the displayed pieces. With an exhibition life cycle of no more than three to six months at a time in any given city and venue, Grande Exhibitions underscores a constant modification of dwelling, perspective, and frames.[15] This international organization, whose dedication to the concept of a traveling exhibition is utmost, operates much like that of American P.T. Barnum's beloved traveling circus, which displayed animal and human oddities beneath its Big Top. Like this circus, Grande Exhibitions ultimately aims to leave a trace of the visual marvels it carries to and displays at each of its stopovers.

Even if modern-day reproductions are visually appealing, intellectually enthralling, and highly marketable, what Grande Exhibitions has achieved are demonstrations of how, in the twenty-first century, mechanical reproduction does in fact cause the productive decay of aura. In the context of their "Da Vinci—A Genius" exhibition, da Vinci's inventions are dissected facsimiles of ideas presented to the viewer. Unlike the *Notebooks* themselves, which are more a specimen of continuous journal-writing and -thinking rather than a comprehensive textbook, "Da Vinci—A Genius" attempts to represent a systemization and totality that was never there to begin with in order to grant privilege to the viewer. Grande Exhibitions takes da Vinci's early cartoons, preliminary sketches, and outlines for a final work and realizes them literally to confirm his genius for the viewer. Furthermore, Grande Exhibitions promotes the sense that to translate da Vinci's works via mechanical reproduction is to place a frame around the multiplicity of meaning found on the disparate folios themselves. However, this frame remains malleable in that it allows for the act of collecting to be on display as much as the collected objects themselves.

As a purveyor for modern cabinets of curiosity, Grande Exhibitions is the quintessential example of a growing twenty-first century mainstream proclivity for interactive technology as the preferred medium through which knowledge is presented to the masses in museums.[16] In all of its current exhibits, Grande Exhibitions takes advantage of various multi-media projections and constructions to rearrange and reframe continuously the relationship between the objects and viewers. Yet this realignment is consistently dependent on the object's aura; the realignment must echo the object in some manner or else the exhibition would fall prey to being a mere spoof and not the "highest quality" it seeks. What Grande Exhibitions accomplishes is thus the privileging of spectatorship over old-fashion veneration; it reinforces a new form of veneration for the museum-goer, one which is based on displacement, resemblance, and reframing, and which emphasizes an anachronistic human experience not unlike the renderings found in the fragment folios from da Vinci's *Notebooks.* Just as da Vinci moved from the stance of collector to that of the collected, or curio, Grande Exhibitions emerges as the curiosity that is itself enframed by its own collections.

CHAPTER TWO

CABINETS IN REVERSE: STAGING THE EUROPEAN BODY AS CURIOSITY IN THE LITERATURE OF NEW WORLD ENCOUNTER

STEPHANIE SHIRILAN

Neil Kenny begins his history of early modern curiosity by noting that the family of terms that make up the semantic range of curiosity "had both subject- and object-oriented senses." In other words, a person could be both curious and a curiosity.[1] This paper foregrounds its study of mimetic desire in representations of early modern contact narratives with the complex figure of the 'collector,' who translated his own curiosity into an object that made him the curiosity of others. Marjorie Swann reminds us that *sprezzatura*, the courtier's seemingly nonchalant grace, aimed to make "all men wonder at him, and he at no man."[2] Drawing on Foucault's genealogy in *The Order of Things*, early modernists have marked the ascendance of a modern episteme in the transition from an economy that privileged the object of the gaze to one that privileged its exercise. Renaissance power, as Stephen Orgel, Christopher Pye, and others have argued, resided in "being looked at."[3] "Modern" (proto-bourgeois and proto-scientific) power, suspicious of the subject's passivity to wondrous displays, adopted the discourse of curiosity in place of wonder.[4]

The cabinet of curiosities unsettles the ease with such epistemic lines are drawn. I suggest that the confusion of the subject and object of the "gaze" is the very animus of the cabinet, and as such the cause of its continued fascination for intellectual historians.[5] Paula Findlen's *Possessing Nature* illustrates how the Italian cabinet served the changing interests of court, market, and the early academies of science. In each instance, collectors curried favors, patronage, or influence by soliciting the wonder of visitors who (it was hoped) would direct their wonder at the displayed marvels towards their proprietor. The collector assembled and published a careful, if seemingly disordered, persona as the purveyor of wonder.[6] Doing so successfully required the translation of the collector's curiosity into a powerful apparatus of wonder-inducement. Such translations are never neat. Here I propose that the depiction of the awe-struck native, a recurring motif in early modern travel literature, displaces European wonder and mimetic investment in the new world onto native bodies instead. The gazing European rhetorically stages himself as the object of the gape.[7] I offer examples of the reversed-curiosity motif in several iconic representations of new world encounters, "real" and imagined: Columbus's letter announcing the discovery, Hariot's *Brief Description*, Margaret Cavendish's *Blazing World*, and Aphra Behn's *Oroonoko*. These texts have been selected to provide generically variant and historically specific instances of a thematic substitution of indigenous fascination for European wonder.

Stephen Greenblatt writes that in the scene of new world contact, Europeans drew on wonder to "cut the complex mimetic knot that links the eyewitness and the world he describes."[8] In Greenblatt's estimation, wonder is a discourse Europeans called upon to disidentify with the indigenes; it is the prelude to appropriation.[9] I argue that European writers did not fashion a discourse of alterity out of their own performance of wonder, but rather that the rhetorical operation of disidentification takes place in the reassignation of wonder to the indigenous "other." Closer examination of the force by which mimetic curiosity is rhetorically transposed from European to Native in early travel narratives complicates our understanding of the place of new world objects in the European cabinet, and, by extension, overly simplified representations of the cabinet as an epistemic prelude to the modern possessive individualism associated with "the collecting habit." I aim to show how the transposition of European mimetic desire takes place through a highly unstable discourse of the value and desirability of the European commodity. I argue that the European body and its refinements are offered as consumable wonders—surrogates for European hyper-investment in the bodies and resources of the new world.

Despite what I will foreground as the centrality of the reversal theme, there remains considerable perception that, as Karen Kupperman writes, "very rarely English writers turned the lens around and conveyed Indian interest in the newcomer's appearance."[10] Mary Baine Campbell notes that while the reversal theme is not unprecedented, it is unusual: "I do not point it out as morally benign or politically progressive but simply as a surprise, a rhetorical moment that…invites a moment's wonder itself."[11] I take up the "surprise" of this rhetorical turn and seek to understand the mechanisms by which wonder and desire (to know, touch and imitate the other) is made to move from the colonizer's body to the body of the colonized.

The paradigmatic representation of Indian curiosity in European objects and exotica goes back at least as far as Columbus, who repeatedly situates the inherent servility of native peoples in their capacity to be awed by the physical objects put on display before them: medallions, bells, images and, later, books.[12] The narrators of these scenes of encounter make tenuous distinctions between the kinds of awe that can (or ought) to be cultivated by "valuable" objects, and the naïve, idolatrous and infantile worship of trifles. According to the interpreters and marketers of new world venture, the thrall that the image of the monarch printed on a gold coin places over the natives testifies to their inherent recognition of rightful authority. Their equal valuation of "broken crockery" and royal images both entices savvy traders and presents a problem that shores up the doubleness of colonial desire so pervasive in representations of early contact: the desire for maximal, indiscriminate profit and the desire to present the native as reasonable and convertible. If the natives with whom they seek to trade are indeed potential Christians, the Spanish cannot seem to trade worth for worthlessness—a scheme Columbus styles himself as being anxious to avoid, even while he repeatedly emphasizes its ease.

> Whether the thing be of value or whether it be of small price, at once with whatever trifle or whatever kind it may be that is given to them, with that they are content. I forbade that they should be given things so worthless as fragments of broken crockery and scraps of broken glass, and ends of straps, although when they were able to get them, they fancied that they possessed the best jewel in the world.... They took even the pieces of the broken hoops of the wine barrels and, like savages, gave what they had, so that it seemed to me to be wrong and I forbade it. And I gave a thousand handsome good things, which I had brought, in order that they might conceive affections, and more than that, might become Christians and be inclined to the love and service of their highnesses and of the whole Castilian nation, and strive to aid us and to give us of the things which they have in abundance and which are necessary to us.[13]

Columbus's description of the natives' appetite for European objects exposes the complex and contradictory logic of the super-valuation of the symbolic commodity over the non-symbolic "trifle." What value can be conferred on the image of the monarchs or regal banners, or the name Columbus gives to the ground he plants them in, if they command equal awe to the trifling objects he and his sailors so easily pawn away?

Already in Columbus's account, the emphasis placed on native appetites for European objects seems to operate in excess of economic expediency. It suggests the narrator's own awareness of the semantic instability between objects of value and everyday objects, and registers his trouble over how to represent the difference between them. Thomas Hariot's annotations of Theodor de Bry's engravings in *America Part I* disclose a similar instability. Hariot annotates one engraving which shows a nearly nude "Chieff Ladye of the Pomeiooc" and young girl holding a European doll and rattle. Hariot concludes his portrait of the mother's and daughter's minimal dress with the remark that they "are greatlye Diligted with puppets and babes which wear brought oute of England."[14] The engraving conveys the propagandist suggestion that the indigenous people of Virginia, like the abundant resources they enjoy, have immediate as well as cultivable value. Hariot's spotlight on native desires for European commodities suggests that the natives sensibly desire the supplementation of European goods while it simultaneously testifies to their naïve valuation of these trinkets over their own natural resources. Hariot and Columbus seek to make the native familiar to Europeans on the basis of their shared appreciation for European goods. The inference in these documents written primarily for colonial stakeholders is that the immoderate appetites of the native peoples for European commodities will make them rapt subjects for colonial investment.

The European commodity first takes prominence in the scene of encounter as an illocutionary object that subdues and even assuages the potential, and rhetorically cannibalistic, violence of first contact. Hariot describes the "great and horrible crye" his party first receives from the Virginians: "as people which never befoer had seene men apparalled like us" (45). The word 'horrible' reflexively connotes both English horror at the sight and sound of the natives as well as Hariot's assumption that the spectacle of the English party provokes horror from the natives who had never before seen their likes.[15] The threat registered by the inscription of the greeting cry as 'horrible' is only revised after the Indians are successfully "called backe" to admire the "wares…glasses, knives, babies and other trifles" (45). Hariot's interpretation rhetorically straddles the suggestion that the natives are both pacified by the power of the commodities on display and that their seeming hostility is a misinterpreted sign of their admiration for the European in all his finery.

The same misinterpreted welcome scene is reproduced nearly identically a century later in Aprha Behn's *Oroonoko*. The arrival of Behn's narrator at the Indian villages of Surinam is also met with a "horrible cry" portentous of real or imagined violence. And, as in Hariot's account, this cry is magically diverted by the enchanting spectacle of the European body and its accoutrements.[16] The narrator prefaces her depiction of the Surinami natives with an explanation that her longing to see 'real' Indian villages had been almost thwarted by the recent threat of Indian uprising. She remarks that the Indians have risen up against the Dutch, "who had not us'd 'em so civilly as the *English*," cutting and stringing women and children "in pieces" and (foreshadowing the story's grisly conclusion) dismembered and nailed the narrator's own footman to a tree (81). In spite of these threats, the narrator is determined to make the eight-day trip to see the Indian villages, and does so in the company of her brother, whose appearance in the text is limited to this one scene where it seems to serve the single narrative purpose of doubling the display of European fashions across the sexes, producing a 'his and hers' touch-and-feel show that makes the male and female body equally available as consumable curiosities. Upon arrival, the narrator and her brother are greeted with a loud cry, which they initially interpret as murderous and almost as quickly reinterpret as one of "Wonder and Amazement":

> We thought it had been for those that would Kill us, but it seems it was of Wonder and Amazement. They were all Naked, and we were Dress'd, so as is most comode for the hot Countries, very glittering and Rich; so that we appear'd extreamly fine. My own Hair was cut short, and I had a Taffaty Cap, with Black Feathers... my Brother was in a Stuff Sute, with Silver Loops and Buttons, and abundance of Green Ribbon. This was all infinitely surprising to them, and because we saw them stand still … we took Heart and advanc'd; came up to 'em, and offer'd 'em our Hand; which they took, and look'd on us round about calling still for more Company, who came swarming out all wondering…taking their Hair up in their Hands, and spreading it wide… as if they would say (as indeed it signify'd) *Numberless Wonders*, or not to be recounted, no more than to number the Hair of their Heads. (81-2)

The Indians grow bold and move from gazing to touching,

> Laying their Hands upon all the Features of our Faces, feeling our Breast and Arms, taking up one Petticoat, then wondering to see another; admiring our Shoes and Stockings, but more our Garters, which we gave 'em and they ty'd about their Legs…In fine, we suffer'd 'em to *survey* us as they pleas'd, and we thought they wou'd never have done admiring us. (82)

It is worth noting the timing of this scene within the chronology of the plot. An atmosphere of climactic threat is temporarily dissolved in the rapture (and if we read it differently, humor) afforded by the European body to native eyes and hands. From dismembered servants the narrative moves to this peculiar *blazon*, a literal undressing and itemization of the body's parts and surfaces, which will be gruesomely reenacted in the spectacular dismemberment of the titular hero, a tableau I will return to for its startling revision of the scene of the "consumed" colonial body.

The encounter in the Indian village follows on the heels of another "encounter" related by the narrator, who has been adventuring through the jungle with Oroonoko, playing audience to displays of his prowess at hunting, fishing and philosophical discourse. Oroonoko has heard of a "numbing eel" and, emulating the seventeenth-century natural philosopher, sets out to test the fish against its reputation, believing it "impossible a man cou'd lose his Force at the touch of a Fish; and cou'd not understand that Philosophy, that a cold Quality should be of that Nature" (80). Oroonoko is nearly drowned by his experiment. Once his fishing rod touches the eel, he is frozen, unable to let go of it, and dragged some distance under water before he is rescued by nearby Indians who themselves become perilously numbed by the mere touch of Oroonoko's body.

Physical contact with the electric eel (the indigenous curio) proves nearly fatal to the African prince turned slave, himself the central "curiosity" of the text. On first glance it might seem that, like the specimens collected in sixteenth and seventeenth-century cabinets, Oroonoko's appeal lies in his remarkable hybridity and the taxonomic confusion of how one might classify a subject whose exceptionality and distinction (in blood, strength, beauty, intelligence) translates across so many categories and conditions. Oroonoko, the one-time slave trader himself, is lured with shows of hospitality and European luxury into an English slave-trading ship where, "having drunk hard of Punch, and several Sorts of Wine" he is put in chains and brought to the New World to be sold. Oroonoko's English owner recognizes his innate nobility and consigns him to be "no more of the Slave but the Name" (69). Oroonoko's natural rank is doubly signified by his vest, a "dazzling habit" he wears from the time of his capture until he begs his new owner to take it from him, seeking to abate the gaze he naively attributes to the curiosity of his clothing. The importance of the vest is its superfluity; it is there to be *divested*, to illustrate the transparency of the quality and distinction of the body that inhabits it. While the English travelers are depicted as enjoying, even soliciting the gaze of the natives, the hero seeks to remove himself from both the gaze and the garment to which it is symbolically attached. In a remarkable reverse fantasy of aristocratic courtly power, Oroonoko cannot strip himself of the gaze. The curio is not appareled to him; he is himself the object and possession, the curiosity that commands our attention, particularly in his acutely mimetic attraction to Europeanness (and Englishness in particular). As a general in Africa, he sought out the company of English slave-traders, learned their language and, even after he is enslaved to them, pursues their company in captivity. Oroonoko discourses on philosophy with his master and devours the narrator's stories of Roman lives and loves—stories that distract him from the plight of his enslavement and the possibility of rebellion.[17]

The conjoined stories of the near-fatal "touch" of the numbing eel and the narrator's reception at the hands of the awed Surinami Indians charge the tactility of contact in this narrative with alternating currents of desire and repudiation that finally explode in the paroxysmal violence of the novella's conclusion. Availing the colonizer's body, especially its garments, to the "touch" of the Indians converts their potentially insurrectional violence into a form of subjugation. Touching the native eel (an almost inescapable equation of encounter with the native other as an encounter with the native phallus)[18] results in the lethal stiffening of the body, a contagious rigor mortis. The touch of the eel transmits its current through the rod, which in turn transmits itself through Oroonoko's body – the threat of contact issuing from body to object to body in a series of proxies that suggests the contaminating force of contact. Despite the repeated infliction of astounding violence to his body, both by himself and others (he later survives his own self-disembowelment), this "touch" is the nearest Oroonoko comes to death until he is finally hacked apart "with an ill-favoured Knife," his dismemberment (the literal removal of his male "Members") commencing a performance that violently returns the mimetic desire materialized by the narrator's reception at the Indian village.

The dismemberment of the spectacularly accommodated European body is restaged in this final scene wherein the body that commands the gaze is itself torn apart and consumed in fire. Oroonoko's execution itself, however, is eerily quiet. The gaze rests uncomfortably on the mute hero who, "having learn'd to take Tobaco," makes his last and only request for a pipe, which he smokes through the ensuing torture.

> …the Executioner came, and first cut off his Members, and threw them into the Fire; after that with an ill-favoured Knife, they cut his Ears, and his Nose, and burn't them; he still Smoak'd on, as if nothing had touch'd him; then they hacked off one of his Arms, and still he bore up, and held his Pipe; but at the cutting of this other Arm, his Head Sunk, and his Pipe drop'd; and he gave up the Ghost, without a Groan, or a Reproach. (99)

Tobacco was known in the seventeenth century for its analgesic effects,[19] but for the stoic general who countenanced so much physical punishment, the resonance of his final request registers something more than the desire for anesthesis. This is the second time that Oroonoko reaches for a New World curiosity associated with its numbing properties.[20] In the first instance, the hero plays the role of the experimental philosopher, pursuing encounter with the native curio nearly unto death. In the final instance, and capping a narrative framed around the cannibalistic economy of slave-produced consumables, the hero smokes while being roasted alive. The fire in the pit and the pipe suggest a consubstantial conflagration at the end of Behn's novella, which is itself a kind of valediction to the English colonial experiment in Surinam.

However tenuous a claim to historical accuracy Behn's *Oroonoko* makes,[21] it is still tethered in time and space to a recognizable scene of the Atlantic world, triangulated between the coordinates of England, Coramantien (Ghana), and Surinam. By contrast, Margaret Cavendish's *The Blazing World* ranges far afield in genre and setting. I raise the comparison to Cavendish's extra-terrestrial fiction last to illustrate how the explicitly fictional lens amplifies and detonates the fantasy embedded in these earlier scenes of projected mimetic fascination. Both Behn's and Cavendish's narratives feature a royal hero abducted from their homelands and translated to a New World. But whereas Behn's hero is burnt alive in Surinam, Cavendish's abducted Empress returns to conquer her native world by means of blazing pyrotechnics and her own dazzling appearance.

For Cavendish, herself a royalist supporter exiled during the civil wars, the imagined spectacle of the triumphant return of the imperial monarch makes aesthetic as well as political sense. What's more opaque is the equation of this spectacular presence—and transfixing luminescence—with devastating powers of destruction. On the morning that the war commences, the Empress appears "upon the face of the waters, dressed in her imperial robes…all of diamonds and carbuncles" (211). The thrall induced by the visual aspect of the Empress is as militarily strategic as it is aesthetically symbolic. The ships of the enemies are immobilized by the appearance of the Empress and her garments. They are rendered powerless to detect the Imperial "fishmen" who have secretly delivered a literally and lethally incandescent firestone that will burn as long as it is kept wet. The enemy ships go up in a great "flaming fire" and her countrymen proclaim the Empress "an angel sent from God" who will not return "until she [has forced] all the rest of that world to submit to that same nation" (211). This she does, in one orgy of fire after another. At the darkest hour of night, the Empress provides the evening's "entertainment," a display of ignited firestones that "put all spectators into an extreme fright, who verily believed, they should all be destroyed." The "entertainment" comes in the relief the Empress provides when, perceiving the terror evoked by the display of her weapons, she replaces them with her own image, dressed "in garments of light" (215).

Cavendish, whose prodigality and eccentricity of dress was well publicized both by her critics and herself,[22] dreams up the body incandescent as a beacon of nuclear light invested with the power of leveling total destruction and invoking absolute subjugation. Rather than endeavor to untangle the knot of author/narrator identification in this narrative,[23] I raise identification as a paradigm through which to examine the performative functions of the fantasy of the spectacular body in these episodes and representations of New World encounter. The obscured identities of these phantasmatic European bodies on display suggest that beyond functioning as imagined devices of subjection they are emblems of mimetic reflexivity—mirrors that "blaze back" the desire associated with their own curiosity.

In *Mimesis and Alterity*, Michael Taussig draws attention to the preoccupation with the native mimic that seems, time and again, to deliberately obscure European explorers' own mimetic predilections. Taussig notes Charles Darwin's eager anticipation of the native's legendary prowess and pleasure in mimicry. Darwin reports that the *Beagle* crew was greeted by Fuegian natives who patted and rubbed their own bodies, then the bodies of the Europeans, and were "highly pleased by the antics of a man belonging to the boat's crew, who danced well and was a good mimic."[24] The mimicry is reciprocal at the very least (the game, it seems, having been initiated by the crewman, not the native). "Who is mimicking whom," asks Taussig, "the sailor or the savage?" (76-7). Likening this question to the linguistic play between adults and infants (does the child learn to speak like a child because the parent mimes child-speech?) Taussig describes the dizzying reflexivity of this colonial performance, which goes "round and round… simulating and dissimulating at one and the same time for the sake of our epistemic health and the robust cheer of realness" (77).[25] He calls Darwin's sailor a reminder "of the pleasure, if not the need, the civilized have of such a savage mirror on the edge of the known world" (78).

For Taussig, mimesis and alterity are conjoined impulses: "a kind of electricity, an ac/dc pattern of rapid oscillations" that arbitrates a "psychaesthenic" experience of subjectivity (192). Taussig borrows the term from an essay by Roger Caillois on insect mimetic metamorphosis. In this essay, Caillois describes creatures that so effectively mimic grass they turn cannibalistic on one another, "browsing amongst their own."[26] Citing Caillois, Taussig describes the European colonist's encounter in the New World as the experience of a body "tempted by space: a drama in which the self is but a self-diminishing point amid others, losing its boundedness" (34). Caillois and Taussig remind us of the relationship between mimicry and incorporation, a drama related to consumption and cannibalism (not only at the entomological level) at the precipice between the self and not self.

In the literature of new world contact surveyed, we see the European chronicler divest the European protagonist of his or her curiosity in the other, collapsing and translating this surplus of mimetic interest onto native bodies instead. As if to temper the delight and awe of the gazing English (both at the scene of the encounter and for those gazing at these engravings at home) de Bry and Hariot place wonder in the hands of the Pomeiooc wives and daughters who are 'deligted' with European dolls and rattles. Behn's Surinami Indians absolve the colonists of their investment in the native body by turning their gaze on the wonder-inducing appearance of the English. Meanwhile, the narrator diverts our gaze onto the spectacle of the punished body—the body as object—that dares to "touch" back. Cavendish's apocalyptic chiaroscuro brings to mind Caillois's striking description of the psychaesthenic experience of being confounded by darkness:

> To these dispossessed souls, space seems to be a devouring force. Space pursues them, encircles them, digests them…It ends by replacing them. Then the body separates itself from thought, the individual breaks the boundary of his skin and occupies the other side of his senses. He tries to look at himself from any point whatever in space. He feels himself becoming space, dark space where things cannot be put. (30)

The psychasthenic's hyper-mimetic sensibility makes him aware of a generalized condition of his own similarity: "He is similar," says Caillois, "not similar to something, but just similar. And he invents spaces of which he is the convulsive possession" (30).

The Empress's ravenous appetite for natural philosophy in *The Blazing World* (which characterizes not only the better part of the narrative, but the expressly philosophical work to which it is appended) either culminates in or is curtailed by—depending on how one reads it—the turn from rampant curiosity to deflective and apocalyptically reflective imperialism. The fantasy of the radiant Empress in command of a nuclear arsenal of weapons made of light enfolds the mimetic urge into its own spectacular repudiation. The body refuses its position as a gazer upon alternative worlds and commands absolute awe instead, bringing the world to its knees in the darkness and holding the specter of its own luminary violence above its rapt subjects. However much the Empress's posture might resemble the posture generically associated with the colonial and, later, the imperial "collection," it calls too much attention to itself *as* posture to be read simply as a staging for the benefit of an awed "native" audience. Like the depictions of projected interest in the European body and commodity, this posture reveals its own discursive production in its deflective abjection of desires. Such abjection must be read as more immediately psychaesthenic and mimetic than simply acquisitive, and thus as more threatening to the histories of the colonial projects with which these early collections of new world objects were associated and the narratives we have come to tell about them.

CHAPTER THREE

THE ARK OF THE MUSEUM: EPISTEMOLOGICAL CHANGE IN JOHN TRADESCANT'S CABINET OF CURIOSITIES

JAN OLESEN

The New Museum of the History of Science has historical roots that can be traced back to the early moments of contemporary western science. The progressive nature of contemporary science often belies its humanist and artistic history. Early modern science worked without an evolutionary theory, and most natural philosophers believed nature recreated itself identically over and over since first creation. The natural world was perfect and eternal. Art urged a similar universalism, not yet "an autonomous sentimental tonality of the particular effect of art, but an indistinct presence of the grace that, in the work, put man's activity in tune with the divine world of creation."[1] In this moment art and science demonstrate deep mutual sympathies: where understanding the world was a process of understanding universal natural principles, appreciating art was a practice of recognizing universal aesthetic principles. Science eventually evolves in a direction quite different from art, but the culture of collection has much to tell us regarding these sympathies and their development. In early-modern England, collections housed both artistic and scientific objects, and the development of science and art can be traced through the practices of collection. This paper will examine the developmental trajectory of what begins as Tradescant's Ark to become *The New Museum of the History of Science*, arguing that it is a cite of the philosophical change from nature and art as universal and eternal, to subjective and contingent.

The earliest cabinets of curiosities grew out of the cult of relics, and contained religious artifacts, natural objects, and artistic productions. The haphazard display in most early modern cabinets of curiosities, or *Wunderkammer*, reflects a specific conception of the natural world and its relationship to art. In "The Cabinet of Wonder" Giorgio Agamben argues that early modern collectors understood the content and form of the natural world in specific ways. When discussing the *Wormianum* Agamben writes,

> Only seemingly does chaos reign in the *Wunderkammer* … : to the mind of the medieval scholar, it was a sort of microcosm that reproduced, in its harmonious confusion, the animal, vegetable, and mineral macrocosm. This is why the individual objects seem to find their meaning only side by side with others, between the walls of a room in which the scholar could measure at every moment the boundaries of the universe.[2]

The famous picture of the *Wormianum* he references is from 1655 (produced one year after Worm's death and after the Danish government took over control of the museum), and while Worm's collection was well known decades earlier, Agamben appears to deploy the term medieval a bit loosely. It's hard to think of any medievalist pushing the temporal boundaries of the period to the middle of the seventeenth century. His description of the presentation of Worm's collection is accurate, however, arguing that there is no particular order to the collection because there is no particular order to the natural world. This assessment does not attempt to order the chaos, but rather understands the chaos as a kind of order. By refusing a taxonomic order within the *Wunderkammer*, Agamben circumscribes the content as well, i.e. there is no reason to aspire to an exhaustive collection because any collection of artifacts reproduces the disorder of the world. There is also no reason to construct scientific or aesthetic categories, since the relationships of things are harmoniously confusing. The structure of the natural world as an ontological introjection (what Lacan would call nature as ego-ideal[3]), rather than a creative projection, leaves nature as objective and inert, removing any notion of aesthetic judgment. There is no subjective "art" impulse in the collection or the viewing. Agamben suggests further that the visitor to the *Wunderkammer* "had the aesthetic impression not that he was viewing a work of art but rather that he was measuring, more concretely for him, the borders of his world."[4]

For Agamben, at this point the perception of the cabinet, nature, and art, are governed by an essence. In "The Man of Taste and the Dialectic of the Split," Agamben argues that in the middle of the 17th century the concept of artistic taste, and a character he calls "the man of taste,"[5] emerges. This shift in the early modern world indicates a fundamental change in understanding art and science. Previous to the man of taste, art and nature are understood to be universal and eternal, and in possession of what Agamben describes as a soul. When art ceases to be a revelation of universal artistic principles the concept of taste springs into being, displacing the soul but creating a subjective presence. With this shift the essence or soul of the natural world begins to shift as well, and natural philosophers begin to understand the subjectivity of nature. Worm's apparent inattentiveness to or disregard for the structure of display is a product of understanding nature as essential and eternal. In this conception, it is important to note that essence reveals itself transparently to the observer. Things in the world are not a matter of perception or opinion, and neither is art. The individual patron to the *Wunderkammer* is not fazed by the construction of the cabinet, nor does he find it peculiar that artistic works are housed next to natural artifacts. At this point aesthetic perception is not personal, but objective. Artistic expression is not a representation of individual aesthetic principles; it is rather the revelation of universal principles. Art was not yet "an autonomous sentimental tonality of the particular effect of art, but an indistinct presence of the grace that, in the work, put man's activity in tune with the divine world of creation."[6] The artistic recreation of this originary moment was not individual expression, but the mimicry of the eternal.

The early modern period in England sees many changes to the concept of nature and art. The work of the apothecary, as with the gardener, was fundamentally underwritten by the belief that nature could be improved both aesthetically and otherwise. Blending certain herbs and plants was a process of manipulating nature to suit human needs, and members of the Royal society took great pride in ornate aesthetics of garden construction. The Royal society devoted itself to the development of Francis Bacon's natural philosophy. For Bacon, nature was not something obvious and self-revealing but protean and opaque. Bacon writes in *The Advancement of Learning* that, "For like as a man's disposition is never well known till he be crossed, nor Proteus ever changed shapes till he was straitened and held fast; so the passages and variations of nature cannot appear so fully in the liberty of nature, as in the trials and vexations of art."[7] Bacon understands nature as varied and passing, something that needs "art" (which in this case means scientific method) to be properly understood.

Francis Bacon's understanding of nature is revived significantly in his mammoth text *Novum Organon*, a text that demonstrates a new practice of understanding the world with homage to the old. Bacon's break with Aristotle's *Organon* precisely asserts that the world cannot be understood through abstract theory, but is instead understood through empiricism and experimentation. Bacon's model for knowledge through experience and experimentation was approved by some, but not all. There were those in the seventeenth century who saw human intervention as a distortion of nature. In "The Mower Against the Gardens," poet Andrew Marvell laments that the human imposition on the natural world will eventually result in a world where "No plant . . . kn[ows] the stock from whence it came."[8] As scientific practices progressed and demonstrated increasingly impressive results, art is increasingly distinguished from the scientific. In what follows, I will show how the collection of John Tradescant spans this aesthetic and intellectual divide, where the universal ark eventually becomes exclusive science.

Tradescant's Ark

What was to become *The New Museum of the History of Science* was initially informed by three central figures: John Tradescant the elder, his son John the younger, and Elias Ashmole. The history of the colourful relationship between these three figures (see below and note 7), and the murky ways in which Ashmole comes to own the collection, has left much open for debate, but the methods of collection of these various owners is relatively clear. Through the first half of the seventeenth century, John the Elder found employment as a gardener and apothecary. Quickly progressing through appointments with a series of wealthy Englishmen, the elder Tradescant eventually gains employment with George Villiers, the Duke of Buckingham from 1623 to 1628. Before his employment with Buckingham, there is no clear evidence that there was an aesthetic structure to the collection at all. At this point Tradescant's collection primarily consists of plant life, and is largely kept outdoors. It is Tradescant's own private collection, and certainly functioned largely as a nursery to supplement and support his gardening tasks. It is only after his move to Lambeth in 1628 that he collects and maintains curiosities in his house. It is also in Lambeth that the collection becomes The Ark. The earliest examples of objects in the Ark attest to a desire for wonder, as Tradescant writes to Edward Nicholas for his desire for "any thing that is strange."[9] As a result, the Tradescants moved far afield in search of rare and strange objects, and "the younger is said to have brought back humming birds and beetles"[10] from the new world.

When Tradescant the younger takes over the museum after his father's death, the Ark has become a well-known collection across Europe. Tradescant the younger was also trained as an apothecary and inherited his father's collection, and critical opinion is divided about who is the more significant collector.[11] The younger is credited with adding fewer artifacts than his father, but is responsible for perhaps the most exotic one, Powhaton's Mantle and Wampum belt.[12] The younger's impact on the Ark and the culture of collection, however, lies as much with his achievements as it does with his mistakes. His plans for hereditary succession for the collection are derailed with the premature death of his only son, John III. With the legacy of the museum in doubt, John strikes up a hasty friendship with Elias Ashmole. The relationship between the two families begins when Ashmole offers to aid in creating and printing a catalogue of the Ark. The *Musæum Tradescantianum, a Collection of Rarities* is published in 1656. Shortly after the publication of the catalogue a deed of gift was presented to Ashmole stating he was to obtain possession of the collection after the death of both John and Hester. The deed explains that Ashmole was a suitable recipient because of his keen understanding of the value of the collection, and his generous help in creating the catalogue. The transition was anything but smooth. On two separate occasions John names different beneficiaries; his first will names the crown but is later changed to either Oxford or Cambridge.[13] After John's death, Hester refuses to acknowledge the deed of gift, and claims it was coerced by John after a night of drinking. But after a short legal battle, Ashmole is named the rightful beneficiary and takes possession two years after Hester is found mysteriously drowned in her pond in 1678.

The biblical echo in the name of the Ark has some misleading implications for the content of the collection and for the philosophy that underwrites its makeup before Ashmole takes possession. The biblical ark has a clear and exhaustive mandate, and its purpose was preservation: Because God was destroying the earth, Noah was to preserve the *righteous people*, two of every clean animal, and seven of every unclean animal (Gen. 7: 2-6, emphasis mine). Tradescant's collection does not come near these mythological dimensions, nor is there a clear edict for collection. The presumed orderliness of the biblical ark is not represented in Tradescant's Ark either. While there are no pictures of the Ark, there are references from those who visited it comparing its structure to other famous Cabinets. In *The Origins of Museums: The Cabinet of Curiosities in Sixteenth- and Seventeenth-Century Europe*, Oliver Impey and Arthur MacGregor suggest that many who visited Tradescant's collection would have been familiar with other European cabinets of wonder. He suggests that geometrician and medical professor Rasmus Bartholin, after visiting both Ole Worm's and Tradescant's collections, vastly preferred Worm's to Tradescant's.[14] This is perhaps not surprising, as both Worm and Bartholin share the same Danish national identity, but his assessment relies on a constitutive similarity to expose a qualitative disparity; the structure and organization between Tradescant's and Worm's collection must have maintained some affinity for a comparison to be made at all. Worm's *Museum Wormianum* is a chaotic assemblage of *naturalia* and *artificialia*, displayed any which way: Stuffed alligators hang from the ceiling, a narwhal horn is next to a petrified egg, which is in turn next to sea shells and assorted plant specimens (see Fig. 3-1). In some cases, as with both Worm and Tradescant, various indigenous peoples are included as part of the collection, stuffed whole or parts pickled.

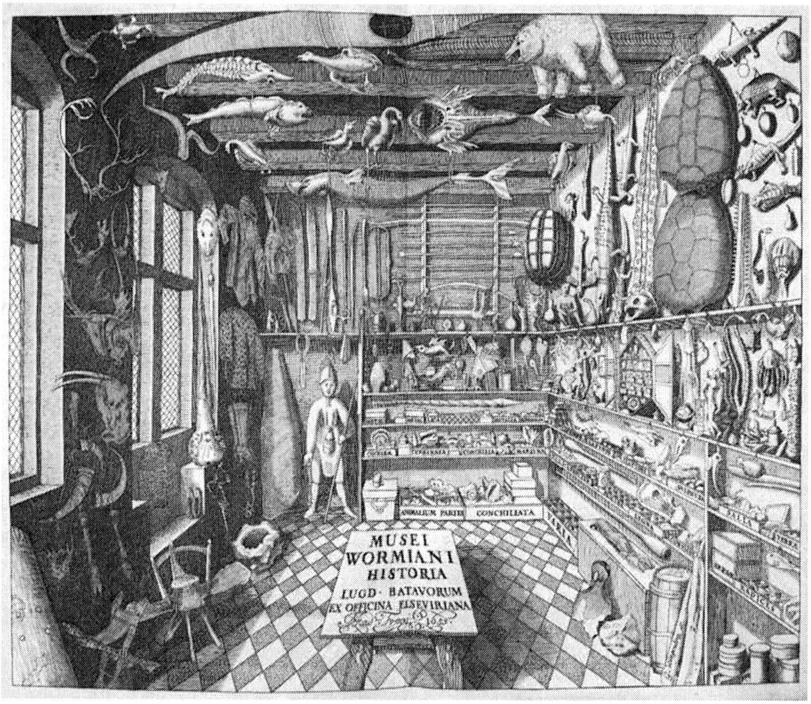

Fig. 3-1: Frontispiece to Ole Worm's
Museum Wormianum seu historia rerum rariorum

Compared with Noah's ark, the concept of preservation clearly takes on an alternate meaning in Tradescant's collection. The slippage in the term turns preservation into death. Tradescant's ark preserves elements of the natural world for knowledge. In the Ark, specimens set immobile on a pin or drowned in the pickling juice lose any subjective presence, becoming objects of study. The artifacts held within the Ark, both plant and animal, are open to the gaze of the visitor. Here, the soul of the artifact is fixed at the moment of death, frozen as a curio for delight, and perhaps confusion, of the intellectual and casual observer alike.

When in the possession of the Tradescants the Ark is ordered in the way Agamben suggests, but it is unlikely that it had any ambitions to present a universal picture of the world. As a commercial venture, a very different set of interests and concerns conscribe the governance of the early Ark. With the move to Lambeth the Tradescants publish a small booklet of the contents, and open the Ark to the public, charging 6d for admission. This is the first instance in England of an advertised and formally enforced entrance fee for admission to a museum, and the fee for admission changes the hierarchy of observation; the museum and its contents become commodities, the content mediated through the ideology of capitalism and collector. When Walter Benjamin reflects somewhat jokingly on the soul of the commodity, he describes the commodity as desiring the consumer, not the other way around: "If the soul of the commodity which Marx occasionally mentions in jest existed, it would be the most empathetic ever encountered in the realm of souls, for it would have to see in everyone the buyer in whose hand and in whose house it wants to nestle."[15] The commodity for the Tradescants is the museum itself, and its desire, along with the Tradescants, is to draw people to pay to see the collection. Thoughts of the collector must necessarily turn towards the audience and an understanding of what delights and draws the multitude to pay-per-view. The concept of the audience takes on a new resonance as well. Oddly enough, this is an instance where commodity culture has a democratizing effect. With the implementation of a mandatory but easily affordable fee for entrance, access to the museum is no longer only the prerogative of experts, academics, and the Tradescants' personal acquaintances. Visiting the Ark soon became less a measure of cultural or intellectual sophistication, than a dalliance for the masses. Because later curators would rely on gate receipts and in-museum instruction for their livelihood, expert opinion of the Ashmolean museum becomes less favorable, in part because of a perceived devolution in its quality, and also because of the necessary undesirable mixing with the rabble. This progresses to the point where German Scholar Zacharias Conrad von Uffenbach reschedules a visit to the museum because the upper room was overcrowded with what he derisively refers to as countryfolk [Weilbsleute vom Lande].[16]

Once in possession of the Ark, Ashmole quickly amalgamates his collection, which consisted mostly of coins and manuscripts, and makes arrangements to donate the collection to Oxford. Conditional for the donation was the construction of a specific building. The collection shifts yet again with this move, from private collection to public institution. This shift had already begun in part with the admission charge to The Ark, the donation of the collection to Oxford formalizes the museum as public space, and marks a move from private to public ownership. The attention to the detail in the physical makeup of the building shows that the disordered order that once reigned in the early Ark is giving way to a notion of taxonomic order. Ashmole's attention to the construction of the museum, creating ten separate rooms, chimneys for ventilation, a series of drawers for smaller curiosities, and specific wainscotting and paint schemes indicate a growing perception of the impact/effect of display.[17] Curatorial directives also change, again from private to public domain. Ashmole writes a constitution governing future acquisitions, and cedes directorship, creating a chair for the museum to curate and oversee collection and cataloguing. The methods of collection, once the sole domain of John Tradescant's personal experience, are now directed by policy. The collection itself, once passed on genealogically is now adjudicated through adherence to a charter. The museum itself becomes more diverse in its interests, using one room for anatomy study, and another for natural history in league with the principles of the Royal Society, and a library where all print media were stored. Here again the development of the museum and display shows a nuanced fissure, where collection moves towards formal principles of collection and with an increased awareness of the aesthetic value of display.

The significance of the charter and the construction of a new building indicates a further shift in the perception of collection. Distinguishing art from science is now in full swing. Where once art and natural objects were housed together without question, now the disciplines of art and science begin to distinguish themselves from one another. Commentary from visitors at the time also shows that patrons were beginning to understand art and science as mutually exclusive entities. When several elements destined for the Ashmolean museum end up at the Bodleian and anatomy museum, Conrad Uffenbach remarks that the anatomy school contained many specimens "which do not belong at all to an anatomical museum, but would be much more suitable to an art gallery like the Ashmolean museum."[18] Tradescant's collection is now understood to be an artistic production, a projection of personal, subjective aesthetic taste rather than a showcase of external, hard reality. The very existence of a mandate for collection demonstrates the idea of transparent collection logically inaccurate. If the natural world fits together in a Deleuzian rhisomatic chaos[19], there is no need to present rules for its collection. If understanding the natural world is as simple as visiting a cabinet of curiosities, through which the viewer could "measure at every moment the boundaries of the universe," there would be no need for an expert curator to guide the visitor through the museum. The moment of the constitution of the Ashmolian museum marks the shift in the cabinet and viewer, where the natural world becomes a subject of study and displaces the eternal essence and soul.

It is this moment where the soul recedes from the object where ethics becomes possible. In *The Coming Community*, Agamben suggests that the idea of ethics can only exist once essence is extinguished. Agamben writes, "if humans were or had to be this or that substance, this or that destiny, no ethical experience could be possible—there would be only tasks to be done."[20] For the viewer in the cabinet of curiosities, or in the more modern conception of historical museum, the absence of essence is the cultivation of taste. Aesthetic education is the beginning of ethics both in the knowledge of the subjective construction of the viewing experience, and the personal response that arises from it. The aesthetic imagination is the key to personal responsibility in the knowledge of the provisionality of this subjective position, a position that is in constant flux.

Regardless of whether Ashmole was the cunning deceiver or an honest collector, the trajectory of what was initially the Ark demonstrates profound changes to the perceptions of art and the natural world. As scientific practices become increasingly compartmentalized, the scientific relationship to art becomes all the more distant. But artistic collections too have diversified in remarkable ways, and collections have shifted from a single space that purports to represent a microcosm of the macrocosm to a myriad of different collections. From museums of culture, art galleries, museums of natural science, to the freakatorium, the interests that underwrite collection are diverse and specific. As collection continues to grapple with its subjective, contingent nature, visitors to respective collections are confronted with the subjective experience, one that should continue to ask patrons to define their subjective position within it. Elias Ashmole's epitaph in Lambeth church eulogizes the collector, stating, "while the Ashmolean museum endures he will never die." And while the idea of an artist living on through the artistic production is not a new idea, the fact that Ashmole, perhaps unwittingly, presented a method of collection in constant change, self reflexively re-evaluating the properties of itself, demonstrates that his gift may lie beyond the limits of the material collection in Oxford.

CHAPTER FOUR

BOTCHED ANIMALS AND ENIGMATIC BEASTS

RACHEL POLIQUIN

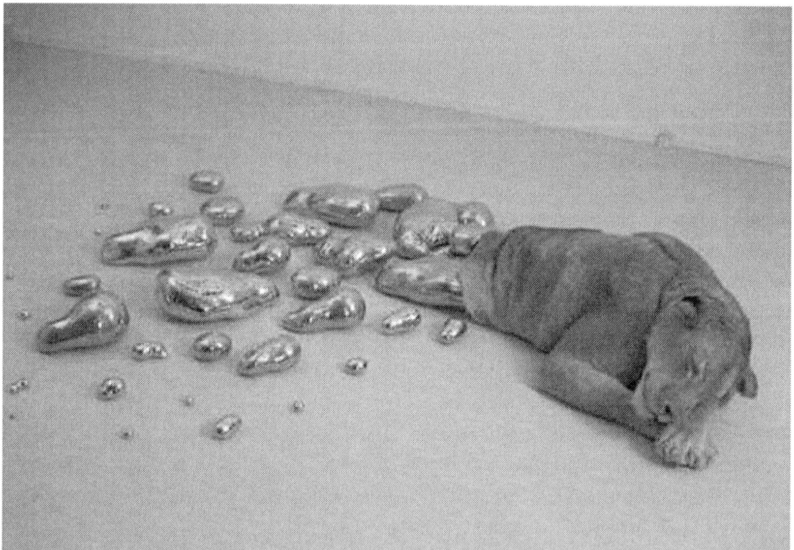

Fig 4-1: Ophelia by the Idiots , 2005. Reprinted with permission by the Idiots.

On the white floor of the gallery, a lioness is sleeping, her head resting on her crossed paws, her ears softly turned downwards. She is relaxed, at peace. But there is only half of her, the front half, beautifully taxidermied, which disappears into—or perhaps emerges from—the globules of gold arcing away from her middle section. Evocatively entitled *Ophelia* after the tragic heroine of William Shakespeare's *Hamlet*, the work is a collaborative creation by Dutch artists Afke Golsteijn, Ruben Taneja and Floris Bakker.

Ophelia brings to mind Stephen Greenblatt's description of wonder as "the power of the displayed object to stop the viewer in his or her tracks, to convey an arresting sense of uniqueness, to evoke an exalted attention." [1] In contrast to Greenblatt's resonance—the way an item engages viewers in the cultural network from which it emerged—wonder arouses a sort of "enchanted looking," a spellbinding visual infatuation. Yet while a wonder might evoke strange imaginings and fantastical visions, it always draws viewers back—binds them, so to speak—to its very real, very concrete presence. In a sense, a wonder hovers between material proof and imaginative possibility, between what the eyes say must be so and what the brain cannot believe is so. And this is certainly the case with *Ophelia.* Escaped from between the covers of a book of fairy tales, the lioness and the gold float between palpable materiality and poetic imagination.

The strangeness of *Ophelia* draws dramatic attention to the ways the aesthetics of an object influence how the object is read and appreciated, that is, to the relationship between the qualities and characteristics of an object's physical form (size, materials, harmony of its parts, craftsmanship, means of manufacturing, beauty, ugliness, etc.) and what sort of information viewers can and do decipher while in its presence. Confronted by half a lioness liquefying into blobs of gold, the empiricist has little to offer. Rather, the allegorist is required, who, in Walter Benjamin's words, has "given up the attempt to elucidate things through research into their properties and relations" and instead "relies on his profundity to illuminate their meaning."[2] Has the lioness fallen under some enchantment or is she dreaming herself into existence? Or is this an alchemical vision of matter being transformed into the purest of elements, or a more sinister transformation of nature's vitality into capital? To read allegory is, in a sense, to learn to dream, to read within and beyond what is visually apparent, to read oneself. After all, the responsibility of elucidating an allegory lies not with the author but with the reader. Its truth cannot be spelled out but realised by a sort of quickening, a flash of experiential understanding. Ultimately viewers are left to make meaning of *Ophelia* from their own reservoir of images.

However and crucially, this dream creature would not be the same if the lioness had been made from ceramics or carved from wood. Paradoxically, without the potent materiality of half a lioness—a genuine, unfeigned, dead creature—*Ophelia* could hardly have cast the same sense of wonder: it is *because* and not despite this raw presence that reason and reality seem to quaver. More precisely still, the visual power of *Ophelia* is due to the artists' flawless construction. If the skin had been badly mounted or the creature's face roughly formed, the spell would have been broken, and the resonance (to use Greenblatt's term) of the piece would have superseded its wonder. The purposeful display of a badly prepared specimen would have drawn attention away from the poetic possibilities of the piece and towards the ethics of animals in art: where did this lion come from, a zoo or the wild? How did it die? How was it prepared? Was it purchased or donated to the artists? In short, the aesthetics of rough and ready taxidermy force viewers to consider the conditions of the lioness' appropriation rather than facilitate an enchanted looking. As Steve Baker emphasizes in his analysis of animals and animal parts in contemporary art, "regardless of any ethical stance, *materials count*."[3] Materials certainly do count, particularly when it comes to organic materials and more particularly with preserved natural specimens. As we will see, the aesthetics of preservation always dictate what sort of imaginative or empirical understandings can be gained.

***

By highlighting the frailty of any line dividing observed reality and poetic imagination, *Ophelia*—an ambiguous animal, a mysterious hybrid—gives twenty-first century viewers a taste for the mesmerizing shock of the unknown experienced by sixteenth- and seventeenth-century collectors of curiosities. By the mid-sixteenth century, a seemingly endless flow of wonderful things from increasingly distant parts of the world spilled out of European ports and into the collections of dedicated naturalists and dilettantes alike. Whatever was rare in occurrence, exotic in origin, or in any way unusual or curious, prodigious or outlandish was avidly collected. The intrinsic visual interest of items such as those in the etching of Ferrante Imperato's cabinet from 1599—a two headed dog, a two-headed snake, an armadillo, a lizard with two bodies—set them apart from the mundane world outside the cabinet's walls and, like *Ophelia*, offered only tantalising suggestions of nature's secret workings.

Over the course of the seventeenth century, cabinets of curiosities developed from wonder chambers to storehouses for empirical investigations about the natural world. The act of collecting became a key component to erudition and an essential practice for naturalists, who hoped, as Paula Findlen underscores, that "their possession of nature eventually would precipitate an understanding of her contents." [4] But how objective knowledge (rather than wonder) was to be extracted from desiccated parts of little known creatures was not immediately evident. While the wonder-effect—that breakdown of reason and understanding—of *Ophelia* stems from flawless taxidermy, the same effect was produced in early cabinets by poor preservation techniques. In this essay, I investigate the sort of information that could be extracted from the animals in early collections and suggest that bad taxidermy and botched animals made for truculent objects. While always offering the anticipation of knowledge, some objects prove too opaque to decipher without a little reverie.

Botched Animals

The collection of the Holy Roman Emperor Rudolf II contained the leg of a cassowary, feathers from at least sixteen birds of paradise, the foot of a sparrow hawk with thirteen claws, and the pelt of a white vulture from India. Among the curiosities in the collection of the Veronese apothecary Francesco Calzolari were a mummified deformed human head, a bat, a flying fish, an assortment of eggs, and a spotted creature with enormous claws. Displayed in the entrance of the Leiden anatomical theatre were an elephant's head, the skin and horn of a rhinoceros, a dog's skeleton, a heron, the snout of an unknown fish, and the bristly skin of a Brazilian beast. Affectionately known as "the Ark," the collection of John Tredescant and his son contained a flying squirrel, the testicles of a beaver, a pelican, a dodo, a wild cat from Virginia, and an egg that was suspected to be from a dragon. The natural specimens listed in Sir Hans Sloane's collection, which established the foundation of the British Museum, were a hair ball from the stomach of a cow, the skin of a polecat, a feather of a condor, a white swallow from Buenos Aires, the bill of a toucan, the back part of an ostrich's eye, the trunk and eyes of an elephant that died of consumption in Middlesex, and two cataracts taken out of the eyes of a blind arctic fox that had lived in Sloane's garden for several years.[5]

As the list suggests, the term "Cabinet of Curiosities" promiscuously encompasses a broad range of collections from princely antechambers and Renaissance cabinets of wonders to early modern repositories of material facts and their varying cultural, ideological, and epistemological motivations for collecting natural objects. Spanning approximately a century and a half from the mid-sixteenth century to the early eighteenth, such cabinets are hemmed by two separate traditions of collecting, the one leading backwards in time to a world resonant with the power of relics, mystical visions, and ancient lore, the other pointing towards what would slowly germinate and sprout into the ordered, systematic fields of science, empirical observations, and facts. Krzysztof Pomian has described this age as an interim period between the authoritative rule of religion and that of science, a period over which curiosity held court, and even more particularly, an age which acknowledged that inquiry necessitated a collection.[6]

Regardless of the impetus for collecting or the ways the objects were deciphered, as Svetlana Alpers has noted, what was gathered into cabinets "was judged to be of visual interest."[7] But, and equally importantly, what lingered on display was dependent on its susceptibility to moths, ants, maggots, rot, dampness, and mould. Whether institutional or private, whether spurred by natural philosophy, wonder, or social prestige, the natural specimens displayed in cabinets remained constant well into the eighteenth century: snouts, testicles, cataracts, feathers, and bristly skins. In other words, bits and pieces of animals that offered the barest glimpse of nature's forms; objects more inclined to breed awe and wonder then natural facts.

Much critical attention has been paid to the cultural and political resonance of these natural artefacts and the expansive intellectual networks within which they were circulated, appraised, and comprehended, but little thought has been given to what the objects actually looked like. Before the widespread use of arsenic paste in the early nineteenth century, which effectively deterred insects, collections always quivered on the brink of dissolution.[8] While minerals, barks, and most plant materials were easily gathered, shipped, and exhibited, fleshy items proved endlessly problematic. Pieces of animals not susceptible to decay such as horns, bones, antlers, teeth, beaks, claws, feathers, eggs, tanned skins, parts preserved in spirits, balls of hair and calcitic deposits were more frequently displayed than complete animals, and the animals that were preserved whole were frequently not well formed. Many creatures were exotic and little known, and the skins shipped back to Europe from abroad were often ambiguous lumps of fur or feathers, sometimes already decaying or infested with worms. As Karen Wonders points out, simply stuffing a skin does not guarantee an accurate re-creation: "[w]ithout having seen the living animal, it was just as difficult to create a life-like mount as it was to represent the animal in a pictorial image."[9] Even with well-known animals, the fleshier parts such as lips, muzzles, and wattles shrunk and cracked with periodic baking, the only known means of curbing insect infestation. With shriveled lips and malformed bodies, sometimes blackened by tar and smoked into filthy lumps, most creatures in cabinets of curiosity were mere caricatures of the animals' former glory.

Bad Taxidermy

The earliest preservation method was mummification by dehydration. Essentially, mummification prevents putrefaction by allowing the body to release moisture slowly; the skin and muscles become rigid, and the tissues shrink, adhering to the skeleton. Most of the fish, snakes, and lizards in early collections would have been mummified, that is, air-dried or slowly baked in ovens, rubbed with various caustic substances, salts, and spices and then lacquered into a hard and shiny shell. Not removing animals' flesh, however, left specimens vulnerable to rot, insects, and fungal attack. Nevertheless, mummification and embalming whole animals with spices continued well into the eighteenth century.

Among the first taxidermy instructions is Friedrich II's description of how to preserve a crane's wing from the thirteenth century. The wing had to be removed from the bird, all the flesh removed, and the skin rubbed with potash to prevent maggots and decay. The wing was then to be "hung in the chimney until the moisture in the flesh has completely evaporated. Although those wings that are not smoked are always more beautiful and glossier they will not last as long."[10] This basic method of preservation hardly advanced over the next three centuries. In 1555, Pierre Belon suggests opening birds longitudinally, removing their innards, spreading salt in the cavity, and hanging the bird to dry, while in the same year Conrad Gessner suggested filling the cavity with wool and volatile oils.[11] Mark Catesby suggested sprinkling snuff inside the gutted bird before baking it in an oven.[12] Naturalists all had their favorite concoction of astringents which included pepper and hot spices like cloves and ginger, salt, sulphur, resinous gums such as frankincense and myrrh, potassium nitrate (known as saltpetre), potash, alum, volatile herbs and oils, snuff, and alcohol. Frankincense and myrrh were the most expensive and effective preservatives. The bitter smell of myrrh masked smells emanating from dead animals while its anti-fungal and anti-septic properties helped maintain the conditions of stuffed skins. Likewise frankincense, a sticky white resin, has a fresh, pine-lemon scent and acts as a natural insecticide.

In the final years of the seventeenth century, the English naturalist and collector John Petiver attached as appendix to a catalogue of his collection one of first extensive preservation instructions for travelling collectors and merchants hoping to profit from the lucrative skin trade. In Petiver's opinion, the best method to protect specimens on long sea voyages was alcohol. "*All small Animals, as Beasts, Birds, Fishes, Serpents, Lizards,* and other *Fleshy Bodies* capable of *Corruption*" were to be preserved in rum, brandy or any other high proof spirit. If no alcohol was available then a strong brine of sea water would do, supplemented with 3 or 4 handfuls of salt to every gallon of water with the addition of a spoonful or two of alum powder if possible. The specimen was then put in a bottle, corked and rosined.[13] The entrails were to be removed from larger birds and their bodies stuffed with flax, hemp, or some other fibrous material mixed with pitch or tar—a mixture known as oakum, the same material that was used to plug holes in sea-going vessels. The bird should be dried in the sun, wrapped tightly, and kept from moisture, the latter being not an easy enterprise on board ship. On long sea voyages, the ruinous consequences of moisture could be staved off by baking stuffed birds gently every month or so, "to kill the *Vermin* which often breed in them."[14] If the bird was too large to preserve whole, Petiver suggested that just the bird's head, legs or wings would suffice. From these murky oven-baked tar-smeared birds and animals, naturalists—perhaps without any idea of the animals' original shapes—fashioned animals for their cabinets. Preservation techniques hardly advanced over the following decades, and well through the eighteenth century naturalists continually lamented the poor quality of specimens on display. Writing in 1770, Thomas Kuckhan deplored the typical specimen as "a poor shriveled-up dried carcase of a bird, in which neither the natural shape, dimensions, or colours are preserved, and which continually excites the disagreeable idea of the poor thing's having been starved to death on purpose."[15]

Of course not all animals were badly prepared. In his travels through England in 1710, Zacharias Conrad von Uffenbach noted "a very beautiful stuffed reindeer" in the Ashmolean collection in Oxford.[16] The Swedish naturalist Peter Kalm was similarly impressed with the birds in Sir Hans Sloane collection during his visit in 1748, noting particularly several stuffed birds that "stood fast on bits of board as naturally as if they had still lived" and hummingbirds "set in their nests under glass as though they had been living."[17] But even the best specimens were sadly short lived, particularly birds whose skins were smaller and more fragile than mammals, and no match for insects and rot. In fact, when Elias Ashmole drew up a set of rules for the governance and maintenance of the Ashmolean Museum in 1686, he included regulations for dealing with the inevitable. Article 6 stipulated that "whatsoever naturall Body that is rare, whether Birds, Insects, Fishes or the like, apt to putrefie & decay with tyme" was to be drawn and coloured by a skilled artist so that if—rather, when—the specimen decayed into nothingness, some document would remain. Article 8 required that "as any particular growes old & perishing, the Keeper may remove it into one of the Closets, or other repository; &

some other to be substituted."[18] As a classic piece of natural history lore, Article 8 was followed too well when in 1755, the curator decided to burn the museum's decomposing or nondescript specimens. Among the victims was a badly stuffed dodo, which was the last surviving taxidermied specimen in the world. Only the charred head and a foot were salvaged.

Imagination and Science

In all truth, the wizened creatures left a lot to the imagination, which was in a sense precisely their power, at least in early cabinets of wonder. While increasingly based on the meticulous observation of specimens, Renaissance speculations about the natural world remained tied to mythology and etymology, poetics and metaphysics, sympathies and antipathies between objects. When it came to zoology, these poetic explanations were encouraged by the raw aesthetics of specimens. With just a beak or a hide or a few brilliant feathers, naturalists were forced to imagine the rest of the creature. Poetry supplemented natural philosophy when objects proved too opaque, and creative interpretation filled in the gaps of limited material evidence. Rudimentary taxidermy opened vistas of allegorical potential and possibility.

Poetic explanations of phenomena were not necessarily incompatible with empirical investigation and taxonomical ordering. As David Freedberg explains in a fascinating essay on Giovanni Battista Ferrari's 1646 treatise on citrus fruits, *Hesperides, sive De malorum Aureorum,* no more exhaustive work on a single family of plant had yet appeared before *Hesperides*. In fact, Freedberg stresses, Ferrari's work stands as one of the most noteworthy taxonomic attempts of any single genus of fruits before Linnaeus. Yet, when baffled by strange citrus forms that seemed to defy all of nature's known laws, Ferrari invented stories to explain them, stories which were frequently fanciful and often derived from literary tradition: "[t]he poetic imagination, harnessed by the rules of rhetoric, became a heuristic tool to supplement empirical logic and the limited evidence of the eyes." [19] Similarly, Paula Findlen has highlighted "the imaginative possibilities of natural phenomena" elaborated in Benedetto Ceruti and Andrea Chioco's overtly baroque catalogue of Calzolari's cabinet published in 1622.[20] Without some form of preservation, many exotic specimens wouldn't have been known at all, but the general inability to maintain the physical condition of wonders from distant lands only increased their obscurity, strangeness, and spell-binding fascination.

Not all seventeenth-century naturalists were as keen to invent and perpetuate mythological explanations, and none less keen than the English philosopher, essayist, and statesman Francis Bacon. Attempting to overthrow ancient lore and deductive reasoning, Bacon's inductive philosophy promoted gathering natural facts through observation, investigation, and experimentation. The new natural philosopher accumulated knowledge slowly and carefully, without preconceptions or prejudice, and especially without rushing to generalisations.

However, not even Bacon was sure which facts would ultimately prove useful, and Bacon determined that all entities and occurrences were worthy of study, material or ephemeral, mundane or rare. No subject was too lowly or coarse to be well observed and marked down in what Bacon termed a Table of Discovery since the importance of things "is not to be measured by what they are worth in themselves, but according to their indirect bearing upon other things and the influence they may have upon philosophy."[21] Bacon's empirical method erected a utopian dream of comprehensive knowledge on a foundation of isolated particulars: knowledge was not garnered whole but was achieved piece by piece, fact by fact. In other words, leg bones, botched taxidermy, and strange animal parts were worthy of serious philosophical investigation.

Bacon's writings were taken as a robust call to action by English naturalists. In great part to perpetuate his philosophies of observation and experimentation, the Royal Society of London for Improving Natural Knowledge was established in 1660. Soon after the Society was settled at Gresham College, members rapidly began accumulating a collection of natural specimens. By 1681, when Nehemiah Grew's catalogue of the Repository was published, the collection housed an unruly swarm of animal morsels: hair balls, the heart of a sea-tortoise, an otter, the "pistle" of a beaver, the leg of a dodo, the skin of a monstrous calf with two heads, various strange hooves, and the tails of a rhinoceros, an Indian cow, and a beaver. Of the animals and birds specimens (not including amphibians and lizards), Grew lists forty-one whole creatures and one hundred and twenty-four parts. Ironically, the new empirical methodology of amassing isolated facts was frequently forced to study mere bits and pieces of animals. So how was knowledge to be squeezed out of these enigmatic shards?

While Grew was faced with the same sort of materially obscure things as those that evoked wonder and allegory from earlier collectors, emboldened by Bacon's philosophy, Grew considered the materials as "a great aboundance of matter for any Man's Reason to work upon."[22] He diligently documentated the length, size, shape, and any distinguishing feature of both whole creatures and their smallest parts. The detail of each entry, however, varies considerably from a single line to several pages, and it is tempting to suggest that length of entry was dependent on the quality of specimen.

Yet Bacon's philosophy did not consist in mere descriptions of things. Bacon encouraged naturalists to look *through* materials in order to access a deeper understanding of processes and laws. For example, in his *Abecedarium naturae* or Alphabet book of Nature, Bacon proposed to pursue nature down to her fundamental building blocks—the letters or laws of nature. While the overly hasty deductive method had drawn conclusions from one or two letters and therefore hopelessly bungled the reading, Bacon insists on the necessity of studying nature piece by piece, letter by letter, observing all instances of such elementary properties as density, vacuity, and whiteness. Such properties, laws, or as Bacon termed them, forms, were endlessly interchangeable and combinable, and like letters of the alphabet, gave rise to all the multiplicity of things and motions in the world.

Strangely enough the material limitations on what sorts of objects naturalists were able to collect and preserve became a step towards comparative anatomy. Rather than attempting to decipher fragments metonymically—as pieces of obscure wholes—naturalists began to approach fragments as illuminating instances of underlying functions and mechanical principles. The tails of the rhinoceros, cow, and beaver in the Society's Repository, for example, gave some idea not of the animals to which they once belonged but of the principles and uses of tails. As Grew notes, a horse "being much pester'd with Flyes … should have a long brush Tail to whisk them off. Whereas the Ass, which either for the hardness and dryness of his Skin, or other Cause, is less annoy'd with them, hath no need of such an one." Likewise, the naturalist who observes that "the ears of a greyhound are pricked while those of a hound hang down" will also be able to reason that the former hunts with his ears and the latter with his nose.[23] Reason was harnessed to imagination, not to invent poetic narratives from animal parts but rather to see through those parts and contemplate the similarities and differences between animals' basic functions, which in turn would hopefully reveal the underlying essences and deeper inner workings of nature's engine.

Although armed with new empirical methodologies and full of optimism, seventeenth-century naturalists nevertheless remained blocked by obscure bits and pieces of botched and decomposing creatures. Materials endlessly dictated the sort of examinations and conclusions observers were able to make; no matter how pragmatically and objectively naturalists approached certain specimens, if those creatures were fragmentary or rotting, little useful knowledge could be squeezed out.

Like *Ophelia*, some objects prove too opaque to decipher by purely empirical means.

From early cabinets of wonder to philosophical repositories, collections of curiosities never displayed knowledge. Rather, they acted as warehouses of potentiality. Each curious fragment individually offered the possibility of some unknown, undiscovered clue about nature's laws, and together a curious collection quivered not with knowledge but its anticipation. Whether naturalists were seeking allegorical or empirical truths, the objects themselves were never transparent enough. Like Noah's ark, that archetypal collection, afloat and swirling on an uncharted sea of thought, without any sure sense of where it was heading, collections of curiosities led viewers on voyages of discovery for which reason and reality needed a little help from the imagination to fill in the bleary shapes on the horizon.

CHAPTER FIVE

A CURIOUS COMMODITY: ANTOINE GALLAND'S *ARABIAN NIGHTS' ENTERTAINMENTS*

AMANDA KENNY

The English translation of Antoine Galland's *Les Mille et une Nuits*, the *Arabian Nights' Entertainments* (1706?-1721), was a popular text that appeared in numerous eighteenth-century editions. It also rewards close literary analysis and comparison to other relevant eighteenth-century works. However, little in the printed reception history clearly shows that eighteenth-century British readers approached the *Arabian Nights* as a work of great literary significance. In fact, much of the commentary and many of the references to it are reductive and vague. There is a sense in the printed record that it was a work many knew about, and perhaps even owned, but few had read in its entirety. Instead, the text seems to become a symbol of the East in the broadest sense, a falsely authoritative source of information on various Eastern nations and cultures, and a way of describing anything out of the ordinary. The book was more advertised than reviewed, until the end of the century, and serious literary critics and notable authors were more likely to be dismissive than celebratory. Henry Fielding, in a famous example, referred to the *Arabian Nights* disparagingly in Book III of *Joseph Andrews* (1742) in his "Matter prefatory in praise of biography." For Fielding it was an example of the literature produced by authors who do not "copy nature" but instead form "originals from the confused heap of matter in their own brains."[1] Reasonable readers might disagree about the justice of Fielding's remarks; nevertheless, his response corresponds to that of many contemporary critics and commentators. Notably, whether positive or negative, early responses to the *Arabian Nights* tended to obscure or fail to mention the details and variety of the text, and many comments even suggest that the person writing had not even read the text. In essence, the evidence suggests that this was a text that was more likely to be collected as a curiosity than devoured as literature.

A Certain Ubiquity

Commentary upon the *Arabian Nights' Entertainments* often emphasizes its common presence in eighteenth-century popular culture. James Beattie, for example, states that "the Arabian Nights Entertainment [sic] is a book which most young people in this country are acquainted with."[2] The *London Magazine*, or the *Gentleman's Monthly Intelligencer* review of Denis Dominique Cardonne's *Miscellany of Eastern Learning* (1771) begins: "The Arabian Nights Entertainments, and other translations from the Oriental Languages, have been received by the publick with an extraordinary degree of favour." The reviewer, without going into details, attributes that favor to "the manner in which they are written" and "the nature of the subject."[3] Readers curious about the manner or subject of the text would have to read for themselves to discover it.

Similarly, an unidentified writer commented confidently in an account of three adventurers and their acquittal at the Old Bailey, "[t]here is no doubt but the reader has perused the History of the seven Champions of Christendom, the Arabian Nights Entertainments, and the History of the Great Man Mountain recorded by Swift, of facetious memory…."[4] The author of the *Loiterer* offers a bit more detail in his mention of the text. He "remember[s] having read in the Arabian Nights Entertainments (and I dare say most of my readers do the same) that Caliph Haroun Alraschid used frequently to go about in disguise, that he might learn what the people thought of his administration."[5] The point of this reference is not, however, to introduce a discussion of the Caliph's significance as a device for the introduction of new narratives. Instead, the author of the *Loiterer* expresses his desire to walk about London, to hear what his readers have to say about his newly published periodical. All of these comments attest to the presence of the text in the talk of the period but offer few specifics about it. It is indeed little more than a curiosity, or a text notable for the mere fact of its existence, rather than for the stories it contains.

A Window on the "East"

The *Arabian Nights' Entertainments* also came to be considered a sort of encyclopedia of eastern manners and mores—in fact, it advertised itself as such on its title page, which describes its contents as "Stories told by the Sultaness of the Indies … Containing A better Account of the Customs, Manners, and Religion of the Eastern Nations, viz. Tartars, Persians, and

Indians, than is to be met with in any Author hitherto publish'd." Galland's "Preface" (1713) repeats and expands upon the title page's claim, noting that the stories in the *Arabian Nights* must be "pleasing" not only for the "Wonders" and "surprising Events" they describe, but also "because of the Account they give us of the Customs and Manners of the Eastern Nations, and of the Ceremonies of their Religion, as well Pagan as Mahometan." Galland assures his readers that these cultures "are better describ'd here, than in any Author that has wrote of 'em, or in the Relations of Travellers." Indeed, if the Preface can be taken seriously, this text not only replaces previously written accounts, but renders "the Fatigue of travel" unnecessary as well because it exposes readers to "all the Eastern Nations, Persians, Tartars, and Indians."[6] In other words, it collects images of strange nations and peoples into a convenient package, designed to appeal to the outwardly inquisitive.

A number of commentators echo Galland's claims to authenticity. Lady Mary Wortley Montagu's *Letters* (1763) affirmed the veracity of fantastic accounts of the East in oriental tales:

> Now, do you imagine I have entertained you all this while with a relation that has, at least, received many embellishments from my hand? This, you will say, is but too like the Arabian tales: these embroidered napkins! and a jewel as large as a turkey's egg!—You forget, dear sister, those very tales were written by an author of this country, and (excepting the enchantments) are a real representation of the manners here.[7]

Other authors took the text seriously as a source of cultural information. Thomas Blackwell even footnotes the *Arabian Nights' Entertainments* as support for his claim about how the Turks, Arabs, and Indians begin to speak, which, according to Blackwell's *Enquiry into the Life and Writings of Homer* (1735), involves a prefatory declaration "that they will open their mouth; that they will unloose their tongue; that they will utter their voice, and pronounce with their lips."[8] While this use of the *Arabian Nights* emphasizes the eighteenth-century view of the text as an authority on Eastern "customs," it is quite inaccurate. It is unclear where Blackwell's reading comes from—most characters in the *Arabian Nights* simply speak in the normal fashion. The text is full of variations upon such words as said, begged, replied, began, etc. Blackwell's misrepresentation of the text obscures the aspects that would have been familiar and appealing to eighteenth-century readers, such as brave merchants and virtuous ladies, and emphasizes its status as an oddity.

John Richardson's *A Grammar of the Arabick Language* (1776), claims that "Even in the Arabian Nights Entertainments, and other Eastern tales, though we may find no necessity to believe in Aladdin's lamp, in the Genie Danhash, or the Faery Peri banou; we shall, nevertheless, discover a truer picture of Eastern manners and beliefs, than in all the Grecian writers; or in hundreds of other books, more generally resorted to as authorities."[9] This idea that the text truly offered an authentic account of eastern customs seems to have prevailed among a number of readers. Even the fairly skeptical James Beattie concedes that the tales, in spite of their French flavor, offer "a pretty just idea of the government, and of some of the customs, of … eastern nations."[10] Beattie does not explain how the *Arabian Nights' Entertainments* accurately portrays these aspects of the East, but the figure of the Eastern despot was well established in writings on the East at the time Beattie wrote. Montesquieu, for example, paints a vivid portrait of the oriental despot in his *Persian Letters* (1721). He writes that though European monarchs possess great power they avoid exercising it, which works to their advantage. In contrast, Usbek writes in Letter XCIX of Eastern despots, "Nothing brings down a Prince so near to the condition of his Subjects, as exercising an extravagant power over them: nothing exposes them so much to the turns and caprices of fortune." Usbek goes on to explain that because a "Persian" subject can be put to death by his sovereign for any reason, no matter how trivial, he has no incentive to avoid committing significant crimes, such as treason. A subject who causes his ruler the "least displeasure" is doomed to die, "and having nothing worse to fear; he is naturally inclined to disturb the peace of the State, and to conspire against his Sovereign; this being the only refuge he has left." Such sovereigns survive only because they "use so many precautions to guard their lives" and employ numerous soldiers, "to tyrannize … their subjects" and preserve their empires.[11] Nicholas Boulanger, in *The Origin and Progress of Despotism* (1764), suggests that Montesquieu's critique was not uncommon. Boulanger begins his treatise by noting that "the oriental monarchs are painted to us as the sovereign arbiters of the fate of the people over whom they reign; and their subjects as slaves devoted from the moment of their birth to bear the yoke of an humiliating and deplorable servitude."[12] The absolute and brutal power of the Sultan of the Indies, and his counterparts in the tales he helps to frame, confirms this view—accurate or not—of the politics of the East.[13] However, this is a reductive reading that fails to account for the complexity of the narratives that Scheherazade weaves, and presents the *Arabian Nights* as a kind of fantastic encyclopedia of the European conceptions of the East.

Galland's association with the text may explain why it had so much credibility on such matters. Readers familiar with his earlier, more factual work, may have assumed that the cultural details of the *Arabian Nights* had the same pretense to authority as his work on d'Herbelot's *Bibliothèque Orientale* (1697). However they came about, these misreadings consume readers in a debate about how authentically Eastern the tales are, diverting attention away from the tales themselves and making the text seem more like an artifact, or an object of cultural significance, rather than a work of literature.

Readers seem to have assumed that not only did the *Arabian Nights' Entertainments* represent the East but that it also perfectly matched the tales told by Eastern storytellers.[14] Different commentators painted an attractive, if anachronistic, picture of eastern men relaxing upon mattresses and listening to a servant or a wife recite passages from the *Arabian Nights*. Alexander Russel, in *A Description of Aleppo, and the Adjacent Country*, writes:

> When the time for repose draws nigh, they sit down on the matrass, and smoke their pipe, till they find themselves heavy; then they stretch themselves out, and leave their woman, or servant, to cover them: many of the people of fashion are lulled to rest by soft music, or stories told out of the Arabian Nights Entertainment, or some other book of the same kind, which the women are taught to repeat for that purpose.[15]

The use of the title *Arabian Nights' Entertainments*, which was a title used only for the English translation published in Britain, suggests that the set of stories the British had access to was the same as those stories heard and told and retold for centuries in various nations across the Middle East. Russel's comment erases the complex transmission history of Scheherazade's stories, and obscures the European aspects of Galland's work and its English translation.

Making the Extraordinary Visible

The text also served as a metaphor for all things fantastic or exotic—this is one of the major uses of the *Arabian Nights* in the writings of others. For example, the author of an article published in *The North British Intelligencer* (1776) on the disturbing and relatively new development of paper money, writes that

> when we see a wise and philosophical nation hugging phantoms for realities, running mad in schemes of refinement, taste, pleasure, wealth, power and greatness, by the sole aid of this civil hocus pocus; when we contemplate paper gold and paper land, paper fleets, armies, and revenues;

> a paper government, and a supreme paper legislature; we are apt to regard the Fairy Tales, the Travels of Gulliver, and the Arabian Nights Entertainments, as grave relations, and historical facts. We are really the true Enchanted Island.[16]

Similar references to the *Arabian Nights' Entertainments* are used in treatises that critique such frightening phenomena as coalition, Berkeley's principles, and the utter ignorance of the British on the subject of the magnificence of American geography.[17]

The text also served as a reference point for descriptions of places and scenes when an image of the fantastic was necessary or when an author's descriptive powers were exhausted. Patrick Brydone depicts a church in Palermo as having an "air of grandeur and uniformity" and then adds that "The roof is hung with innumerable lustres filled with wax candles, and, I am persuaded, when the whole is lighted up, it must be equal to any palace either in the Fairy Tales or the Arabian Nights Entertainments."[18] In a similar vein, the *Ambulator*, a travel guide to London, notes that the illumination of Vauxhall "at 10 o'clock put the reader in mind of the magic representations in the Arabian Nights Entertainments."[19] Even the most unlikely tourist destination, a salt pit, is pictured in terms of the *Arabian Nights*. The following recommendation to potential travelers appeared in *The London Magazine* for 1780:

> I tell you, that of all subterranean curiosities in this island, this is probably the best worth seeing. Were I in a romantick humour, truth would support me in almost any thing I could say of it; but I am tired to death with description—it is a most laborious business. Seize, therefore, upon the Arabian Nights Entertainments, and pick out the dazzling palace of some genii, and there transport yourself in imagination: this will give you some idea of it; inadequate perhaps, but sufficient in some degree, to answer the impression I am desirous you should receive.[20]

Somewhat more plausibly, the use of glass chandeliers in "some London shops" is compared to "an enchanted palace in the Arabian Nights Entertainments."[21] This fascinating use of the *Arabian Nights* as a sort of proxy text speaks to its intelligibility—these authors clearly assumed that the descriptions present in the *Arabian Nights* would be understandable to their readers. However, this accessibility or familiarity extends only to vague fantastic descriptions.

Fictional travel writers drew on the *Arabian Nights* in similar ways. In Smollett's *Humphrey Clinker* (1771), Lydia writes to her primary correspondent, Miss Letitia Willis, upon her visit to Ranelagh:

> All that you read of wealth and grandeur in the Arabian Nights' Entertainments and the Persian Tales, concerning Bagdad, ..., Damascus, Ispahan, and Samarkand, is here realized.... Ranelagh looks like the enchanted palace of a genie, adorned with the most exquisite performances of painting carving, and gilding, enlightened with a thousand golden lamps that emulate the noonday sun.[22]

Smollett's reference indicates his view of the *Arabian Nights*. Lydia's exaggerated, enthusiastic, girlish excitement provides us not with a recommendation of the text, but with a picture of the perceived reader of such texts. Smollett's particular usage here also suggests that he may not have read it—Lydia's remarks follow in the vein of the many writers who used the *Arabian Nights* as a reference point for the fantastic. Jane Austen used an allusion to the *Arabian Nights* in precisely the same way, putting it into a speech from the silly and verbose Miss Bates in *Emma* (1816).[23] Thus, in this type of reference to the *Arabian Nights' Entertainments*, we see it serving as a kind of repository of fantastic description. It functions as an example of the curious, and as a means for explaining other curious objects.

Review and Advertisements

According to Antonia Forster "reviewing, in anything approaching the modern sense of the term, began in the eighteenth century, with the *Monthly Review* in 1749." The *Critical Review* followed in 1756, and the two journals were the most influential for a quarter of a century.[24] Neither periodical reviewed the *Arabian Nights' Entertainments* until a new and corrected translation appeared in 1799 from Longman, translated into English from a Paris edition of 1786. The *Critical Review* begins, with tepid enthusiasm, "We only notice this edition of a performance which alike delights the innocence of youth and the experience of age, on account of the new preface," although the reviewer goes on to praise the new translation. [25] That year also saw reviews of the new translation in the *British Critic* and the *Gentleman's Magazine*.[26] All four reviews are notable for their limited discussion of the importance of the text in question. They serve primarily to alert readers of the introduction of a new translation, and, in the case of the *Gentleman's Magazine*, to list previous, recent translations. The *Monthly Review* spends more time speculating about the possible origins of the text than discussing its potential merits as a work of fiction, but notes "the curiosity and interest which they so powerfully excite" and the "luxuriant descriptions with which they abound."[27]

Almost without exception until the end of the Eighteenth century, the *Arabian Nights' Entertainments* receives passing mentions and advertisements without extensive serious critical attention. The text appears frequently in lists of "books recently published" and, interestingly, was advertised several times in the Proceedings of the Old Bailey. For example, the eighth volume appeared in a list of "Books printed for Andrew Bell" underneath advertisements for remedies for the gout and toothache in the Proceedings for Wednesday 27 April 1715. The inclusion of the *Arabian Nights* in circulating library catalogues adds to its commodification and classification as popular fiction. According to Barbara Benedict's study of "Jane Austen and the Culture of Circulating Libraries," libraries were overtly commercial, listing books alongside "various fashionable goods" such as, in the case of Harrod's 1790 catalogue, "medicines, stationary, 'Dewdney's Powder for cleaning Leather Breeches,' 'Terra Cotta Inkstands,' and 'Riley's coloured Pencils for drawing upon Silk....'"[28] The presence of the *Arabian Nights' Entertainments* in this type of venue, in addition to other contemporary comments made about it, seems to suggest that it was a fashionable and popular text, consumed in a manner similar to that of other fashionable commodities. It seems not to have been recognized as important literature, and it becomes clearly an object to collect rather than a book to read.

Critical Commentaries

Critics of the *Arabian Nights' Entertainments* also focused on its fantastic nature without delving into the diversity of its contents. Charles Gildon, in the Preface to *The New Metamorphosis*, calls the work a "sick Dream."[29] Voltaire, praising tales from China, states that in Chinese fables, "We meet with very little of the absurd or incredible, like the metamorphoses invented by the Greeks, and imbellished by Ovid, the Arabian nights entertainment, and the fables of Boiardo and Ariosto. The invention of the Chinese fables seldom departs from verisimilitude, and always has a moral tendency."[30] Voltaire also reproaches the Greeks for their polytheism and condemns such figures as Neptune, Vecta and Mars as "fit only for the Arabian Nights Entertainments."[31]

James Beattie, an early literary critic of the *Arabian Nights*, ultimately dismisses the book. He condemns its "great luxury of description, without any elegance; and great variety of invention, but nothing that elevates the mind, or touches the heart. All is wonderful and incredible; and the astonishment of the reader is more aimed at, than his improvement either in morality, or in the knowledge of nature." Having condemned the

Arabian Nights as a whole, he goes on to confess that he nonetheless admires some aspects of it:

> there is somewhere in it a story of a barber and his six brothers, that contains many good strokes of satire and comick description. I may add, that the character of the Caliph Haroun Alraschid is well drawn; and that the story of forty thieves destroyed by a slave is interesting, and artfully conducted. The voyages of Sindbad claim attention: they were certainly attended to, by the author of Gulliver's Travels.[32]

Beattie's reluctant admiration constitutes the most detailed reading of the text until the twentieth century. However, even that reading leaves us with more questions than answers. What are the "strokes of satire" he sees in "The Story of the Barber" and those of his brothers, and how are they deployed? What makes the Caliph a "well drawn" character? What is artful about "The Story of Ali Baba, and the Forty Thieves Destroyed by a Slave"?

Defenses of the Fantastic

The *Arabian Nights'* appeal is partly contained in the fantastic—something to which not all readers objected. David Fordyce discusses fables and their role in education:

> The Mind must have its Gambols and Flights as well as the Body.... I see no harm in going beyond the precise Bounds of Nature, in emblazoning Facts, and giving strong Caricatures of Things, so as to strike and astonish the Mind, which is yet raw and unformed; provided still the Moral be good that is couched under them, and there be nothing in them to corrupt and vitiate the Taste. Therefore I see no harm if the Voyage to the Moon, the Persian and Fairy Tales, the Arabian Nights Entertainments, and the like, are put into the hand of Youth.[33]

Vicesimus Knox commended the *Arabian Nights* as "well calculated to kindle a flame in the bosoms of boys" and to inspire them to make use of "their portion of genius."[34] This view corresponds to Bruno Bettelheim's theory about the purpose of fairy tales, which, in order to "enrich [a child's] life" must "stimulate his imagination; help him to develop his intellect and to clarify his emotions; be attuned to his anxieties and aspirations; give full recognition to his difficulties, while at the same time suggesting solutions to the problems which perturb him." In addition, they must "entertain" and "arouse … curiosity."[35]

John Hawksworth makes an even stronger argument in favor of the fantastic. In *The Adventurer* No. 4 he contends that though novels attempt to portray reality, they necessarily fail: "The Novel…is confined within the narrower bounds of probability, the number of incidents is necessarily diminished, and if it deceives us more it surprises us less." Hawksworth favors the fantastic, and notes that as long as fantastic texts, like the *Arabian Nights' Entertainments*, preserve a logical internal consistency "the mind is satisfied." For example,

> when the agency of Genii and Fairies is once admitted, no event which is deemed possible to such agents is rejected as incredible or absurd; the action of the story proceeds with regularity, the persons act upon rational principles, and such events take place as may naturally be expected from the interposition of superior intelligence and power….

When once we accept the fantastic we are "abundantly rewarded by the new scenes to which we are admitted, and the unbounded prospect that is thrown open before us."[36]

Richard Hurd also offers a spirited defense of what he calls a "Faery way of writing" in his "Letters on Chivalry and Romance":

> But the source of bad criticism, as universally bad as bad philosophy, is the abuse of terms. A poet, they say, must follow *nature*; and by nature we are to suppose can only be meant the known and experienced course of affairs in this world. Whereas the poet has a world of his own, where experience has less to do, than consistent imagination. He has, besides, a supernatural world to range in. He has Gods, and Faeries, and Witches at his command….
>
> Thus in the poet's world, all is marvelous and extraordinary; yet not *unnatural* in one sense, as it agrees to the conceptions that are readily entertained of these magical and wonder-working Natures.[37]

It was not unheard of, therefore, for critics to defend the value of the fantastic in literature. Richard Hole's *Remarks on the Arabian Nights' Entertainments* (1797), however, takes a different approach, and argues that the book's fantastic elements are real.

Hole's thesis defends the *Arabian Nights* against charges of inauthenticity, inaccuracy, and unrealistic depictions of the world. He argues that the tales are truly eastern in origin, not European, based on "internal evidence." Moreover, he has found "No allusion to modern customs, to modern events or characters" to discredit it. Having established the tales' genuine nature, he attempts to prove that the geography of Sindbad's journeys is based in the real world and might be relied upon, with the caveat that the Arabs had no compasses and were "very inaccurate geographers." He also excuses the fantastic elements of the text through a connection to natural philosophy. "Sindbad's monsters of the deep," according to Hole, are accounted for in Pliny under different names.[38] This comparison, or defense, affirms the text's encyclopedic reputation among some readers.

The *Arabian Nights* proved useful as a repository of curious scenes. Addison, in *The Spectator* No. 195 (1711), uses "The Story of the Grecian King and the Physician Douban" as an introduction to an essay on the importance of exercise and moderation in diet.[39] Interestingly, Addison's essay argues that "Physick, for the most part, is nothing else but the Substitute of Exercise or Temperance."[40] In the part of the story that Addison retells, however, "Physick" plays an important role, seeming to contradict his thesis. The physician orders the King to exercise with a ball and a mallet of wood, which are filled with medicine. The King is cured, Addison states, through "the Vertue of the Medicaments perspiring through the Wood."[41] Exercise, in this instance, serves merely as a means of delivering medicine, not as a superior method of preserving health. This excerpt of the *Arabian Nights* has little relevance for Addison's argument, and may even contradict it. It served, most likely, as a device to engage the reader's curiosity.

Conclusion

What is striking about most eighteenth-century references to the *Arabian Nights' Entertainments* is their lack of particularity. The text is either grouped with a number of other texts supposedly of a similar type, or the reader is asked to imagine "some palace" or "some scene" from the *Arabian Nights*. In the vast majority of references to the tales in the eighteenth century, no specific tale or character is mentioned, not even Scheherazade. Most references could be written or read and understood, in fact, without the writer or reader having ever opened the *Arabian Nights' Entertainments*. Even James Beattie's brief analysis, though more detailed than most, fails to account for numerous aspects of the text. The many editions published in the Eighteenth century suggest it must have found its way into the hands of many readers. The reception history, however, highlights its status as little more than a curious object that describes curious places and things. It seems to have been worthy of collection, but not necessarily valued as a literary text. Interestingly, it is only recently that critics of Galland's version of the Arabian Nights have moved beyond their eighteenth-century counterparts,[42] and much room remains for additional work that seeks to unpack the many narratives contained within it. Thus far the text has largely denied serious critical analysis, most likely because of its daunting length and complex translation history, leaving it to remain a curious commodity for the twenty-first century reader.

CHAPTER SIX

CAPTAIN COOK'S CABINET: THE MAKING OF AN ARCTIC IMAGINARY

JANELLE A. SCHWARTZ

> … Skins of various animals, such as Bears, Wolfs, Foxes, Dear, Rackoons, Polecats, Martins and in particular the Sea Beaver, the same as is found on the coast of Kamtchatka. Cloathing made of these skins and a nother sort made, either of the bark of a tree or some plant like hemp; Weapons, such as Bows and Arrows, Spears &c Fish hooks and Instruments of various kinds, pieces of carved work and even human sculs and hands, and a variety of little articles too tedious to mention.
> —Captain James Cook

> The ship is the heterotopia *par excellence*.
> —Michel Foucault

Like Ferrante Imperato's sixteenth-century *Dell'Historia Naturale* and Ole Worm's seventeenth-century *Museum Wormianum*, traditional cabinets of curiosity all but defied categorical order. Contained in people's homes, displayed in/as what would become national museums, exhibited in/as public gardens, even presented in the form of small, private curio boxes (to cite only a general sampling), these cabinets or wonder-rooms offered both wide and narrow glimpses of a kind of encyclopedic episteme. By collecting together all shapes and sizes of *artificialia* and *naturalia*, these spaces attempted to corral knowledge into a physical configuration, at once suggestive of totality and revelatory in its fragmentation. In short, such cabinets provided a visible and seemingly instantaneous panoramic demonstration of how much was "known" (read collected) of our rapidly expanding world. Notably, the objects making up these collections often came from voyages of discovery, on land and at sea. They came, that is, from colonial efforts, which in turn helped to fuel the collecting frenzy that surged in the eighteenth and nineteenth centuries and continues into today. What almost all such cabinets of curiosity have in common is the fact that they retain a stationary location. They are essentially immobile. In this sense, the cabinet is not merely a space for collected items, it *holds* an actual place. The *Museum Wormianum*, for example, could be originally found and visited in a wonder-room built by Worm himself. It was built so that others could view it, experience it. And its popularity soon caused this private collection to be made public, becoming part of the Royal Danish Kunstkammer in Copenhagen in 1665. Worm's collected curiosities thus enjoyed not only the care of a curator's hand; his pieces enjoyed the stability of an accessible venue. But what of a wonder-room that lacks this stability and accessibility? What if, for example, the cabinet were put to sea?

At 8 o'clock in the evening of 12 July 1776, a Saturday, Captain James Cook of the British Royal Navy set sail out of Plymouth Sound, England—"with a gentle breeze at NWBW"[1]—on what would be his third and final voyage. Yet one more explorer in a centuries' long list, Cook doggedly made his way to the polar north in search of the elusive Northwest Passage connecting the Pacific and Atlantic oceans. His route took him first south around the Cape of Good Hope, Africa, then east toward Van Diemen's Land, Australia, north passed Tahiti, Christmas Island, and Hawaii, until finally he reached the North Pacific and what is present-day Cook Inlet. He reached this south central point of Alaska toward the end of May 1778, almost two years after his initial embarkation. He would spend the next six months navigating the arctic sea, charting and recharting the vast landscape, and trading with indigenous peoples, before turning back to Hawaii (where he would be killed), all in an effort to find the by-now mythic open polar sea.[2] Although this sought-after trade route would not be successfully traversed until the opening years of the twentieth century (by Norwegian explorer, Roald Amundsen), Cook's late eighteenth-century travels to the far north did succeed in correctly identifying Alaska as a landmass connected to, rather than separated from, the North American continent.[3]

This extremely abridged history of Cook's last expedition, which will be filled out and explored in what follows, is meant to underscore the idea that Cook himself was a seeker. He relished opportunity after opportunity to encounter and record the not-yet-completely-known or as-yet-unknown. It is therefore my contention that Cook's penchant for exploration, his penetrating empiricism, and his meticulous journaling (always with an eye toward publication[4]) cast him as a collector. By inhabiting the roles of climatologist, cartographer, natural historian, anthropologist, economist, envoy, and journalist, not to mention his titular role as ship's captain, Cook effectively pieced together a cabinet exhibitive of an arctic imaginary. He partakes in what Barbara Stafford delineates as the "prismatic nature" of research, which "span[s] disparate and fluid areas, each with its own languages, master queries, and traditions," in an effort to develop a space in which "noncompartmentalized interaction might fruitfully occur."[5] An examination of the contents of Cook's journal from his Third Voyage, specifically his observations and experiences and the patterns of his record-keeping during the final third of his journey (March 1778 – January 1779), assembles the North Pacific into an incongruent panorama: a seemingly immeasurable place nevertheless stuffed with natural elements and synthetic objects, indigenous peoples, settlers, and traders. The frozen north is presented—cliché notwithstanding—as a hotbed of activity; this representation challenges the reader to reconcile a mythologized scenic wonder with the shipman's collective empirical gaze. This is the arctic imaginary put on display through the writings of Captain Cook.

Significantly, then, this chapter is not solely about Cook the captain. His story as an arctic explorer is a story bound up with the movements and activities of the ships he commanded, with the ebb and flow of the imperial tide, and with the bewildering sea- and landscapes (most often uncharted or barely, erroneously so) to which he was sent. In effect, this chapter is also about the ship that carried its captain, an English bark christened the *Resolution*, and its sister ship, the *Discovery*—both of which ferried the curious into, just as they themselves appeared as curiosities against, a vast frozen setting. These ships represent what I am calling "floating cabinets," or points of collection contingent on the instability, or more accurately, the mobility of both the physical container and the interpretive gaze constitutive of it. They depend as much on time as they do on space, and thus can be read as what Foucault identifies as "a place without a place":

> If we think, after all, that the boat is a floating piece of space, a place without a place, that exists by itself, that is closed in on itself and at the same time is given over to the infinity of the sea and that, from port to port, from tack to tack, … it goes as far as the colonies in search of the most precious treasures they conceal in their gardens, you will understand why the boat has not only been for our civilization, from the sixteenth century until the present, the great instrument of economic development, but has been simultaneously the greatest reserve of the imagination. The ship is the heterotopia *par excellence.*[6]

Characterized as "absolutely different from all the sites that they reflect and speak about,"[7] Foucauldian heterotopias invert our understanding of utopias. If, as Foucault states, "utopias are sites with no real place," then heterotopias are places "outside of all places, even though it may be possible to indicate their location in reality."[8] For example, the myth of a temperate polar zone figures as the utopia in this scheme, like that which Walton went in search of at the North Pole in *Frankenstein*[9] and Cook himself debunked at the South Pole during his Second Voyage.[10] By contrast, Cook's ship can be read just as Foucault reads any ship: as a heterotopia "that exists by itself, that is closed in on itself and at the same time is given over to the infinity of the sea." Although both Cook's ship and its sister ship, as well as the indigenous canoes, effectively serve as supply ships to the arctic imaginary, it is chiefly the *Resolution* that serves as the nexus of exchange necessary to its formulation. Because its route took it into uncharted (or, again, poorly charted) waters, the *Resolution* can be read as an outsider working to collect and transmit meaningful data of a foreign or "other" space. In this way, readers of Cook's journal are also positioned as outsiders, so that both Cook and his readers are able to construct the ship as a space "given over to the infinity of the sea" while still viewing it as a delimited "reserve of the imagination." Buoyancy thus denotes the vital tension between a ship's density and that of the arctic sea as much as it characterizes the palpable tension between the real and the imaginary.

After all, Cook's ship was set in the Arctic, a verified space—as opposed to any so called temperate zone—occupied by a multitude of elements both natural and synthetic. It was always "possible" to pinpoint the *Resolution*'s position—however *passing* it may have been. In this way, the primary vessel of Cook's expedition is uniquely situated as a heterotopia due to its intrinsic transience. It is meant to be able to pass *by* the land it is sent to survey, and to pass *over* the water serving as its transportative, connective medium. It is also meant to pass *into* and *through* the various harbors and ports for resupply and continued exploration and, most significantly, trade. The ship acts as a plot-able site at which and from which to witness the Polar North.

Likewise, the secondary vessel, the *Discovery*, can be read as what Foucault articulates as a "counteraction" to the primary one: it acts as a mirror image of the *Resolution*. The *Discovery* does "exist in reality," but it functions more as a reflective surface, underscoring the *Resolution* as "at once absolutely real, connected with all the space that surrounds it, and absolutely unreal, since in order to be perceived it has to" emerge under the gaze of a distinct, other point—in this case, another ship.[11] I argue then that the floating cabinet is not a *product* of the arctic expedition; rather, it is a *processual construction* defined as much by its physical movements through a watery medium as by its fluid transitioning between three interrelated aesthetic modes: the ark, the cabinet proper, and the bridge.

> MONDAY 10th [June 1776]. Took on board a Bull, 2 Cows with their Calves & some sheep to carry to Otaheite [Tahiti] with a quantity of Hay and Corn for their subsistence.
>
> TUESDAY 11th [June 1776]. Received on board several Astronomical & Nautical Instruments which the Board of Longitude intrusted to me and M^{r}. King my second Lieutenant.
>
> TUESDAY 9th [July 1776]. Received on board the party of Marines, consisting of a $Lieut^{t}$ Serjeant 2 Corporals one Drum and 15 private…
>
> SATURDAY 13th [July 1776]. Added two young bulls, two Heifers, two young stone Horses, two Mares, two Rams, several Ewes and Goats and some Rabbits and Poultry, all of them intended for New Zealand, Otaheite and the neighboring islands, or any other place we might meet, where there was a prospect that the leaving of some of them might prove usefull to posterity. [12]

The four journal entries above quickly demonstrate what Gananath Obeyesekere observes in *The Apotheosis of Captain Cook* as Cook's "self-conscious" recognition of his ship "as a Noah's Ark."[13] He produces a catalog of the supplies taken aboard for both sustenance and science, so that in addition to its role as observatory the *Resolution* recalls Noah's efforts at conservation. However, the eighteenth-century ship replaces divine sanction with trade incentive. As a selective repository and transport for the interests of the British Empire, the *Resolution*, like the biblical ark, is less a cabinet of curiosity than a cabinet of necessity. Just as the Ark's purpose was to preserve God's creatures, the *Resolution* maintains a particular telos: to locate and traverse the pacific route of the Northwest Passage. In other words, the *Resolution* was to aid in the preservation of the British Empire by expanding trade possibilities. At the same time, however, the European collectors on board the *Resolution* (especially its thoughtful entourage of naturalists, botanists, cartographers, astronomists, etc.) inhabit an impossible subject position if the ship is indeed compared to the Ark.

If the Ark itself is read as an archetypal cabinet for/from God's eye, leaving Noah to be the principal specimen among an exclusive crowd, then the *Resolution* would need an equally omniscient conductor/audience to secure a parallel interpretation. This it does not have. Instead, the *Resolution* collapses the principal collector into his cabinet—i.e. Cook must be seen as the lead actor in the undertakings of the *Resolution*, not as an all-knowing creator. Consequently, the *Resolution*-as-ark lacks a structuring outside (the *Discovery* serves only to signal, by virtual mirroring, the existence of the *Resolution*); all knowledge of its existence, its make-up, its movements, and its interactions comes from the inhabitant(s) within it. Cook's journal entries in particular, which in themselves are an amassing of his polar vision, serve as the structuring force. This emphasis on an interior space as the potential site of meaning suggests in turn that this so called ark still be read as a traditional cabinet, replete with a pell-mell catalog of its contents.

> A great many canoes filled with the Natives were about the Ships all day, and a trade commenced betwixt us and them, which was carried on with the Strictest honisty on boath sides. Their articles were the Skins of various animals, such as Bears, Wolfs, Foxes, Dear, Rackoons, Polecats, Martins and in particular the Sea Beaver, the same as is found on the coast of Kamtchatka. Cloathing made of these skins and a nother sort made, either of the bark of a tree or some plant like hemp; Weapons, such as Bows and Arrows, Spears &c Fish hooks and Instruments of various kinds, pieces of carved work and even human sculs and hands, and a variety of little articles too tedious to mention. For these things they took in exchange, Knives, chissels, pieces of iron & Tin, Nails, Buttons, or any kind of metal. Beads they were not fond of and cloth of all kinds they rejected.[14]

Recalling the first epigraph at the top of this chapter, the above text illustrates the variety of goods often traded between the Europeans and the ever-present "Natives." While "Natives" in this context undoubtedly point to the indigenous inhabitants of the arctic region, the use of this word also serves to complicate the already murky subject position of Cook and his men. Simply put, the crew of the *Resolution* are native to their ship, just as the "Esquimaux" are viewed as native to the arctic land and sea. Thus, when Cook relates the "trade [that] commenced betwixt us and them," he immediately calls attention to the tenuousness of the hierarchy he has attempted to construct in this deceptively undeveloped region. "Us" suggests that the Europeans are insiders, native to their floating space, while "them" implies a people existing outside of this space. Consequently, the indigenous peoples are portrayed as being both natives and outsiders (and thus perhaps more "at home" in a place wholly dependent on the external environment). They are displayed in "a great many canoes" around the periphery of Cook's ship, which Cook often records with meticulous precision,[15] as if to portray an exotic scaffolding marking off the arguably normative boundaries of imperial control. Heterogeneous space, observes Foucault, is defined by "sites which are irreducible to one another and absolutely not superimposable on one another"[16] (Foucault 23). Not only then do the objects traded—e.g. "the Skins of various animals… Cloathing… Weapons… human sculs and hands… or any kind of metal"—fall together into a cabinet of practical and novelty objects; the perspectival slip between inside and outside demands that such a floating cabinet always be read two ways: indigenous peoples collected from Cook just as he collected from them. Cook's ship is thus as much a cabinet of curiosity to the people of the Arctic as the Arctic itself is to Captain Cook. Perhaps this accounts for Cook's overwhelming use of the word "trade" and other related terms ("traffick," "complement," "barter," "exchange," as well as "token," "present," "thievery") throughout his journal entries. While some are more or less charged with colonial innuendo than others, the emphasis on giving and receiving builds a significant tension into Cook's representative cabinet of the Far North.

Buoyancy is a necessary quality of any sea-worthy vessel. The ability for both the *Resolution* and the indigenous canoes to float—to maintain their surface tension with the oftentimes calamitous tidal swells and shifting pack ice of the North Pacific—is tantamount to their function as water-borne crafts. Buoyancy supports essential mobility. But this buoyancy is also a quality intrinsic to our understanding of the floating cabinet as a symbolic construction.

"It must not be understood that I supposed any part of the ice we had seen fixed, on the contrary I am well assured that the whole was a moveable Mass."[17] Cook wrote this statement into his journal on Friday, 21 August 1778, when sailing amidst the thickening pack ice of the Arctic Sea—just eight days before his decision to give up the season's search for the Northwest Passage and return to Hawaii.[18] The water-cum-ice became ever more treacherous and unstable with the onset of winter, and often trapped the European ships without warning (due in large part to the remarkably mobile quality of the pack ice). Given this characteristic lack of fixity in the Polar North, the environment was as attractive to the European imagination as it was repellent to its actual experience.[19] But the experience itself was also often recounted with heroism and tragedy,[20] while the arctic imaginary preserved the notion of a pure space, of a space somehow undisturbable by industrial man and therefore resistant to his heroic efforts. There clearly was—and is—a magnetism about the polar regions that extends across literal and figurative realms.

Heterotopias, explains Foucault, "have a function in relation to all the space that remains. This function unfolds between two extreme poles."[21] Taken literally, this phrasing points directly to the Arctic and Antarctic regions as positional anchorages, and to the ship carrying Captain Cook and his men as a heterotopic space ("a place without a place") to be studied in connection with the "extreme poles." But this is an ironic anchorage, as much "at sea" as the ship attempting to reach it and the pack ice often concealing it. As Sarah Moss highlights in *The Frozen Ship*, "the axis wobbles, the poles move in relation to each other, and the point around which our planet's magnetic field is arranged is not the same as its axis."[22] This very real fluctuation, while not completely understood during the eighteenth and early-nineteenth centuries, nevertheless caused compass readings to vary from one expedition to another and longitudinal lines to shift. The natural magnetism of the poles was thus at odds with its synthetic counterparts. It left captains like Cook without a steady guide or reliable map for their expeditions. "We were upon a Coast," wrote Cook of his Third Voyage, "where every step was to be considered, where no information could be had from Maps, either modern or ancient: confiding too much in the former we were frequently misled to our no small hindrence."[23] His interactions with contemporary Russian settlers on the Aleutian Islands, for instance, revealed how at odds the physical geography was with contemporary maps and map-makers:

> If *M*r. *Stahlin* was not greatly imposed upon what could induce him to publish so erroneous a Map? in which many of these islands are jumbled in in [sic] regular confusion, without the least regard to truth and yet he is pleased to call it a very accurate little Map? A map that the most illiterate of his illiterate Sea-faring men would have been ashamed to put his name to.[24]

As a consequence of this "regular confusion," the voyage of the *Resolution*, guided in large part by the eye of its captain, was forced to collect natural markers such as mountain ranges and volcanic plumes,[25] stands of fir trees or rocky beaches,[26] even "a shag, or Cormorant,"[27] in order to determine the appropriate configuration and hence navigation of the variable expanse. But natural landmarks could be just as misleading as the maps attempting to chart them. Between 17 May and 1 June 1778, for example, the *Resolution* was forced to turn around continually in a large river near Cook Inlet, after being frustrated again and again in its efforts to find northern passage. Cook named this river "River Turnagain" (present-day Turnagain Arm, just south of Anchorage) and declared the following:

> If the discovery of this River should prove of use, either to the present or future ages, the time spent in exploring it ought to be the less regreted [sic], but to us who had a much greater object in View it was an essential loss; the season was advancing apace, we knew not how far we might have to proceed to the South and we were now convinced that the Continent

> extended farther to the west than from the Modern Charts we had reason to expect and made a passage into Baffin or Hudson bays far less probable, or at least made it of greater extent. But if I had not examined this place it would have been concluded, nay asserted that it communicated with the Sea to the North, or with one of these bays to the East.[28]

Cook's "regard to truth" as a cartographer is clearly paramount in contrast to the *Wunderkammer*-like "jumble" of earlier maps, so that from the perspective of the *Resolution* the Arctic is represented as what Foucault describes as "a space that is other, another real space, as perfect, as meticulous, as well arranged as ours is messy, ill constructed, and jumbled."[29] Thus is Cook's ship also a revision of the traditional cabinet of curiosity into not only an appropriately stocked space, precise in its order and purpose, and suitably cared for, but also a space displaying the attempt to unravel the chance and waywardness of an arctic expanse. It is not merely a conservationist's ark, it is a cabinet actively working to impart order onto seeming chaos. As a heterotopic site, the *Resolution* is "not freely accessible like a public place."[30] And so the real challenges of arctic navigation and the imagined potential for charting the Northwest Passage must be made to maintain a crucial tension in order to create the representative buoyancy of the floating cabinet.

It is worth repeating here that Cook's nautical achievements brought him and his fellow sailors into regular—albeit transient—contact with an arctic nature. Descriptions of the climate, topography, flora, and fauna were catalogued alongside such details as the number of canoes often surrounding the *Resolution* and the physical appearance of the "Natives" contained within them.[31] Cook himself consistently articulated tableaus of the natural world that confronted him. "Like a hawk hungry for prey," wrote Vanessa Collingridge in *Captain Cook: A Legacy Under Fire,* [Cook] lived through his eyes."[32] He scoured the coastlines looking for signs of traversability and the availability of resources. For example, on 16 May 1778, just prior to the oppressive circularity in River Turnagain, the *Resolution* found itself "surrounded on every side by land" and thus forced to take harbor "in a place which in the Chart is distinguished by the name of *Snug Corner bay*." Remaining true to its name, this bay was a "very snug place," "sheltered from all winds," and dangerously shallow ("hav[ing] in it from 7 to 3 fath. water a Muddy bottom").[33] The land that extended out from the shore, however, clearly provided what Cook felt were useful, if not entirely accessible, supplies—e.g. timber and fowl. And on 26 June 1778, while sailing off the coast of Unalaska island, with the weather "so thick that we could not see a hundred yards before us,"[34] Cook reported that "there were several breakers about [the ship] and yet

Providence had conducted us through between these rocks where I should not have ventured in a clear day, and to such an anchoring place that I could not have chosen better."[35] After emerging from this Odysseus-like trial, Cook found that the cove in which they set anchor contained "some tolerable good grass and several other small plants, one of which was like Parsley and eat [sic] very well either in soups or as a Sallad."[36] These and other such accounts of Cook's interaction with the arctic landscape add to the buoyant bind of the real and imaginary that of the sea and land. Just as the open ocean provides for the mobility of the *Resolution*, its catch of fresh halibut fish, and a neutral meeting space for the Europeans and the Arctic's indigenous peoples, so too does terra firma provide much needed sources of potable water, the possibility of extending the footprint of the British Empire, and the resources for both sustenance and the ship's upkeep. The boundary between sea and land cannot, therefore, be breached if the *Resolution* is to retain its identity as a visionary cabinet projecting "new," unpredictable frontiers.

However, as Cook's journal exposes, this boundary was indeed often violated: "[By] the inattention and neglect of the Man at the lead, the ship struck and stuck fast on a bank that lies nearly in the middle of the River."[37] Or, "As we found the ship again very leaky in her upper works, the Caulkers were set to work to caulk her and repair such other defects as were wanting."[38] Although the *Resolution* had been refitted from the Second Voyage to the Third, Cook did not supervise the renovations and so they were poorly done. Add to this human error and the variable weather conditions, oftentimes drastic in their fluctuation from an obscuring fog to a fragile "Calm" to a wind that "blew very hard and in squals with rain and thick hazey weather… a perfect hurricane," [39] and Cook's journal can be read as a sensational inventory of the damage that plagued his ship.

> At this time [during the "perfect hurricane"], the Resolution Sprung a leak which at first alarmed us not alittle; it was found to be under the Starboard buttock, where from the bread room we could both hear and see the Water rush in…"[40]

As one of a multitude of separate damage reports between March 1778 and January 1779, the anecdote of the leaky buttock instantly reveals precisely how tenuous a command Cook's ship had over the "absolutely [in]different" site of the Arctic. Rushing water can tear apart a ship as well as sink it—either way such a floating cabinet would be *medially* lost. That is, the floating cabinet would be lost through its own medium (water), dismantled in both real and imaginary spaces. This transgression of the external medium into a protected interior space[41] discloses the floating cabinet as both repository and vomitory; it threatens always to eject the very matter of its collection. The *Resolution* is therefore the vessel out from which collections can be observed and through which collections pass. It does not simply attract and absorb the gaze of the curious; it projects the curious gaze itself. It is the ultimate point of reference—a moving, permeable one—that sutures together time and space along with the objects and elements set within these dimensions. As a floating cabinet, the *Resolution* is above all an interdisciplinary space. It is, finally, an epistemological bridge between an historical empire and what today is still recognized as The Last Frontier.

CHAPTER SEVEN

COLLECTING ANIMAL IMAGES: A NATURAL HISTORY OF CINEMA

WILLIAM NOLAN

The nineteenth-century emergences of photography, proto-cinematic technologies and cinema itself abound with animals. Whether under a scientific scope, within a photographic frame, or in cinematic space-time, animals populate the history of photography and the emergence of cinema as if they had been there all along, awaiting the arrival of a device that could register their vitality. In a sense animals were excellent subjects for the emerging forms of representation simply because they move, but their location in the early cinematic and proto-cinematic frame is never unambiguous. In works that are neither more zoological nor cinematographic, and that just as well straddle the border between photography and cinema, Eadweard Muybridge and Etienne-Jules Marey produced series of animal images that sought to find the representability of life at its most elusive. The presence of animals in the frames of this historical arc toward motion photography reveal cinema's participation in the nineteenth century culture of the collection and display of life and foreground its participation in regimes of vision in which categories of life, humanity, and animality are at stake.

Significant work in the study of early cinema in the late twentieth century released our understanding of the historical emergence of the cinematic apparatus from both the rigid history of technological evolution and the history of western narrative. Such work argued that we understand early cinema, if not its whole history, better by setting its emergence alongside a broader set of cultural practices and values. In seeking to consider early cinema outside of its ultimate transformation into narrative cinema, these studies have positioned it within the realm of public spectacle, popular throughout the nineteenth century, urging not only comparisons of cinema with museums, circuses, and world's fairs, but also comparisons of these public spectacles with all of the proto-cinematic devices emerging in anticipation of cinema itself. Tom Gunning's "The Cinema of Attractions"[1] was groundbreaking in opening up the categories of visual display with which early cinema might be associated. Vanessa Schwartz subsequently genealogized the emergence of cinema by considering the extent to which certain public spectacles and institutions in late nineteenth-century Paris exhibit a cinematic experience prior to cinema's technological appearance.[2] Likewise, Jonathan Crary complicated the technological evolution of visual representation and display by analyzing these instruments and their popularization in terms of the cultural demands to which they respond—most important of which for him is the mounting desire to see vision.[3] These works collectively loosen cinema's ties to narrative and allow for thinking through various questions about cinema according to the regimes of looking they enact. In this piece I will argue that practices of collecting and looking at animals, the need to reincorporate them into a nineteenth-century culture that has largely effected their exclusion, as well as the hope such practices offer to a mounting collective concern that western culture, specifically through its representative practices, has become increasingly disconnected from a natural world, all importantly inform the specific emergence of the proto-cinematic technologies developed by Muybridge and Marey.

As an avatar of cinema, the emergence of the zoological space responds to a problem of scope in the study of natural history. In the late eighteenth century, naturalists who went out into the world and observed animals in their natural habitats found themselves at odds with the cabinet scientists who studied preserved, dead specimens. On both sides of the debate, proponents argued that the other failed to observe that which was truly important in studying animals. The field naturalist argued that animals must be studied in their natural surroundings in order to be properly understood. The cabinet scientist argued that in nature one could scarcely get close enough to wild animals to learn anything of substance, and nothing at all of its physical anatomy. If the scope of the field scientist was too broad, then the cabinet naturalist's was too narrow. Hence, the study of animals in captivity buttressed itself against two more established modes of animal science. In his article "Ethology, Natural History, the Life Sciences, and the Problem of Place," Richard Burkhardt investigates the historical emergence of specific spaces for scientific research and the authority those spaces grant the science carried out within them. Bernardin de Saint-Pierre, in his decision to establish a menagerie at the *Jardin des Plantes,* and Frederic Cuvier, in his role as director of the Paris menagerie, articulated the arguments by which the zoological space insinuated itself as a middle ground in the late eighteenth- and early nineteenth-century debates surrounding the study of the natural world. According to Burkhardt, Saint-Pierre struggled to establish a menagerie at the *Muséum national d'Histoire naturelle* at odds with cabinet scientists who saw the menagerie more as a holding area for soon to be preserved specimens, rather than a place that would enable important scientific research. He responded by emphasizing the vital importance of studying the *life* of animals and the limits of the dead specimen:

> Saint-Pierre responded by allowing that it was not enough to study dead plants in herbaria or dead animals in a natural history cabinet. What appealed most to the lover of nature, he insisted, were *living* things. "The best prepared dead animal," he wrote, "presents only a stuffed skin, a skeleton, an anatomy." The *life* which had been the creature's principle feature was missing.[4]

Following Saint-Pierre's tenure as director of the menagerie, Frederic Cuvier took over the directorship in 1808 and held it until 1838. Though Cuvier must also have found it necessary on occasion to defend the place of the menagerie within the Museum complex, the *Jardin des Plantes* had established itself as a unique and important place of scientific inquiry during his time as director, and had become the clear inspiration for the creation of the London Zoological Gardens in 1828. By 1825 Cuvier "went so far as to suggest that menagerie studies would ultimately render field studies unnecessary."[5]

> [T]he menagerie could be for the zoologist, Cuvier argued, what the chemist's laboratory was for the chemist. It was a place where one could see not only what does happen in nature, but what could take place in nature. … The reason contemporary ideas of animal intelligence were so inadequate, he maintained, was because they were based on isolated facts involving free-living animals, and systematic experimentation with free-living animals was simply not possible.[6]

The study of animal behavior thus simultaneously carved out a space in which one could observe animal life and a space of discursive legitimacy in the debates about the study of animals. It was not merely a matter of contextualizing the animal—though it certainly was that—but matter of limiting that context and adjusting the scope of animal observation in order to see animality to what was then deemed the greatest extent possible. The zoological space galvanized these debates by focusing on questions of vision and imbricating in those questions the value of observable life. By both (re)animating and framing the scope of the study of animal behavior, the zoological space spectacularized the observation of animal life. Such a spectacularization cannot be understood outside of the mounting obsession with vision and the proliferation of regimes of looking so characteristic of European cultures of collection and spectacular display in the nineteenth century.

A comparison of the zoological gardens and the emergence of cinema in the latter half of the nineteenth century draw our attention to qualities that zoos and film in the late nineteenth century alone share. They are spaces in which the unfolding of animal (and human) life in time is put on display. While the space they carve out is designed specifically to capture a slice of natural, unmediated, animal reality, ultimately the structures that produce the possibility of this observation condition the spaces they engender. What's more, they offer a marked difference to their respective precursors, i.e. the natural history museum and still photography, by not simply capturing and framing, but animating the objects they display. More than simply arresting life, cinema and the zoo attempted to harness the unfolding of time. As we shall see, the cinematic space emerges through an adjustment of scope remarkably similar to the creation of the zoological space in order to better observe animals. What zoological impulse does the drive toward motion photography retain?

Though Eadweard Muybridge is a crucial part of any account of cinema's prehistory, the common description of him as the man who developed a sort of photography that would later become crucial to the invention of cinema proper perhaps too quickly glosses his pursuits and contributions to the history of the emergence of motion photography. Not only did he produce various mechanisms for capturing movement in rapid successive exposures, he invented the zoopraxiscope for projecting these images—a development which, however skeletal, arguably constitutes the invention of motion pictures and in any case constitutes the initial voyages into and experimentations with a cinematic space.[7] Rather than contribute a third figure to the debates over the inventor of cinema, though, I'd like to conceive of the emergence of the cinematic apparatus as a several decades long process, wherein Muybridge is not so much an inventor of cinema, but a figure deeply emblematic of that cultural/technological/spatial emergence. An analysis of Muybridge's photography and technological developments condition a further claim, which will be the focus of my argument here: when humans step into the object position of a moving picture camera, they are stepping into a space already well staked out, and in many ways fashioned, by animals. The enormously popular practice of looking at animals in zoos loom large here, but, more specifically, this animal space is carved out as such in three ways: (1) by the focus on animals as photographic objects, (2) by the conflation and commingling of animality with mechanicity, and (3) as a result of the "animal nature" of photographic representation, in contrast to a system of human signification in crisis. As a space carved out and marked by animality, I suggest that when humans step into the space, it holds the promise of revealing and recuperating their own lost animality and connection to the natural world. Stripped of language as well as clothes and virtually every other mark of culture, the cinematic space that Muybridge's experiments bring about offers an escape from an industrializing civilization increasingly detached from the natural world and mired in slippery signification. It offers a return to a grounded world of movements, gestures, and looks.

There is no overlooking the presence of the animal in Muybridge's work or terminology. Muybridge described his work as "zoopraxography"—the picturing of animal motion or, more literally, the writing of animal praxis. Further, he named his invention the "zoopraxiscope"—an instrument for looking at animal motion. While the obvious reference of these names in the prehistory of cinema is the zoetrope, we mustn't forget that contemporaneous with the emergence of photography, the West had witnessed the proliferation of zoological parks across Europe and the United States. When photography was invented, there were only three zoos in Europe; by the emergence of the cinematographe in 1895, there were nearly one hundred throughout Europe and the United States.[8] More importantly, the clearly stated motivation for Muybridge's pursuit of series photography was the desire to see animals, specifically a horse, more clearly. Indeed, like the emergence of the zoological space, Muybridge's invention was conceived of as an apparatus that allowed humans to see animals in a way that preexisting technologies and strategies of looking did not. As the story goes, because Leland Stanford's horse, Occident, was such a fast trotter, human vision was insufficient to clearly determine the position of the animal's legs at any one moment, and more specifically to see if all four of its feet left the ground at any one point.[9] In this leap forward for visual technology—lining a track with cameras, having the horse trigger the shutters as it ran past them—photography was quite expressly conceived of and employed as a supplement to human vision: it could see that which was hidden from the naked human eye. The apparatus thereby takes on its own animal status, performing a biological function for which the human organ is insufficient.

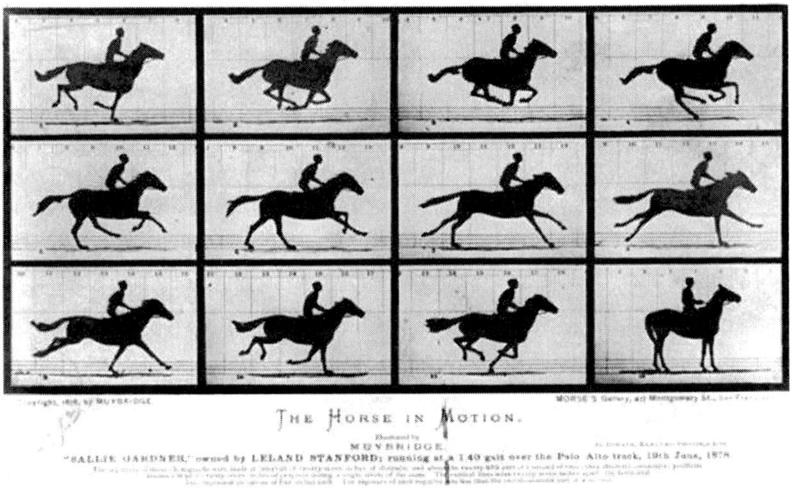

Fig 7-1: Muybridge's first published study of animal locomotion.

What is often overlooked here is that there are two challenges, both crucial to the emergence of cinema, posed by capturing a moving animal. First, one must stop the animal, freeze its movement in a single exposure, which involves both increasing shutter speeds and manufacturing plates light-sensitive enough to record the image with such short exposure times. This is a distinctly animal challenge, indeed a problem posed not only by a moving horse but by animals more generally. Prior to these technological advances, photography was somewhat limited to landscapes and portraits, precisely because everything in the frame had to remain still. Given that landscapes don't move and people can be told to sit still for the duration of an exposure, up until this point animals were literally and figuratively somewhat of a cloudy spot in the history of photography.[10]

Muybridge's decision to line a track with cameras in order to capture successive images of the trotting horse at very short intervals was the second, better-known innovation. Though various methods were used to trigger the shutter, such as strings across the track tripped by the horse's legs and the sulky wheel connecting a circuit, all of the initial means employed the animal's movement itself. Thus, in a manner of speaking, the horse was taking pictures of itself. Such an act not only appears to produce its own instantaneity, it gathers its movement into the intervals between those instants, which cinema would later redeploy. As such, both of Muybridge's innovations, viz. the cinematic reorganization of time and space, are responses to animal life. Not only was he able to see what had previously been the secret of the horse—indeed, all four legs left the ground at once—he instrumentalized animal agency in order to reveal that secret and create a new form of human representation. Whatever the involvement of the animal in the evolution of photography prior to Muybridge's experiments at Palo Alto, from this point on the animal, and more generally animality, would become inextricably bound up with motion photography. On top of that, it is at this moment that photography (still and motion) becomes an instrument that reveals the unknown secrets of the natural world. Again, it captures that which the naked eye cannot perceive.

The role of animals in the emergence of cinema is not however limited to a circumstantial experiment undertaken for Muybridge's chief supporter and financial backer. Not only did Muybridge dedicate most of the rest of his life's work to the study of human and animal motion with various photographic apparatuses, Muybridge's study of animals would inspire collaborator Etienne-Jules Marey to invent the chronophotographic gun. By turning his attention to birds, Marey deployed the problems posed by capturing animal movement as a motivation for yet another crucial development in cinema's prehistory. Because one could not reasonably expect birds to trigger shutters or move in a predetermined direction, Marey developed a photographic gun, which captured several successive images at predetermined intervals. Further, it was handheld and thus could adjust to the unpredictability of bird flight. Thus, it is precisely through the commingling of animal and machine that cinema continues to emerge.

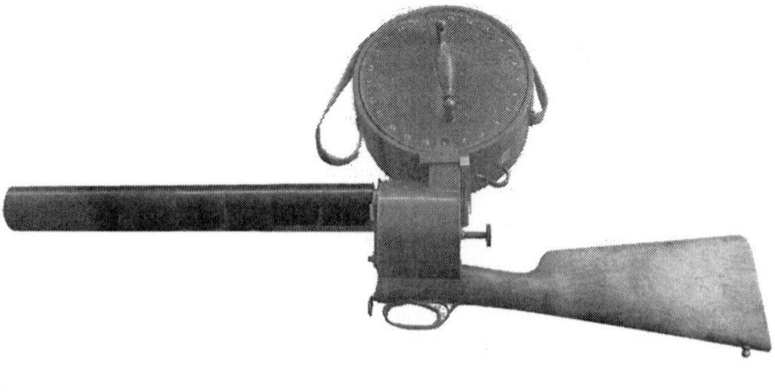

Fig 7-2: Marey's Chronophotographic Gun. Image by David Monniaux. Used under the GNU Free Documentation License.

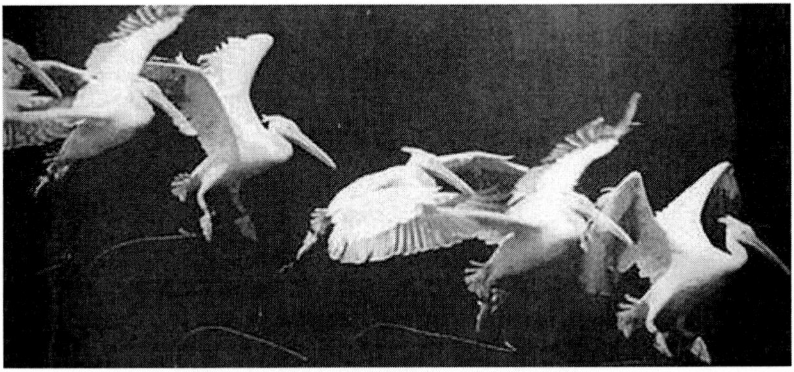

Fig 7-3: One of Marey's studies of bird flight.

In his first book, *La Machine Animale*, Marey writes "Living beings have frequently and in every age been compared to machines, but it is only in the present day that the bearing and the justice of this comparison are fully comprehensible."[11] Though Marey was likely referring to animals and humans as the animal mechanism in order to suggest the mechanicity of living things, we might just as well choose to read him back onto his own machinery. Though he saw them more or less as different ways of performing the same measurement, in many ways Marey actually privileged his graphic method of capturing animal movement in which animal movements were literally measured and graphed by the instruments attached to the subject's body.

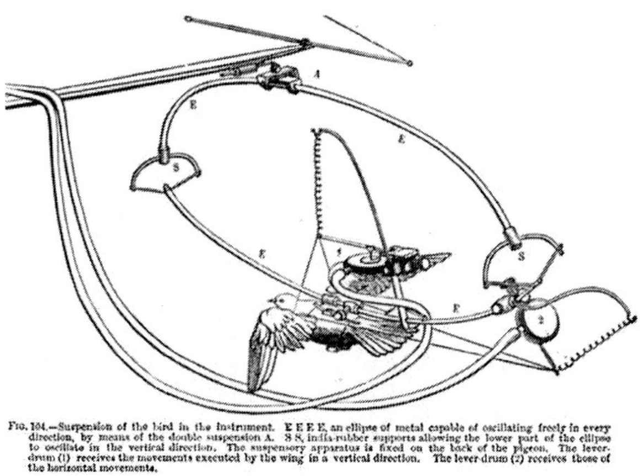

Fig 7-4: A pre-photographic motion study, from Marey's *Machine Animale*.

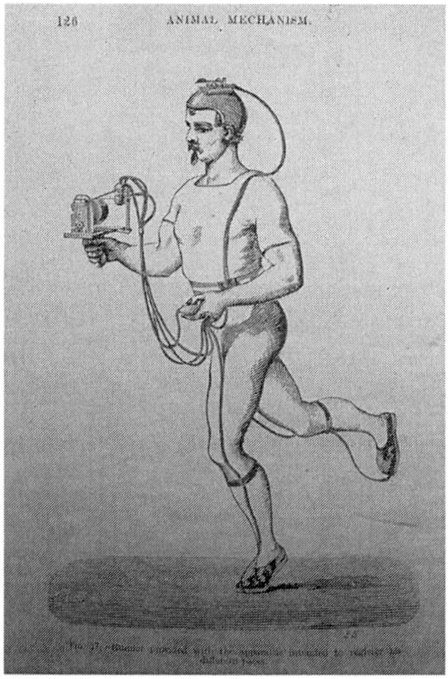

Fig 7-5: Marey's study of human motion, from *Machine Animale*.

What is achieved in both methods, however, is a clear commingling of animal and machine, an apparatus which adapts to the body, meets it at its borders, and extends out of it. This is to say, as suggested above, there is something distinctly animal about the photographic apparatus, Muybridge and Marey's proto-cinematic technologies, and cinema itself, in not only the focus on animals and their distinctive role in its development, but insofar as the varied apparatuses operate as supplements to or replacements for human vision.

Both the zoological park and cinema appear to ground human practices of representation in the world as much by the nature of the representations they produce as by the nature of the apparatuses they employ. The zoo and the cinema appear to recapture and recuperate an increasingly distant natural, living world; in so doing they respond to and reveal an emerging crisis in representation. The markers of this crisis are to be found in the mechanisms and architectures with which these practices hope to collect, contain, organize, and display the living as well as in the desire to participate in a mode of representation not subject to the slipperiness of signification. Film and photography appear to counteract this slipperiness because the mode of representation depends on the light reflected by the *imaged* object. This type of sign was described by Charles Sanders Peirce as the index—"a representamen which fulfills the function of a representamen by virtue of a character which it could not have if its object did not exist."[12] The connection between representation and the world is physical, the image insists on what *must have been*; though it can be deeply manipulated, the film image always bears some trace of the object it has captured. To remove that connection between image and object is to step outside of photographic representation. Though perhaps the zoo is not precisely indexical, the zoo animal is at once powerfully real and, in its decontextualized performance of its species and its colony of origin, reduced to a harmless trace. Like the photograph and the actualité, the zoo as well insists on what must have been—e.g. an Africa, a hunter, and a lion. Insofar as these representational practices offer a way of signifying that is at once non-arbitrary and yet available to the human subject, they appear to offer redemption to a system of signification in crisis. They offer hope that things might again have meaning in and of themselves—a return to Adamic language, the *call of the object*. As the animal is involved in any return to paradise, the nature of animal language, or the imagination of such, is not separate from the issue of indexicality. In *The Electric Animal,* Akira Mizuta Lippit has argued that animal language differs from human language in that animal communication has an almost indexical relationship to the state of the animal situated in its perceived environment. By contrast the relation between referent and signifier in human language is arbitrary, conventional, and thus subject to slippage.[13] While animals can lie, they cannot fabulate; as such, their utterances, gestures, and looks remain connected to the world. This understanding or imagination of the animal raises a number of questions unique to the analyses of the zoo and cinema. Namely, considering their investments in the display of real life, what does it mean, in the zoo and the cinema, to represent animals (and humans) in an animal, that is indexical, way?

The nineteenth century witnesses both dramatic developments in visual culture and the removal of animals from modern daily life. John Berger, in his book *About Looking,* has pointed out that "Public Zoos came into existence… at the beginning of the period which was to see the disappearance of animals from daily life."[14] Lippit expands on this point and argues that a deep correlation exists between "the disappearance of wildlife from humanity's habitat [and] the reappearance of the same in humanity's reflections on itself … such as the telephone, film and radio."[15] These phenomena suggest a deep-seated cultural need to recover the loss of the animal at the moment of its relegation. More importantly, it suggests that both the zoo and cinema occupy similar positions as responses to a loss of the animal—the recuperation of such in its indexical trace. For Lippit, the culmination of this loss and work of recuperation is the electric animal, but perhaps more potently for this analysis, it is the image of the animal, the *animal-image.*

Muybridge's work externalizes and simulates the human perceptual apparatus and produces images of animal and human life unfolding in time. His work promises to reanimate human representation by giving it life through the movement it captures and recreating it in a mechanical apparatus. Two important characteristics distinguish Muybridge's work at the University of Pennsylvania a decade later from his initial studies in animal movement. First, 16 of the 781 plates of the later study demonstrate a distinctly different approach to the issue of capturing movement in time. These 16 plates display sets of images that differ from one another not by the passage of time but by differences in camera position. Taken simultaneously, these images effectively replace the scale of time with space, thus radically destabilizing the perceptual order. As Crary has written of the earlier studies, so too, I would argue, these studies "posed plural scatterings of attention and the possibility of unforeseen perceptual synthesis outside of any disciplinary imperatives."[16] Well aware that his images could recreate motion through projection with his zoopraxiscope, Muybridge foresees the ability of the cinematic apparatus to once again supplement human vision. Projected, these images simulate a cinematic arc around Muybridge himself but since the images are taken all at once that arc does not extend in time, but rather moves through a single moment. The unfolding of time is arrested and redeployed into space and we are presented with a deep analysis of a single instant.[17] Such a manipulation of time and space once again supplements human vision, accomplishing what the naked eye cannot and hoping to reveal what is hidden from it, namely, the instant itself. Like the horse producing its own instantaneity and gathering its movement into the intervals, Muybridge inserts a distinctly human time into the space of a hybridized animal/ mechanical movement.

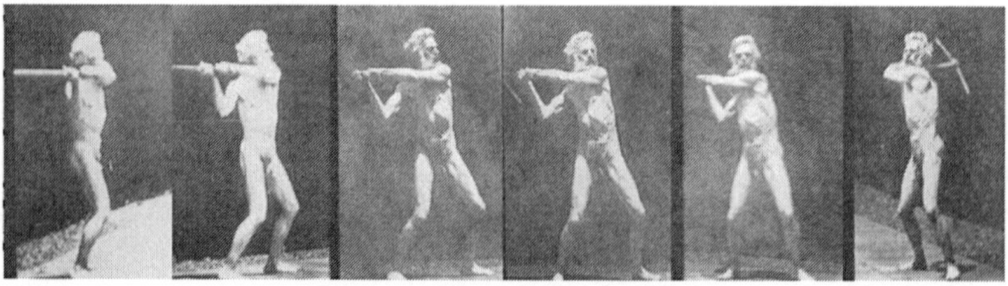

Fig 7-6: Muybridge's self-study

Second, this new method of capturing movement is exclusively focused on human figures and the balance of human figures to animals in *Animal Locomotion*, the publication of Muybridge's work at the University of Pennsylvania, is virtually the reverse of the earlier Palo Alto experiments, which focused primarily on animals. Though a number of technological factors contribute to an explanation of this shift—for instance, the ability to produce prints detailed enough to show the contours of the hairless human body—it is more important to understand this step into the object position of the motion picture camera as a double move of both technological advancement and mourning the deepening separation of humans and animals. Whether it is by virtue of Muybridge's earlier experiments, Marey's inventions, or the observational spaces created by the zoo, the space created for the observation of the unfolding of life is a space deeply marked and carved out as animal. These experiments contribute to the breaking down of human movement and to the subjection of the body to Taylorist regimes of industrialization, so that they appear to strengthen modernity's grasp on human subjectivity. However, by escaping referential signification, destabilizing the perceptual order, and occupying the site marked as the animal object position, these same experiments seem to open up a line of flight into the deterritorialized space of the animal.

In conclusion, consider one more piece of Muybridge's biography—namely, that he was indicted for the murder of his wife's lover, tried, and acquitted on the grounds of temporary insanity. In fact, Muybridge never denied the chain of events: learning of the affair, getting his gun, taking the several hour train ride, and finally shooting his rival. He maintained, however, that this succession of events somehow did not determine guilt, that there were extenuating factors that ought to exonerate him. Though he never actually gave any account of his reasoning, claiming instead a poor memory due to his disturbed state, his lawyers contended that he ought not be held responsible for his actions.[18] Tom Gunning has argued that with the inventions of still and motion photography, the body "became a transportable image fully adaptable to the systems of circulation and mobility that modernity demanded."[19] Beyond rising capitalism and industrialization, Gunning argues that this imaging and measuring of the body replaces marking it as a means of control. Specifically, it subjects the body to new regimes of determining guilt, of which the subject is often unaware and unable to hide from. Gunning writes: "In both the legal process of detection and its fantasy elaborations in detective fiction, the body reemerges as something to grab hold of, and the photograph supplies one means of gaining purchase on a fugitive physicality."[20] Under such a regime of examination, "The body has become a sort of unwilled speech, an utterance whose code is in the possession of a figure of authority rather than controlled by the enunciator," [21] a criminal captured "in an act of unconscious revelation."[22] In one of the images from the experiment described above, we find Muybridge, pickaxe in hand, wearing a menacing countenance and nothing else. He has turned his camera, his revealing apparatus, back onto himself. He has stepped into a space both animal and criminal, a space that reveals what the subject either cannot or will not. This particular arrangement of space and time delves deeply into a single instant, reanimating that which the camera freezes—how could this figure before that apparatus not hope to reveal that which no human eyes could see? Does he feel guilty at not having paid for his crime and thereby seek to reveal it in other ways? A sort of obsessive confession? Or does he look to answer to something outside human judgment? The sadness of this photo—and it is sad—is its manifold mourning of the loss of so much innocence: of animality, of a fallen language, of a murder that can't be confessed, and of an apparatus that can't reveal anything more than what it already has, an apparatus that ultimately can't return humans to an Edenic paradise. In any case, the scientist Zoopraxographer has subjected himself to his own instruments of observation, heralding the inward turn of both anthropology and psychoanalysis.

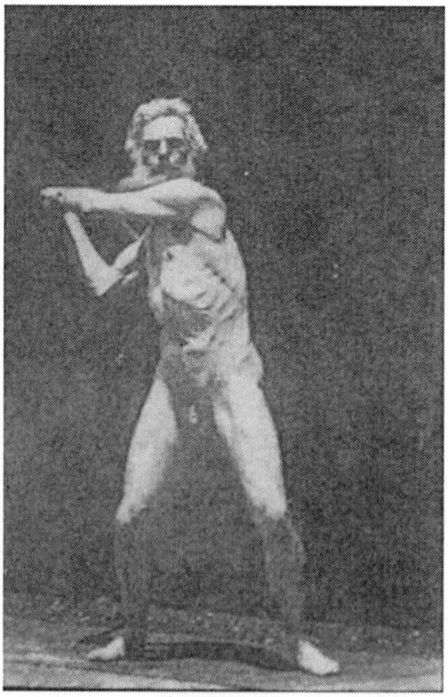

Fig 7-7: A single image taken from Muybridge's self-study above.

CHAPTER EIGHT

AN INCOHERENT COLLECTION? ANDRÉ DU BOUCHET'S *L'INCOHÉRENCE*

MICHAEL SOHN

> Ce qui est soustrait—à la lecture se soustrait comme en hauteur—une parole ponctuelle, un moment, le soutiendra… parole ponctuelle arrêtée, de même que son lecteur, sur la cassure. Mais les points d'arrêt eux-mêmes sont en déplacement… témoins—sur une interruption—en déplacement…
>
> [That which is taken out—from reading taken out like at a height—a punctual speech, a moment, will support it… punctual speech stopped, the same as its reader, on the breach. But the stopping points themselves are in displacement… witnesses—on an interruption—in displacement…]
>
> —André du Bouchet, "Hercules Segers"[1]

In 1979, French poet André du Bouchet (1924-2001) published two books, *Laisses* and the aptly titled *L'Incohérence*[2]. In the former, he collected what, for the most part, look like poetic texts, be they in verse or in prose or in some combination of the two. In the latter, he gathered a disparate group of prose texts and translations, many of which he had published years earlier in various reviews. What makes *L'Incohérence* unique from what du Bouchet had published up to this point is, frankly, its incoherence *as* a book. Five years earlier he had published another diverse collection of prose, *Qui n'est pas tourné vers nous*[3]. The texts, spanning twenty years and ranging from more straightforward art appreciation or criticism to prose poems and meta-poetic texts, all address in their various ways the work of du Bouchet's good friend, the sculptor and painter Alberto Giacometti. *L'Incohérence* has no such unifying object even if, to take a phrase from the epigraph to another very disparate collection of prose, Stéphane Mallarmé's *Divagations*, the texts collected "traitent un sujet, de pensée, unique,"[4] or at least can be made to do so[5]. All the other prose collections du Bouchet has published since *L'Incohérence*, with the possible exception of *L'emportement du muet*[6], group texts on related subjects (Reverdy, Tal Coat). Even *L'emportement du muet* limits its range to critical texts addressing other writers (Baudelaire, Leiris, Stétie) or painters (Poussin, Tal Coat)[7]. Why, then, the incoherence of *L'Incohérence*? And what does such incoherence do to the unified object that is—should be?—a book?

Asked by journalist Monique Petillon about the title, du Bouchet explains that

> [i]l y a peut-être dans *L'Incohérence* une contradiction qui se retrouve dans le titre lui-même. Au fond, c'est un livre qui, d'une certaine façon, me paraît très construit tout en échappant à l'ordre de la succession. Le livre n'est pas paginé. Un texte mène à un autre, une page se lit en regard de l'autre, et pourtant on pourrait commencer le livre par le milieu ou le lire à rebours dans tous les sens.[8]

If pressed, we can certainly see such construction. *L'Incohérence* opens with a prose poem which du Bouchet tells Petillon has to do with the relationship between writing and the voice, and then moves on to a dense prose meditation on painter Pierre Tal Coat, then to a brief text thinking about poetry, followed by a magnificent long reflection on 17th century Dutch painter and engraver Hercules Seghers. Next du Bouchet has inserted a whole section "on" translation: translations of Hopkins, Pasternak and Hölderlin, in the center of which is du Bouchet's important speech on translating Hölderlin, "Hölderlin aujourd'hui." A text reflecting on the "meaning" of the events of May 1968 comes next, followed by a prose poem in turn followed by a short statement about painting (Michel Haas/Cézanne). Du Bouchet then places a couple of pages transcribed from one of his notebooks, a text on painter Bram van Velde and, finally, two more prose poems. Clearly, a very constructed book: two pairs of texts on painting "frame" a central section dealing with translation, and the texts that remain (which I have called "prose poems" for lack of a more precise descriptive, "meta-poetic texts" might be more accurate) all reflect on language, are filled with landscape imagery, and therefore echo many of the concerns of, if not actual passages from, the texts on art and on translation[9].

It seems hard, then, to disagree with how du Bouchet describes *L'Incohérence*, but what does such a description indicate about the book and how we are to read it? That is, if we agree that the book is "very constructed all the while escaping the order of succession" and therefore exists as something other than, to return to Mallarmé's epigraph to

Divagations, "[u]n livre comme je ne les aime pas, ceux épars et privés d'architecture"[10], how do we nonetheless reconcile this structure with the lack of succession? How can we have a book without having the one and the other? And why, all possible irony aside, give the book such a title? Of course, du Bouchet might have in mind Heraclites' claim that the most beautiful order in the world is a pile of rubble, thereby placing *L'Incohérence* in a larger "philosophical" context by connecting it to the disorder of the world[11]. But even then, du Bouchet could have just called it "Proses", much like the anthology of diverse texts he will assemble in 1995 and simply title, *Poèmes et Proses* [*Poems and Prose*][12]. What, beyond a possible Heraclitian paean, does the title "incoherence" describe?

This common structure, or common lack of it, between the disorder of the book and the disorder of the world recalls Giorgio Agamben's description of the medieval cabinet of wonder: "Only seemingly does chaos reign in the *Wunderkammer*, however: to the mind of the medieval scholar, it was a sort of microcosm that reproduced, in its harmonious confusion, the animal, vegetable, and mineral macrocosm."[13] I am not claiming, of course, that *L'Incohérence* functions as such a cabinet, and there is no reason to describe its contents in this way just as there is no reason not to. Nor is there or isn't there an inherent reason to invoke Heraclites as a way to undo that "order of succession" that we expect from a book. The problem with this book (and there is no doubt that it *is* a book) is one of *description*, of where description in its effort to contain what it describes necessarily becomes, at least in part, its own content. After all, the title describes (or can be made to do so) what I have described as the disparate nature of the book. Yet, as du Bouchet states seven years later in his long and magnificent meditation on translating Hölderlin and Paul Celan, "Tübingen, le 22 mai 1986", when it comes to language, we cannot so quickly separate the container from the contents: "la langue—contenu, déjà, du poème en cours: au départ, le contenu n'était pas la langue. mais ce qui déborde la langue, aussitôt qu'elle a pris figure de poème, alors se découvre en sous-œuvre, et le poème enfin—lui-même un contenu à son tour."[14] As soon as we write, we are also *in* writing, the words referring as much to themselves as to outside themselves, and that outside a container in turn.[15] To call the book, then, "Incoherence", or to describe it as a *Wunderkammer* giving shape to that incoherence, is to have already forgotten how such words participate in the very shape they purportedly name. Does this mean we can only think about *L'Incohérence* in the terms implied by du Bouchet's own title? What are those terms? And if the title, as a word, cannot claim even a liminal existence but is already in and of the book?

As an epigraph to the book, du Bouchet places this small "poem": "… l'incohérence/ des parties de l'eau."[16] The lines echo many in *Laisses* and appear to provide a metaphor for *L'Incohérence as* a book: the uneven surface of rushing water exhibits various "nœuds dans le courant"[17] which constantly appear and disappear, seemingly without an order but nonetheless revealing on the incoherent surface the unseen structure of the depths. The apparently incoherent "parts" of the water, by recalling their adhesion to a torrent that "avoids the order of succession," reveal that the water is multiple precisely in being one, in-coherent and indivisible. Another Heraclitian hunch and one inscribing the title deeper within the book[18]? Actually, the epigraph is not a poem but the *example phrase*, first appearing in the 5th edition of the *Dictionnaire de L'Académie française* (1798), for the word "incohérence": "INCOHÉRENCE. s. f. Qualité de ce qui est incohérent. *L'incohérence des parties de l'eau. L'incohérence des idées.*"[19] At the threshold of the book, then, part of a definition, and that part which, rather than defining the word, shows it in action, puts it in motion, functioning as an example, as a phrase, already not completely part of the definition, subject to theft, to transformation. Are we to see the book as another such example phrase, putting into action the *quality* of the incoherent? The title would no longer function then as a description or as a definition, but rather as that quality precisely escaping the container it names: not the incoherent as category or categorical, but what *appears* to be, like parts of water.

That *L'Incohérence* functions as an example of (at the very moment it names) what appears incoherent *and* as the "example phrase" describing the quality certainly alters the way we read the book as a whole. This means that at no moment can we really isolate any one text without losing the in-cohesion that allows the book to escape linear progression and to nonetheless appear as jaggedly whole as a pebble or a mountain: "brisé et indivis comme le caillou (caillou nommé Sainte-Victoire, ou dans l'air montagne non moins privée de nom qu'au sol le caillou)."[20] As soon as we look to only read about Pierre Tal Coat or Bram van Velde or Hölderlin, we return these texts to their origins outside *L'Incohérence*, ignoring how their place in the book has already touched to the quick their status as unique and individual texts.[21] When we allow the texts to remain in apposition/opposition, the unique consistency of du Bouchet's language and attention threatens the specificity of each text. Thus, once incorporated into the book, each text is, to take a phrase from "Transcrit d'un calepin", "Individu. Indivis."[22] We can only read each against and with the other, each as and as not the other, less that they all treat "a subject, of thought, unique", than that they refuse, in the space of the book, to treat anything other than the *attention* at their origin. Talking to Petillon about the diverse subjects—particularly written or art work—addressed in *L'Incohérence*, du Bouchet admits: "qu'il s'agisse d'œuvres de Tal Coat ou de Segers, ou de pages écrites par Pasternak, Hölderlin ou Hopkins, ce sont des œuvres qui existent tout à fait indépendamment. Je les prends en charge avec toute l'attention dont je dispose, mais dans cette attention elles se perdent aussi."[23] The separate, independent works are lost precisely because du Bouchet attends intently to them, are lost not only *in* an attention suddenly translating its objects into a language profoundly foreign to them, but lost *to* such attention, as if the best way to focus on a work were, paradoxically, to turn away from it. "Si j'ai envie de parler d'une œuvre ou de traduire un texte," he tells Petillon,

> c'est que sa vivacité m'incite à un déplacement. C'est un sentiment que j'ai souvent dans une exposition de peinture. Si un tableau me touche vivement, il m'incite plutôt à m'éloigner à grands pas pour poursuivre, dehors, ce que le tableau a pu éveiller en moi. C'est un rapport d'éveil : je vais plus loin, pour vérifier.[24]

Such a "turn away" does not mean that one ceases to attend. Rather, the attention no longer arises when one confronts the object but takes root in the confrontation now *remembered*, a profoundly different circumstance for attending to an object. Of course, writing that attention down assumes, if not such a turn, at least a certain temporal and spatial distance, for other than notes taken in the heat or the cold of the moment, one writes always at a certain remove. Du Bouchet describes such a remove and a reprise of motion when he writes of a Bram van Velde retrospective:

> En face de peintures de Bram van Velde réunies en assez grand nombre, l'épanchement du trop-plein de la couleur allant son chemin, moi-même cheminant du mien—passé, je me souviens, comme à côté, puis au loin. Je me souviens de la disparition de toute figure dans la chaleur de ce passage précipité, laissant à chaque pas sur le regret de n'avoir pas fait, et même à nouveau, demi-tour (le tour entier ne pouvant être effectué que beaucoup plus loin). Mais de face, cependant, aller—comme la couleur—son chemin, est aussi se soustraire à l'immobilité du rapport de face qui arrête les figures… […]
>
> [In front of the paintings of Bram van Velde reunited in a fairly large number, the spilling over of the overflow of color going its way, myself going mine—passed, I remember, as if besides, then far away. I remember the disappearance of every figure in the heat of the precipitated movement, regretting at every step not having, and even again, turned around (the

> entire turn only being able to be carried out much further on). But in front of, however, to go—like color—one's way, is also to subtract oneself from the immobility of the frontal relationship which stops the figures … […][25]

Du Bouchet charts a mutual countermotion between his attention and Bram's paintings, more specifically the paintings' most salient feature, color. Both he and the paintings "go their separate ways," but in that separation he remembers (and writes) what he saw, and less what he saw than the motion that allowed him, for instance, to note "the disappearance of every figure." In this sense Bram's work is "lost" *as*, rather than *in*, du Bouchet's movement in front of and then away from the paintings,[26] just as his attention shifts from the retrospective itself to the turning away that defines, for him, total attention. "Loin de la peinture," he writes at the bottom of the same page, "et jusqu'à la perdre de vue — si ce que je vois m'a atteint."[27]

If being touched by the work necessitates taking a sudden distance and mutual remove "in order to verify", this proximally produced distance allows writing to move forward.[28] When Petillon asks, thinking of du Bouchet's prose, "[j]usqu'à quelle limite peut-on pulvériser le texte, distendre le fil qui relie les mots", du Bouchet admits that,

> [à] la rigueur, si on voulait se livrer à un travail de réflexion critique, une pensée sans lacunes pourrait être reconstituée. Mais cette reconstitution, je dois dire," he quickly adds, "ne m'intéresserait pas beaucoup. Ce qui me paraît plus intéressant, c'est le sentiment d'un mouvement qui ne minimise pas l'oubli, qui n'estompe pas les contradictions, les incohérences, qui ne nous retranche pas de l'instant irréductible.[29]

By claiming that the texts *appear* full of lacunae as long as we let them go their own way, du Bouchet repeats the epigraph: the incoherence both is and is not of the surface, is on the surface because of an underlying structure. The book "escapes the order of succession" because of this "depth," because the relation of the surface incoherence to the underlying structure is, as the metaphor implies, vertical, cutting across and against the horizontal continuity of writing and of the book.

Yet what seems to me the most interesting element of du Bouchet's remark is not the gap between seeming/appearing and being, between words and world,[30] but "the sentiment of a movement" incorporating what writing at a remove implies: remembering, certainly, but also the lapses of memory and the contradictions that come with them *as* the feeling of movement. In fact, as readers, we can only experience such lapses and the incoherencies that underlie them (like the forgotten riverbed "remembered" by the parts of water above) as sudden shifts in our reading, since whatever they were at the origin, these contradictions have now become part of the *texture* of the writing. Du Bouchet sees such a distance from the origin as part of how poetry takes place. Poetry, he affirms in "Image à terme",

> est comme décolorée par la rapidité avec laquelle elle s'éloigne de la circonstance qui lui avait conféré semblant de justification. Si loin qu'elle apparaît nette de passé, qu'on la retrouve au-devant de soi comme non avenue, son point d'origine ne se laissant localiser que dans l'instant, et dans un instant qui la dessaisit, coup après coup, des significations auxquelles on peut l'avoir assujettie.[31]

Although the texts in *L'Incohérence* aren't quite poems, as his remarks to Petillon indicate, in those remarks and in "Image à terme" he stresses the precipitation with which words move away from their initial circumstance. This means precipitating away from meaning, or at least those significations, speaking of poetry, "to which one was able to subject it."[32] We can understand this precipitation "à l'écart, soudain, de la signification," to take a phrase from "Hölderlin, aujourd'hui,"[33] in many ways and across du Bouchet's career. In the two passages in question, du Bouchet singles out the disarticulatory power of what he calls, when speaking to Petillon, "the irreducible instant." The instant remains at the origin and is therefore twice inaccessible—as the origin, and as, instant, irreducible. A few years later in *peinture* du Bouchet will put it bluntly: "le présent: une séparation."[34] Henri Maldiney sees such an inaccessible present as part of language itself. In order to argue that "[l]oin d'être une aberration grandiose et difficultueuse, la poésie d'André du Bouchet réactualise, à chaque pas, une situation universelle inscrite dans les plus anciennes racines de la langue,"[35] Maldiney turns to the Indo-European root *per*.

> *Per* indique aussi bien—dans les divers systèmes construits des langues—l'éloignement dans l'espace et le temps (passé ou futur) et le rapprochement, la direction où l'on va et celle d'où l'on vient, l'autre côté et le voisinage, l'affrontement et la proximité, l'enveloppement et la transgression, le passage ou la percée… […] Loin, en avant, par-delà, auprès, etc… sont indivisiblement unis dans l'articulation d'une même tension spatio-temporelle, qui caractérise l'être à l'avant de soi : la présence (*prae :* datif de direction de *per* et *sens :* participe du verbe *esti*, être). C'est la structure dimensionnelle de la présence d'avoir à se rejoindre, elle *et* son monde—comme un navire, à l'impossible, sa proue.

> [*Per* indicates as well in the diverse constructed systems of languages—distance in space and time (past or future) and bringing together, the direction one goes and from which one comes, the other side and vicinity, confrontation and proximity, enveloping and transgression, passage or breaking through... [...] Far, out in front, beyond, near, etc... are indivisibly united in the articulation of the same spatial-temporal tension which characterizes Being out at the front of self: presence (*prae*: dative of direction of *per* and *sens*: participle of the verb *esti*, to be). It is the dimensional structure of presence to have to rejoin itself, itself *and* its world—like a ship, impossibly, its prow.][36]

For Maldiney, presence is already a separation, regardless of the language in which you express it. I am less interested in the phenomenological and ontological consequences he discerns by describing presence as such than in how we can see this type of rupture in du Bouchet's texts. What does it mean to see the instant as such an inaccessible breach? How write—in—this separation? Du Bouchet rarely speaks of "presence" but, as in the oracular statement from *peinture*, of "the present," merging "being" to time.[37] We cannot apprehend the present, at least we cannot speak such apprehension—all we have access to is the past and the presentiment of the future, the present being a syncope as soon as we wish to think it. "[L]e souvenir n'est que la conscience du présent," he states in *peinture,*[38] and at best we can have "the sentiment of a movement which does not minimize forgetting, which does not smooth over the contradictions, the incoherencies," since the present as such disrupts any attempt to pin it down, much less to express what such a separation is like. The present is brutal for du Bouchet, destructive of anything constitutive and continuous since it interrupts and leaves us on the edge of such an interruption. It interrupts language along with the self, forcing each to "turn back" and confront, in the breach, a materiality and temporality outside of signification. Yet such a "punctual" moment paradoxically frees us, if we can still speak of an "us," "Gangue: moi qui ne peux le dire—me dire—qu'en l'éclatant: moi", he writes in "Là, aux lèvres," Or, in "Hercules Segers": "là je suis, je ne suis pas là..."[39]

How does writing, then, fit into such a "syncopated" experience? Does it merely mark the edges of the breach, a sort of cartography of the unsayable? Writing in "... sur un coin éclaté" that "[l]a pensée à froid (je me souviens de la chaleur) la pensée à froid est contrainte ici de passer par les chemins du langage qui n'est pas le sien. D'ailleurs, il n'y a pas de chemins, pas de langue,"[40] du Bouchet indicates that a syncope also exists between thought and language. Yet if language is never owned by or subject to thought, what place does poetry or writing have? Is it, to return to *L'Incohérence*, a question of offering another *example* dangerously close to figure (as in the tension between thinking coldly and a memory of heat)? Does writing, then, provide "le dosage d'un matériau conducteur de la perception pressentie—à communiquer sans qu'elle se perde, ou qu'elle ne soit pas seule tout à fait à se perdre—aussitôt confondu avec ce qui aura été perçu"?[41] In a text occupying the margins of "Sous le linteau en forme de joug," a prose meditation on Tal Coat's art, du Bouchet hints at an answer: "... l'articulation d'une pensée, où elle s'enclenche, apparaît de nouveau enfouie, comme reprise dans sa gangue, inapte, de nouveau, à indiquer.../ je reconnais, je ne connais pas."[42] The way thought articulates—and it is not by chance du Bouchet uses a verb with mechanical overtones like "s'enclencher"—has little to do with *indicating*, with indexicality, with confronting, in an etymological sense, the phenomenal world of which we and our words are a very physical part. Thinking fallen back into its fleshy gangue, we can now recognize without knowing. Recognition does not need to pass through a name,[43] perhaps happens faster than we can name, has little to do with the immobile structures implicit in knowledge and, more importantly, exists in the present moment *as* anteriority,[44] since we never recognize for the first time. Unless, of course, such recognition outside anteriority is poetry: "Le mouvement: par poème qui renvoie à une pensée,—et la pensée, à ce qui demeurera irréfléchi."[45] Poetry—and writing—cannot escape thinking, but we can miss recognizing the *movement* that alone opens language to what exceeds and precedes it. The poem may point towards a thought, but that thought must lead us to what will have already remained outside of reflection. It is this movement that alone gives the sentiment or, better yet, the "presentiment," of what language and thought cannot encompass, subject, enclose.[46]

How in *L'Incohérence* do we recognize this movement of language beyond language, at least in a way that does not just cite du Bouchet's descriptions as I have here and there? *L'Incohérence*'s content does not fundamentally differ from the poems and metapoetic prose du Bouchet will continue to publish up until his death in 2001. The book does differ, however, in the degree to which the movement and the turn away physically punctuate the pages, as if the "quality" of the incoherent were not so much what *L'Incohérence* says than what it shows, not so much what we do or do not understand than what we see. And what do we see? Prose to be sure, frequently looking like prose. But in some of the texts, the paper punctures the paragraphs, cutting in from either or both margins, sometimes pushing up through the very middle of a word or line. It thus transforms the paragraph into something resembling a "text-block" more than the even rectangle we expect from prose. And in those text-blocks we find parentheses that open but never close, we find blocks opening and sometimes closing with ellipses, sometimes sentences within blocks opening and/or closing with ellipses. The space between text-blocks varies, and sometimes blocks or series of blocks are separated by three dots, seeming to imply sequence or segment when the forward motion of the text brooks no pause. All these visible incoherencies remain fairly consistent in the texts du Bouchet published both before and after *L'Incohérence*, differing at most by degree and not kind. However, literally alongside these visible disruptions of the text, we also see text-blocks in smaller point and in italics congregating in the margins, sometimes just in one and sometimes in both, sometimes in isolated text-blocks and sometimes in sequences running across several pages, sometimes seeming to comment on the main text and sometimes going their own way. In "Hercules Segers," these marginal blocks spill out of the margins at the end of the first and third sections, pouring onto the page and into configurations unlike any other to my knowledge in du Bouchet's work.

Certainly, all these textual asperities—the incoherence of parts of water?—slow reading down by constantly interrupting meaning, at least the kind of meaning fixed by what Mallarmé called "le va-et-vient successif incessant du regard, une ligne finie, à la suivante, pour recommencer."[47] We must constantly stop to regain our bearings, to make sure we have correctly read a phrase, to decide whether we are to continue down the main text or to slip over to the margins or pause to think about how we should connect adjacent text-blocks if at all. What du Bouchet writes about translating Mandelstam rings true about reading his own work: "là, j'ai—marquant la page, voulu faire halte. comme, plus loin, sur l'arête de la fraction, fixer le sens. mais il ne se fixe pas."[48] When we stop to "pin down the sense," we risk, like du Bouchet, the works to which he attends, losing the movement which alone constitutes a direction (the other meaning of "sens"),[49] since each time the text's physical configuration interrupts reading we might suddenly find ourselves facing a new "point de départ."[50] We also find ourselves confronting the *fact* of our reading, as if the way du Bouchet works his pages has somehow solidified, made opaque, the very act that gives a book meaning and purpose. The figure of the reader actually appears in "Hercules Segers" where du Bouchet indicates that "... lecteur lui-même en cours n'est qu'un signet... [...]."[51] Reader, I move through a text, marking at any moment my stop rather than my step, at least every time the brute fact of the book interrupts my reading. That is, reading, the book never "disappears" like it is supposed to since the visible incoherencies and a sense "which cannot be pinned down" keep pulling the page back up to its surface.[52] Reading du Bouchet, we can never, or at least not completely, separate reading from seeing. We recognize the book, the page, the words and what they mean when we articulate and what they offer when we do not,[53] but we do not know how to proceed.

Yet "[c]e qui est soustrait—à la lecture se soustrait comme en hauteur — une parole ponctuelle, un moment, le soutiendra… parole ponctuelle arrêtée, de même que son lecteur, sur la cassure. Mais les points d'arrêt eux-mêmes sont en déplacement… témoins—sur une interruption—en déplacement…".[54] Whatever, reading, we cannot read, whatever interrupts our reading *as* reading, nonetheless finds footing in the very speech seeming to breach a sense we can now only see. It is the "punctual" nature of a word, the "existence singulière […] du mot qui se détache lorsque, notre attention portant sur lui, on s'y arrête plus longuement que son emploi ne le veut"[55] that both supports and breaches, that renders the syncope itself a support. Du Bouchet shows us such a syncope breaching and supporting in the last two pages of the first section of "Hercules Seghers"[56]:

> … *d'une lettre à une autre,* oui
> *et* non…
>
> (*interlettrer…*
>
> … oui *et* non *que l'œil*
> *appréhende à travers l'alignement qui*
> *se constitue, lettre aérée contre*
> *lettre, en un mot…*
>
> oui, *le* nul
> *se déplace sans aucune indication de*
> *mouvement.*
> *Une source n'est pas un*
> *signe…*
>
> … nul
> *est une source…*
>
> (*signe—pas plus que par le*

travers d'un mot horizontal, lettre
succédant à lettre alignée, celui
qui l'articulera debout...

Ce qu'il a sous les
yeux, étant là, échappera au
spectateur de la parole écrite,
mais il en ressent, feuilletant
le volume mal refroidi, aussi
le manque—comme en avant
de lui sa main...

(*d'un mot à l'autre, comme il est chaque*
fois possible—avant de parvenir à
l'autre—de se perdra...

oui *et*

non : *maillon confondant...*

... ici je perds, demeuré sur
son intonation, le mot qui
suit...

... perdu, c'est ici.

At first glance, du Bouchet seems to straightforwardly describe the experience of moving from word to word, if not from letter to letter. As soon as we recognize that movement, we discover gaps between letters, see "blanks" between words and lines and paragraphs. Through these gaps we glimpse the paper, but only at the expense of what had been letters and words and paragraphs. We oscillate between "yes" and "no," affirmation and negation, as between letter and letter and word. All this is in the page, *is* the page, is what "the eye apprehends through the alignment which constitutes itself, letter aired against letter, into a word." We move cleanly through the body of the words as long as the paper, immobile, doesn't punctuate, remains, in a sense, invisible despite its very material presence as what allows us, after Mallarmé, to pursue black on white.[57] The paper, not seen, is null, yet anything but inert: "the *null* is displaced without any indication of movement." Du Bouchet sees this "null" as an active source preceding and underlying the letters and words that we align into some sort of sense. As we read and write, we risk getting lost in these blanks since there is no guarantee we will arrive at the following word.[58]

We could—and many critics have[59]—spend a lot of time thinking about what du Bouchet implies here and how the white paper functions physically and metaphorically in his work. I would like rather to consider briefly limiting myself to the text at hand, how du Bouchet allows the paper to figure a whole panoply of "things," and what such figuration intends for reading and for meaning, if not for *L'Incohérence* more generally. On the previous page of "Hercules Segers," for example, the "null" is translated as "le muet"[60]:

> *Le muet—ressource du mot…*
>
> *… avant la lettre, comme à même le*
> *muet…*
>
> *à la main qui délite ou*
> *menuise, fraîcheur d'avant la lettre…* […]

Anterior to words, the "mute" supports them, fills them, especially for the hand that takes apart, like the eye that will later align. "Le muet" is a key word in du Bouchet's work, connected as here to language's source and support as to the paper against which we can see the words. He makes such figural connections explicit towards the end of the last section of "Hercules Segers"[61]:

> *parole :*
>
> *Le support emporte…*
>
> *l'air*
> *interrompu*
> *appelle…*
>
> *… l'air, de même que le papier, représentation de l'air,*
> *avant de l'emporter, traversera la parole qui s'y place…*
> *terrasses—*
> *représentation équarrie du papier (l'air, je ne le renvoie à rien, le laisse, aphone, à ses froissements—ainsi que moi-même, porteur parfois—sans un mot — de paroles…*
>
> *[…]*

… sans un mot brûle aussi bien que brûle sous les mots le papier…

"L'air," too, is another key word in du Bouchet's work, and we can understand why he sees paper as representative of it: breath is the body and support of our speech just as the paper "underneath" the words gives body to writing, regardless of whether we actually speak or put words to paper. Both the paper's white and our breath "traversent," cross, punch through the letters and the words that they support. Not only are words and their meaning at risk on the paper and in breath, but we are ourselves. For, as du Bouchet indicates in the third part of "Hercules Segers," this support is also what is beyond or before or not even the human[62]:

(mots ou hommes oblitérés, lorsque leur support inhumain, s'étant fait jour, achève—mots ou hommes—à nouveau sa traversée…

… et le mot dans sa voix—comme je vais outre—plus vite encore : la parole…

… en face est de l'autre côté…

… et confondus… paroles et hommes, par instants confondus— muets—au support inhumain soulevé lorsqu'il se fait jour (j'ai dormi dans l'amas des montagnes —au réveil comme défait—ayant eu appui, repos…

… interstice
de cette blancheur
par le travers de signes
qui
s'y inscrivent,
inentamée,
puis s'interposant, comme
au
froid du carreau l'haleine
ou une nue…
muet, l'opaque
sur quoi j'écris,
transparaît…

Du Bouchet brings together in this passage all the figures we have seen so far: breath and air and the white of the paper figuring breath and air. He also describes the mute and meaningless phenomenal materiality of "our" support, figured by the earth when it, like the paper burning up through the words, obliterates any human trace. The opening text-block of this third section describes such a support—and the figural confusion—clearly: "… l'inhumain élargit: aussi inégal qu'entre mots ou mains le papier… par leur travers, aussi, ce papier—ou, plus haut, le roc, lorsqu'il affleure, mêlé aux résidus de murets ceinturant le versant des Auch…".[63] The act of reading, when interrupted by any of the incoherencies we have seen, allows us to sight all those other supports of which we are a senseless part: the earth under our feet, the sky against which we are visible and, since we are a "chose parmi les choses,"[64] a sort of undifferentiated ontological materiality that, for du Bouchet, is "monde" ["world"] where "words and men, by instants mixed together—mute—with the inhuman support raised up when day breaks."

I have moved rather quickly through these passages, but what du Bouchet calls "la puissance de la figuration du papier," like sense, cannot be pinned down.[65] Even if we can list the terms du Bouchet uses to describe it, "là, ce que j'ai voulu dire, le papier, mieux que moi—et avant moi, l'éclair."[66] That is, whatever we want to make of this shifting figural splay, the paper itself is never multiple, never exceeds its simple (if not brute) physical fact. We can certainly understand this "brutality" as another figure, if not another quality of the incoherent, but it is now a *visible* one literally passing *through* the words rather than figured by them. In this sense, it means nothing, is for nothing[67]; simply, "... il y faut ce vide... et, au travers des signes aérés en quoi, un moment, la figure d'un mot, se constituera, comme sur un grincement place nette... le vide... fraîcheur qui disperse les signes...".[68] We can see this "cleared place," precarious, in the pages from "Hercules Segers" cited in block above, and we can see how malleable it is, never settling on a visual figure. From the rather rectangular blocks of text butting up against one or the other margin, almost like smaller pages in the page, as in the first citation, to the more "free-form" lines describing the paper as air in the second and third, to the text-blocks competing with more text in the margins in the fourth—what we see *as* page shifts, what we see *in* the page shifts, although the page itself never shifts, remains page and paper, ground against which we see the words and material support always threatening to overwhelm them. How, for example, to read a page where one, if not both, of the margins are themselves filled with text? Do such pages demand that we be, to take a title from du Bouchet, "here in two"? We cannot read these texts without also coming face to face with the act of reading, a way perhaps to figure the blind spot of our own vision, the face underlying our gaze, neither of which we can ever actually see.[69] Is this another way to recognize but not to know? But reading, I do know: "là je suis, je ne suis pas là" since "n'étant pas assuré de ma place ici comme sur le papier, je me suis interrompu pour commencer."[70]

CHAPTER NINE

ANATOMY OF AN EXHIBITION: W. G. SEBALD'S *THE RINGS OF SATURN*

AMY JOHNSON

The Museum Effect

Paul Valéry, a resolutely artistic rather than theoretical theorist of perception, is useful as a precursor to W. G. Sebald; in their common interest in the act and effect of perception, they each turn to the museum as exemplary. In Valéry's 1923 essay "The Problem of Museums," he describes the difficulties presented by the museum's demands on its visitor. Sebald's narrator's walking tour in his novel *The Rings of Saturn* (translated to English from the German in 1998)[1] likewise leads to much the same result as Valéry's museal difficulties do—intellectual, emotional and physical exhaustion accompanied by a pervasive sense of loss—for the narrator experiences the world as a giant museum. Valéry explains:

> [O]ur heritage is a crushing burden. Modern man, worn out as he is by the immensity of his technical resources, is also impoverished by the sheer excess of his riches.... All things end up on the wall or in a glass case.[2]

Not unlike Sebald's narrator, Valéry "staggers out of this temple of the loftiest pleasures with a splitting head—an extreme fatigue, accompanied sometimes by an almost painful activity of mind" (Valéry 205). Valéry's melancholia announces that the arrangement of aesthetics—and that our consideration of aesthetics and aesthetic objects—may be a matter of, if not life and death, the difference, then, between health and sickness. "All things end upon the wall or in a glass case" is the melancholy, irritated conclusion Valéry comes to, and this is the problem Sebald will reiterate at the beginning of his novel with his description of the window frame in his hospital room. Valéry suggests that objects ending up on a wall or in a glass case separates us from the ideal perception and thus experience of them, particularly when those objects are arranged higgledy-piggledy in a heap.

Sebald takes up the process and structure of the museum—its collections, its frames—as a version of the problem presented by perceiving the world around us, particularly the traces (or the absence of indications) of things past. The immediate concern voiced at the beginning of the novel, that of being overwhelmed by what the museum of the world has to offer, made bodily in the experience of melancholy, is blinding. If we are overwhelmed by the experience of the museum, what is it, precisely, that overwhelms us—what we see or what we can no longer see?

The Museum as Frame

Approximately one third of the way through *The Rings of Saturn*, while resting on Gunhill in Southwold, Sebald-the-narrator recalls a moment from a previous trip (Sebald 80). He had made that trip "especially" to visit the Mauritshuis in Holland, in order to see Rembrandt's 1632 painting *The Anatomy Lesson*. The narrator remembers that after having a bad night, however, he had been "so out of sorts" the next day at the museum, he was "quite unable to harness [his] thoughts as [he] looked at the body being dissected under the eyes of the Guild of Surgeons" (82). Nor is this recollection the first time the narrator has been concerned with being unable to focus on something. Before a separate and more extended rumination on *The Anatomy Lesson*, the novel opens with a description of the narrator's collapse after the walking tour plotted by/in the novel, when he is taken to Norwich Hospital in a state of "almost total immobility" (3). During this stay, he says,

> I became overwhelmed by the feeling that the Suffolk expanses I had walked the previous summer had now shrunk once and for all to a single, blind, insensate spot. Indeed, all that could be seen of the world from my bed was the colourless patch of sky framed in the window. Several times during the day I felt a desire to assure myself of a reality I feared had vanished forever by looking out of that hospital window. (4)

All reality—the world outside—is now framed, like the works of art he has meditated on during the previous year. The hospital window, "which, for some reason, was draped with black netting," is pictured in the text, framed by the black of the poorly lit room (4). This netting, which duplicates the framing in miniature, and to which Sebald calls our attention, first seems simply a detail provided for realism—a reality effect, emphasized, or "demonstrated" by an accompanying photo—but the netting will have reappeared by the end of this chapter (as well as throughout the book), its squares turned sideways into the interlocking diamonds of the quincunx of seventeenth-century naturalist, doctor and writer Sir Thomas Browne. These opening frames are immediately followed by a series of repetitions and revisitations, a frame that is itself an iterated pattern that ties the apparently rambling fictional travelogue together.

The framing of that hospital window is the novel's first indication of what I argue is its prevailing model for understanding—or framing—the world: museums. The museums the narrator visits may seem no more explanatory than any other stop he makes, yet because, as I will argue, museums are houses of melancholy, they allow Sebald to offer his reader a new way of looking. Museums are constituted by incomplete narratives, gesturing towards forgotten or destroyed aspects of the past. While this melancholia inhabits all kinds of museums, whether or not the arrangement of exhibits is self-conscious of it, melancholia—the refusal of closure, the insistence on narrative as incomplete—is especially acute in museums that preserve or exhibit the traumatic past. For Sebald, the emblematic collection is that of a cabinet of curiosities, or *Wunderkammer*, because the objects collected are not arranged teleologically nor do they form a narrative of progression.[3] Cabinets in particular were born of the "impulse to slot each item into a vast network of meanings and correspondences" in order to reveal a "fundamental unity beneath this welter of multiplicity" and the "desire to exhaust to the full every aspect of the real world, and to contain it within a finite space."[4] Cabinets were evidence that "[e]verything has its allotted place, answering to everything else in an unbroken chain" (34). In this way, cabinets guaranteed the authority of their owner-arranger, just as contemporary museums appear to guarantee the authority of a particular vision of history. One came to a cabinet "looking for symmetry, analogy," just as one must learn to read Sebald's novel looking for analogies. Cabinets were designed to recoup an "ancient, 'lost' body of learning," to establish the unbroken chain between "art and nature" (35). The different kinds of value ascribed to objects—scientific, artistic, religious—are "not easily distinguishable," especially if one is looking for analogies (73). As the "impossibility" of such an undertaking became increasingly clear, collectors began to use objects as lessons, as *memento mori*, or instruction in appropriate behavior and attitudes, just as later museums, such as Britain's South Kensington Museum, were organized to educate their visitors about anthropological and ethnographic "facts" (43).[5] Some items were, indeed, made into other items—shells and minerals, for example, might become portraits. Such collections, then, emphasize the transitions from one object to the next, the logic of the collection itself.

This kind of seeing reveals what we have lost due to human destruction, natural destruction and the passage of time.

Museums house and arrange objects and texts—historical or artistic—that offer a narrative of the past, of people, of the world around us. Sebald is fascinated by museums because they are the place where we think about the relationship between art and life, representation and experience, and they are thus essential to his project. Questions about this relationship suggested by the frame—Is the comfort of art an illusion? How does art affect how we see the world?—form the foundation of the novel. The book's first image, the hospital frame that is at once comforting in its evocation of reality and problematic in its obfuscation of what remains outside that frame, is indicative of the paradoxical relationship Sebald suggests life has to art. Institutionalized art is at once a way of knowing the world and also a way of effacing the reality of the world outside the frame. Like museums, Sebald's novel attempts to recreate complete narratives, but unlike most museums, does so by creating a perspective that is at once human and inhuman—made of the real, of facts, and given life through the embellishment of fiction, the artificial. Rather than passing themselves off as fully restored, Sebald's narratives insistently point to themselves as melancholic, incomplete or somehow fictitious. This sort of self-consciously artificially enhanced narrative, one that produces a critical discomfort or friction, Sebald argues, is the sign of narrative health, of an ethical attempt at knowing the past.

In this essay, I follow the thread of Sebald's comments about art—the making, marketing, and displaying of art—as his narrator tries to articulate what we see and don't see, and what the consequences of different kinds of seeing are. What museal knowledge suggests, and what Sebald's novel demonstrates, is that it is in our methods of perception and our consciousness of them that the possibility of the ethical lies. What I call the museum effect is, for Sebald, not merely the result of putting something on a wall or in a glass case, but a way of seeing that creates or facilitates uncertainty about its own accuracy by calling attention to the artificial design of all art and history. For Sebald, the ethical is a combination of uncertainty and the melancholic response to loss of all kinds—of knowledge, events, places and objects as well as people. Writing melancholia literarily reproduces the figure of the quincunx, both connecting things and leaving a space between them—a pattern, like the pattern of woven silk, another of the novel's tropes.

Museum as Metaphor

The novel reproduces the narrator's experience of the world as an exhibit, an experience that claims the body is the connection between representations of the past and the past itself. Is the narrator's problem, his sickness, a result of having seen "too much," as Valéry seems to suggest, or is the illness due to the *way* the narrator has been seeing? Perspective, arrangement's partner in determining how we see, is a result of where we stand, where our bodies are located as we look—in history and in space. The bodily effect of seeing is recorded not only in the narrator's own body, that is, his melancholia, but also through his perspectives on the art he examines.

In its evocations and memories of the past, mixed with the narrator's musings on the present, reading the novel is not unlike perusing a museum exhibit. The narrator is on a walking tour, and so we "walk" with the narrator. The novel insists that readers connect various parts of the book (and various pieces of evidence or exhibits) to each other in ways that are very much like the way museums direct or order the visitor's experience, dictating to some degree the narrative that the reader can construct, both on the level of chapters and across the novel as a whole.[6] While museal orderings are generally linear, chronologically progressing through a historical era—be it one of art, nature or science—and generally progressive or teleological, Sebald's ordering extends in all directions, like a cabinet of curiosity. It is neither linear nor progressive; rather than privileging particular historical moments, *The Rings of Saturn* attempts to construct a synoptic vision. The arrangement of "evidence" in the novel—its unmarked quotations from books as well as from people the narrator meets, its mini-narratives, its photographs, reproductions, objects and memories—suggests the catalog and arrangement of a museum exhibit, a system that is itself narrative. Historical museums, for example, are collections of objects whose relation to each other demands explanation by their very proximity, so that via its organization the display of a collection becomes a narrative of the past. All museums can function narratively in this way, but Sebald has the novel function like a museum.[7] Rather than having the museum "masquerading in the narrative as the past, [in order to] facilitate [a] critique of the present," however, as Barbara J. Black argues H.G. Wells and other Victorian authors did,[8] *The Rings of Saturn* takes museums as its model of arrangement to explore what art and its arrangements tell us about our relationship to the past, how the past is represented to us, how we perceive it and what we miss. In other words, a way to pattern the visible with the invisible.

The concept and structure of museums makes visible otherwise invisible connections between the narrator's "exhibits" because, Sebald proposes, museums are places where we must infer the connections between fragments. Those fragments, museums argue, are evidence of an allegedly once-coherent narrative that we are asked to reconstruct from what is left. Inferring here is an active process, asking of us the difficult task of inventing without being seduced into believing our own invention. Rather than a random assortment of events, places, memories and objects, as many critics have suggested, *The Rings of Saturn* is a carefully, complexly arranged exhibit designed to make visitors see its objects in new and meaningful ways.

The combination of a *fin-de-siècle* understanding of art and life as inextricable with an entirely twentieth-century skepticism about museums as institutional presentations of art and history[9] produces Sebald's "museum effect."[10] Like a museum, Sebald's novel narratively reorganizes the world in the effort to represent certain events, objects, and people as interconnected, a representation Sebald suggests is an ethical one, or at least an ethical attempt at representation. Sebald's novel, like a museum, has a structure rather than a specific plot, which is perhaps one reason it is thus far his least talked-about novel. The many museums the narrator visits, as well as the novel's museum-like structure, encourage reading the otherwise "random" links in *The Rings of Saturn* this way—as exhibits in a museum the narrator follows both physically on his tour, and mentally across his wide-ranging and often arcane knowledge. Rather than a collection's individual objects, however, Sebald's museal concern is with the larger issue of exhibits or collections, the narratives they tell and, perhaps most importantly, the other narratives they have, by process of selection and arrangement, obscured.

It is by stressing the structure of his novel that Sebald calls attention to the arrangement of its exhibits and their interrelationship. The novel's objects have an order to which we are unaccustomed, but which it is essential to see in order to understand the novel itself.[11] As an institutional model, the museum explains both the novel's project and its method. Historical museums, seven or eight of which the narrator visits, also attempt to make the invisibilities of the past visible through displays of evidence. The novel argues that such museums invariably tell us more about our relationship to the past and our ideas about it than they successfully recreate that past. "Natural" history museums and realism in art both work to elide the fact that we can no longer fully or accurately perceive the past. It is precisely a museum's or particular work of art's inability to revivify the past that should remind us of what is lost.

Artificially rearranging objects, events and people creates an otherwise impossible (unnatural) structure of things that we could not see simultaneously, creating imaginative supplements and connections between things where only gaps remain. Sebald's museum effect thus knowingly employs artifice in order to depict representationally problematic events ethically, that is, one that acknowledges what we can no longer know and mourns its loss. The ethical dimension in representation, for Sebald, is one that creates or facilitates uncertainty about its own accuracy by calling attention to its own design. Its self-conscious artifice thus creates a surplus of meaning, making what is being represented a figure of loss through the acknowledgment of the artifice required to represent it at all. In doing so, the representation avoids creating an emotional effect that makes viewers or readers feel—falsely, and in the case of traumatic losses like those of World War II, dangerously—that they can encompass or know what is being represented, despite the imperative to understand such events. The ethical dimension is thus truly in the response, ultimately, not in the representation, but it is the representation that either facilitates or obscures that response.

A View of the *Lesson*: What We See When We Look

What kind of stories can a museum collection tell? That is, if "[a]ll things end up on the wall or in a glass case," what are the ethics of that perspective? The narrator's discussion of *The Anatomy Lesson*, framed at the Mauritshuis and juxtaposed to the very different *A View of Haarlem with Bleaching Fields*, anatomizes the painting to suggest that, having framed a perspective, it demands that we think critically, perhaps subversively, about that perspective. "Demands" because Sebald not only wants us to *see* as much as possible of what the painting records, both in its content, its structure, and what isn't there, but each of the novel's exhibits suggests that he believes we have an ethical obligation to the people of the past to do so. The narrator remembers that, on his first trip to the Mauritshuis, "without knowing why, I was so affected by [*The Anatomy Lesson*] that later it took me a full hour to recover, in front of Jacob van Ruisdael's *View of Haarlem with Bleaching Fields*" (83). It is no surprise when Sebald notes that *The Anatomy Lesson* "would continue to occupy me considerably over the years to come" (82), given the two separate ruminations on the painting here, the first on pages 12–17, including a reproduction of Rembrandt's painting, and the second on page 82, presumably the fruit of the thinking he has been doing about it since. The juxtaposition of these two paintings leaves us with two major questions.

What is it that so "affects" the narrator? And, what does this have to do with *Bleaching Fields*?

The narrator describes in detail this second painting, Ruisdael's *View of Haarlem with Bleaching Fields*, yet this painting is *not* reproduced in the text.[12] Why reproduce Rembrandt's portrait, but not Ruisdael's landscape? Perhaps it is because presented in this way the narrator's description doesn't have to compete with what it describes. But it is precisely the second painting's perspective that makes it both palliative and suspect for Sebald. Perhaps its realism is so familiar that the painting does not seem to need to be literally visualized; perhaps he did not want to allow his readers the same pernicious respite afforded him in the museum.

Most of the description is given over to the painting's perspective:

> The flatland stretching out towards Haarlem is seen from above, from a vantage point generally identified as the dunes, though the sense of a bird's-eye view is so strong that the dunes would have to be veritable hills or even modest mountains. The truth is of course that Ruisdael did not take up a position on the dunes in order to paint; his vantage point was an imaginary position some distance above the earth. Only in this way could he see it all together. (83)

Ruisdael's perspective is impossible because it is "an imaginary position" from which the painting can claim to "see it all together." This phrase calls to mind the narrator's description of Rembrandt's perspective, which he earlier suggests is equally impossible. Sebald is ultimately more sympathetic to Rembrandt's impossible perspective because, while it is no less "imaginary" in what the narrator claims is its anti-rational anatomy, it is the perspective of an individual, an individual who was there; its perspective is grounded in the human form, both in subject and object. If Rembrandt's vision is preferable, however, what in *The Anatomy Lesson* so affected the narrator that he needed to recover?

What is preferable is also what makes the painting disturbing: its sympathetic speculation forces the viewer to focus not simply on an abstract lesson, but on the lesson as a material object, that is, the dead body of Aris Kindt. The narrator claims that in *The Anatomy Lesson* Rembrandt has painted the corpse's hand—the part being investigated first, out of the prescribed order of an autopsy[13]—as enlarged and anatomically backwards, precisely in order to call attention to the body, and away from the ostensible subjects of the commissioned portrait, the Guild of Surgeons. Rembrandt, the narrator speculates, calls attention to the body because it is in fact the body that, despite being the lesson, is the thing that has become invisible to spectators. The corpse, the narrator goes on to explain, is that of Kindt, a pickpocket executed that day in 1632 for his crimes. At the time, executed criminals and the destitute were the only corpses available for public autopsies or medical training, and so the moment of dissection becomes one of triumph over the criminality embedded in the body as well as over the mysteries of Nature.

The narrator argues that Rembrandt has purposely shown us the dead pickpocket's hand "not only grotesquely out of proportion compared with the hand closer to us, but…also anatomically the wrong way round.…In other words…a crass misrepresentation at the exact centre point of its meaning, where the incisions are made" (16 – 17).[14] For the narrator, then, the "exact centre point of [the painting's] meaning" is the pickpocket's hand. It isn't merely that the hand represents what Aris Kindt did when he was alive, but also that he is being punished beyond death for those crimes. The painting was commissioned by the Guild of Surgeons as their portrait, and while the narrator here implicitly argues that Rembrandt has committed a subterfuge and instead painted a portrait of Aris Kindt, what is perhaps more important to Sebald is that this vision, *The Anatomy Lesson*, is also a representation both of the achievement of knowledge and its cost.[15] It is not merely the record of a lesson for the medical students then present, but a lesson about the ethical imperative involved in looking at art. Rembrandt's painting memorializes the achievements of science while exposing the overlooked or forgotten individual destruction that is its price. To take the narrator's speculation a step further, if Rembrandt's commission were paid with monies generated by the public autopsy lesson, then this is another of the novel's many instances of art laundering blood money.[16] Part of the *Lesson* is that meaning is only created "where incisions are made." It isn't that the more you see, the more you risk your vision "shrinking," as Valéry suggested, but that the more you see *seeing* as an ethical endeavor, the more difficult because the more disturbing seeing itself becomes.

Rather than a "crass misrepresentation," then, the painting is a representation of something other than what it at first appears to be, and, according to the narrator, of what the commission paid Rembrandt to paint. Rembrandt, the narrator suggests, has imaginatively supplemented our vision in order to help us see what we otherwise wouldn't, what, the narrator claims, Rembrandt alone saw: "that greenish annihilated body… the shadow in the half-open mouth and over the dead man's eyes" (17). In his lengthy meditation on Rembrandt, historian Simon Schama claims that Rembrandt is, in fact, the first painter of an anatomy to do so.[17] Though the painting is realistic, Rembrandt's exaggerated "blunder" in painting Kindt's hand backwards forces us to see what the painting's realism cannot represent—that is, Aris Kindt, the person, as well as the system which has served his body up to enlightenment. A willingness to combine what is real with what is artificial allows Rembrandt to demonstrate what would otherwise be effaced. In its self-conscious artifice, Rembrandt's representation effectively conveys something that would otherwise be lost, while Ruisdael's representation works to elide its own artificiality, encouraging the viewer to imagine the landscape as a possible perspective rather than an impossible one dependent on its own artifice.

Sebald thus suggests that the power of the mind to create literature—to imagine another way of seeing—rather than merely a fiction, is a necessary element in creating any ethical semblance of the past. Rather than creating a "false intimacy" with the dead, it attempts to put "the beholder into an uncomfortable kinship with the dead as well as with the living," as Schama claims Rembrandt does. The ethical discomfort, that melancholy "uncomfortable kinship with the dead," is produced by uncertainty, the friction of fact and artifice.

Synoptic Vision

In collapsing the spectacle of a museum and a theatre of anatomy—a room in which people paid to watch the dead dissected before their eyes—the novel early on suggests its skepticism about strategies of visual display. This is the first hint that, as Sebald elsewhere puts it, "The accounts of individual eyewitnesses, therefore, are of only qualified value, and need to be supplemented by what a synoptic and artificial view reveals."[18] This, I would argue, can be taken to be Sebald's whole *modus operandi*, and what follows in *The Rings of Saturn* is precisely that—a series of artificially enhanced views combined with "the real" in an effort to produce a synoptic one, just as *The Anatomy Lesson* is here followed by the *View of Haarlem with Bleaching Fields*. Only in this way, the novel suggests, can we see it all together—that is, to see that we cannot see it "all." Rembrandt's painting is at once an anatomy lesson—what the Guild saw, a momentous scientific occasion to be memorialized; what the audience saw; and a moment of punishment and destruction, what the narrator claims Rembrandt saw. Each of these views can furthermore be aligned with a particular class perspective, a particular disciplinary perspective (philosophy, art, medicine), and different moments of time. The painting collapses the moment of incision and the time of painting, as well as pointing to the moment of Kindt's death and the existence of the Guild—dressed as they are in their unbloodied finery and likely not what they were in fact wearing at the lesson.

Both *The Anatomy Lesson* and *View of Haarlem with Bleaching Fields* hang in the Maruitshuis but are separated in the novel by 70 pages and in the museum by at least two rooms. *The Anatomy Lesson* is, in this sense, both separated from and next to Ruisdael's *Bleaching Fields.* Sebald has rearranged the Mauritshuis in order to make a new exhibit, one devoted to a consideration of what exhibits actually show us. As Sebald notes in respect to the Ruisdael landscape, in order to "see it all together" one must take or create an "impossible perspective," that is, a perspective which partakes of the artificial or fictional. The two paintings are two different versions of "impossible perspectives." Here indeed, the links are not at all random. These two pictures hang together because they share the same theme. Furthermore, it is the narrator's chronologically later response to *View of Haarlem* which allows his rumination on the ethics of Rembrandt's perspective in *The Anatomy Lesson* at the beginning. Each episode is concerned with questions of perspective and of what one is able to see, as much as it worries over what we cannot see. Indeed, it is impossible for the reader to grasp the full import of this without making these links back and forth throughout the text, weaving together episodes that are linked not by proximity or cause and effect but in other ways—by place, but across centuries, or by time, but across great distances, by similarity of shape or description, and so on. Again these are not random links, but links of resemblance—the kind of resemblance that, according to Foucault, "played a constructive role in the knowledge of Western culture" up to the end of the sixteenth century, specifically, *analogy*, *adjacency*, *emulation* and *sympathy*.[19] Sebald's links function similarly, illuminating connections that, in what Foucault would call our twentieth-century *episteme*, have become otherwise invisible. These links construct a kind of knowledge, a pattern that can accommodate both the visible and the invisible—the unknowable or unspeakable of the past. The distance between *The Anatomy Lesson* and *View of Haarlem* suggests that there is a necessary ethical, as well as historical, dimension to understanding the past.

Sebald's descriptions of both paintings are themselves lessons in how to see the ethical—or the lack thereof. Though both paintings embellish their views, the meditation on the disturbing picture yields an ethical dimension that seems lacking in its neighbor. And it is the ethical dimension—the meaning at the point of incision—that disturbs, and that Sebald returns us to again and again. The attempt to represent the world as though we are not embellishing it in doing so, the way Ruisdael does, is beautiful and undeniably soothing in this instance (though not, say, in the instance of a Zola novel). But, as Sebald's narrator comes to suspect, such subterfuge can also be unethical. The virtue of art, its right to exist, according to Sebald, is making us see in a way we normally cannot, one that specifically reveals or makes visible an ethical dimension. Realism depicts the existing conditions, but, as Oscar Wilde wrote, "it is exactly the existing conditions that one objects to; any scheme," and for Sebald, this includes any literary style, "that could accept those conditions is wrong and foolish."[20] To reproduce via realism is only to perpetuate the problem. For Sebald, artists of all kinds need to resort to the artificial, to obtrusive or excessive style, in order to call attention to the process of seeing.

In order to better call attention to this process, Sebald uses what looks like the epistemology Foucault describes as the "Renaissance *episteme*." At the end of the first chapter, Sebald turns to fellow polymath Sir Thomas Browne, who describes this way of seeing in *Religio Medici* (1643):

> [I]n this masse of nature there is a set of things that carry in their front, though not in capitall letters, yet in stenography, and short Characters, something of Divinitie, which to wiser reasons serve as Luminaries in the abyss of knowledge, and to judicious beliefes, as scales and roundles to mount the pinnacles and highest pieces of Divinity. The severe Schooles shall never laugh me out of the Philosophy of *Hermes*, that this visible world is but a picture of the invisible, wherein as in a pourtract, things are not truely, but in equivocall shapes; and as they counterfeit some more reall substance in that invisible fabrick. (74)

This antiquated way of seeing means understanding the world based on various kinds of resemblances, as cabinets of curiosity do. According to Foucault, "It was resemblance that largely guided exegesis and the interpretation of texts [during the Renaissance]; it was resemblance that organized the play of symbols, made possible knowledge of things visible and invisible, and controlled the art of representing them" (Foucault 17). "Resemblance" thus presents seeing as reading a kind of code, a science of echo, juxtaposition, adjacency, analogy, and sympathy. Everything is linked, everything contains a hidden meaning; it is merely a matter of figuring out which kind of resemblance is at work.[21]

This episteme of seeing and representation borrowed from Browne helps Sebald create a pattern in which we can see events that otherwise seem very much like dissociative breaks—calamitous events so unspeakable they seem unconnected to life as we know it—from war to natural environmental destruction. Sebald's arrangements link episodes of destruction to each other, putting them in a context in which we can begin to think about them. Yet the pattern he creates also requires leaving certain parts of that representation unfinished—in other words, speculative. These are the components that, for Sebald, makes a representation ethical, a representation that does not try to pretend we can ever fully recreate what has been destroyed.

Melancholy History in the Museum

The museum effect Sebald employs—the rearrangement of objects, events, people, and memories into an impossible perspective of the sort we are generally given in museums—does not allow us to see what is otherwise unrepresentable (for example, the past or a particular traumatic event), which is, nowadays, generally thought to be one of the functions of museums. Instead, Sebald's museum effect asks us to envision what relationships we are *not* seeing. Ultimately the gaps between the exhibited objects make room for the unrepresentable—the obscured or sacrificed that can no longer appear, even from an impossible, artificially enhanced perspective. According to Sebald, we have an ethical obligation to perpetually mourn what used to exist in those gaps, which we cannot even imagine fully or accurately. To mourn without end, in Freudian terms, is to suffer from melancholy, and it is an obligation to melancholia, to mourn the absence of even a trace of the destruction, that Sebald requires. Melancholia is the appropriate response to the ethical vision of a Rembrandt. For Sebald, it is the artist's obligation to bring before the eyes of the viewer-reader this critical melancholy, even making himself sick in the process. Thus, a certain kind of illness—a critical melancholy—is in effect a sign of ethical health, and one shared by almost all the many writers referred to in the novel.

It is only in museums that human beings, otherwise bound by the limits of earth and mortality, can "see" history, across time and place, past our own ends. Museums provide a bird's eye view of the world by juxtaposing its remnants to create a narrative, which we refer to as history.[22] In doing so, museums do not overcome the limits of perspective or accurately or ethically narrate events. Rather, they are a demonstration, an enactment, of the problem, but an enactment that, like fiction, frequently presents itself as a solution, or indeed, effaces the presence of a problem. Sebald's narrator is troubled by such ways of seeing, by how microscopes and telescopes may not complement each other but exist in a more hostile relationship, obscuring each other's vistas.[23] The narrator is attracted by bird's-eye views, but also worries over what such panoramic perspectives make too small, too far away for us to see, just as individual perspectives may make larger contexts invisible. Visits to museums in the novel, then, are not simply excursions to find the past; they are ruminations both on the relationship between museums and their spectators and what that relationship can tell us about the past and how we understand it. Humanity has longed for and created a world of views from above, attempting to give ourselves the ability to see everything, all at once. Rather than asking what these perspectives make visible, Sebald suggests that the question we should be asking is, *What does this view obscure? What has been, is being sacrificed in order to make this view possible?*[24]

Ultimately, all such bird's-eye perspectives are death-like in their attempt to see beyond mortality, to see in an unhuman or supernatural way—we either "stand on a mountain of death," such as colonialism, a recurrent topic in *The Rings of Saturn*, to see beyond, or we are ourselves dead when we can see beyond (125). The ethical is perhaps then something beyond human capacity, something for which we must always strive, though we are fated never to achieve it.

An Ethics of Perspective

Recent thinking about categorization and display in museums reminds us of this older way of understanding objects and relating them to each other and ourselves. In their taxonomic systems, museums make visible the ways in which we look at the world. In an exploration of what he calls "Foucault's Art of Seeing," John Rajchman says the philosopher claimed,

> There is a history not simply of what was seen, but of what could be seen, of what was *seeable*, or visible.... His idea is that not all ways of visualizing or rendering visible are possible at once. A period only lets some things be seen and not others. It 'illuminates' some things and so casts others in the shade.

Yet what is truly invisible is not those things cast into shadow, but "the light which illuminates things or makes them visible" (Rajchman 91–93). Rajchman's main argument is that, for Foucault, this philosophy of the visible, "to see what was unthought in our seeing, and to open as yet unseen ways of seeing," was an *ethical* one, and Sebald makes the same connection between the visual and the ethical in *The Rings of Saturn* (96). The linking, over time, of how we see to the question of ethics, might in fact be one way of describing the book's plot, that is, that it plots an uneasy connection between ethics and visuality. The idea that ethics is a visual category is hardly new—the ancient understanding of "beauty" in its ethical sense is, quite obviously, visual. Foucault attempted to "see the events through which things become self-evident" so that he might "see in what ways they may be *intolerable* or *unacceptable*… to try and see how we might *act* on what cannot yet be seen in what we do."[25]

Though Sebald has said that he does not believe "one can write from a compromised moral position,"[26] he simultaneously insists that we acknowledge that "Art is a way of laundering money" and literature is no different. Thus, to write literature is at once to manufacture a compromised moral position and depart from the literal truth, and yet, *The Rings of Saturn* suggests, literature—specifically a literature that "demand[s]… departures from the source material… [and is] drawn from memory and imagination, indivisible as they are"[27]—is perhaps the only way to ethically approach the human history of destruction, and to remind readers that the approach itself is obligatory but not enough. Departures from source materials and the emendations of memory and imagination ensure a measure of uncertainty rather than melodrama. And, to imply that we can know with any certainty the experience of the dead is precisely to presume not only a false intimacy with the dead, but with history itself. Sebald's prose works hard to negotiate the compromised moral position of literature, making visible things that have been invisible; but the ethical feat that it accomplishes is to keep what is unspeakable and unrepresentable that way while reminding us it is nevertheless our responsibility to keep trying to imagine the unrepresentable. As Sebald suggested, "There are many forms of writing; only in literature, however, can there be an attempt at restitution over and above the mere recital of facts, and over and above scholarship."[28] Facts need fiction to flesh them out, as it were, but fiction must be transformed into literature with the help of facts in order to be ethical.

Stories of Silk: Melancholic Writing

In the last chapter of the novel, the narrator considers the metaphor of weaving as a way of articulating the effect on authors of trying to get the right thread in representation, of the despair that such a representation is possible, and of the ethical obligation on the part both of the reader and of the writer to keep working at it anyway. The last museum of the novel—the "small museum of Strangers Hall," which houses pattern books from the local silk industry—is perhaps the most revealing in this sense. That this is a museum of or for "strangers" perhaps suggests that the bits and pieces of the past, as well as its people, are strangers, that is, those from whom we are now estranged, while we are also simultaneously ourselves strangers in the "museum"—that is, among the patterned bits and pieces of evidence we have left of the past.

The unexplained purple silk first surfaces in Browne's *Urn-Buriall*, a response to the discovery of ancient urns in Browne's area of Norfolk—not coincidentally the neighborhood where Sebald begins his walking tour. Browne's own skepticism in the treatise about what the urns "mean" historically or humanistically matches Sebald's concern that we take what is left—the objects or traces of the past—too literally, forgetting the gaps. Browne's is an earlier instance of skepticism about how objects and events become museum pieces and about the stories we can make them tell. The silk is itself an unearthed burial, symbolic of the veiling and unveiling of what remains, woven throughout Sebald's text in references to silk, silkworms and cultivation, and weaving. The silk offers remnants of the past but no certainties about it.[29]

Melancholy, the description perhaps most often (and most often without explication) applied to Sebald's works, is, for Sebald, the most ethical position—that of not letting go. Melancholy, the perverse insistence on keeping an emotional wound open, is the refusal to mourn, for mourning implies an end, an acceptance of the past. Memory remains an open wound. Melancholy is thus not an active remembering, for it does not, it cannot, piece together what has been dismembered into a coherent narrative. In this case, melancholy is precisely the refusal to accept a story pieced together from memory as commensurate, as enough.

And melancholia is perhaps nowhere more evident than in the drive to tell and retell stories—stories without ends.

> That weavers in particular, together with scholars and writers with whom they had much in common, tended to suffer from melancholy and all the evils associated with it, is understandable given the nature of their work, which forced them to sit bent over, day after day, straining to keep their eye on the complex patterns they created. It is difficult to imagine the depths of despair into which those can be driven who, even after the end of the working day, are engrossed in their intricate designs and who are pursued, into their dreams, by the feeling that they have got hold of the wrong thread. (Sebald 283)

The worry of having the "wrong thread," that one's efforts are doomed to inadequacy means the work of memorializing, of melancholy, is never at an end. In a Beckettian gesture, Sebald claims, "Writing… is a dubious business, merely more grist to the mill. And yet, considering the superior force of objectivity, it is even less defensible to refrain from writing than to go on with it, however senseless it may seem" (*ONHD* 155). For Sebald, the feeling that he must go on is an ethical one.

Rather than writing as something which solves loss, writing becomes a record of the attempt to do justice to what is lost. Whereas at the beginning of the novel we are inclined to see Sebald-the-narrator's melancholy as individual, by the end of the novel, we are asked to understand this melancholy as a reaction not to an individual loss, but to that which we have all lost—the past, its culture, its people. The melancholy that appears framed, and thus limited, by the hospital window at the beginning has shown itself to be everywhere by the end.[30]

Literature as Quincunx

Sebald has clearly woven a pattern in which all of this evidence now exists in the "impossible perspective" of the novel. If we tried to visualize it, this pattern might look something like the quincunx that is at the heart of Browne's treatise *The Garden of Cyrus*, and reproduced in Part 1 of *The Rings of Saturn*. The quincunx both connects things and leaves a space between them—it catches things as in a net, but also lets what is finally unrepresentable slip through, thus giving us a larger context in which to place what seemed outside of all experience and perception without falsifying the unknowability of the past, the unspeakability of destruction or the mystery of death.

We might also identify it in the woven silk that recurs throughout the novel. When we look at it, silk appears to be solid form, but looked at differently, it is a pattern of holes joined together by the silkworm threads. Insofar as the novel provides an answer to the question of the piece of silk, it is simply this different way of looking at the silk, as a pattern of holes. Viewed from this perspective, silk is a quincunx, a pattern imposed over what remains, just as the purple piece of silk covers the remains in the "Homericall urn of Patroclus."[31] The cover—that is, what would hold the contents together—in Browne's Norfolk urns is missing; the silk is what remains and represents what cannot be recovered or remembered, or unearthed once it has been buried. All of the objects, events, and people—the exhibits—the narrator refers us to are somehow like that somber and mysterious piece of silk. They are unfathomable in themselves; they mean only when set in relation to other objects or events, when put in a collection. The only way we can construct any sense of the past, and any ethical relation to it, is to arrange and rearrange and imagine what we have left; in other words, we construct a museum.

In *The Rings of Saturn*, the example of cabinets of curiosity places what remains in a pattern, connecting what remains while also accommodating the unanswerable questions. The quincunx, the connections, these other ways of seeing function somewhat the way Foucault described his own philosophies: "Maybe at best they have allowed one to think in another way what one already thought, and to see what one has done from a different vantage point and in a clearer light" (Foucault, *The Use of Pleasure* 11, qtd. in Rajchman 109).

The netting Sebald lays over his collection, connecting each thing to another, works to suggest that we are encircled by fragments all the time, whether we see them or not, fragments that seen together represent a vanished presence. Echoing—or possibly quoting Browne—Sebald writes, "The greater the distance, the clearer the view: one sees the tiniest of details with the utmost clarity. It is as if one were looking through a reversed opera glass and through a microscope at the same time. And yet, says Browne, all knowledge is enveloped in darkness" (Sebald 19).

The darkness that we must admit surrounds our knowledge—both in its getting, as depicted in *The Anatomy Lesson,* and in its representation—is embodied in the objects that begin and end the novel: apparently lost museums. Unlike the real museums that house melancholy in the spaces among what is left, what is exhibited, what is known, lost museums are repositories of nothing but those gaps, imaginatively filled with invented objects and events. At the beginning, the narrator searches unsuccessfully for the Norfolk & Norwich Hospital's medical museum, where he hopes to see Sir Thomas Browne's skull, while the last section of the book begins with a rumination on Browne's *MUSÆUM CLAUSUM*, or *Bibliotecha Abscondita*. In being framed by two lost museums, the novel acknowledges the loss of what we have traditionally thought museums preserved for us, yet it simultaneously suggests that a twentieth-century and liberally museal way of thinking, a quasi-Renaissance episteme, provides us with a valuable way of seeing, of relating to and understanding the world. Museums, as we have seen, claim to construct otherwise lost or invisible wholes from parts, to tell a coherent story based on the selection and arrangement of its exhibits. *The Rings of Saturn's* use of museums points to the novel's structuring (and structural) irony: Obsessed with what is lost, we appropriate the structure of a collection of found objects.

The museum offers a meaning other than that which it claims to offer, like Sebald's narrator's reading of *The Anatomy Lesson*. The museum cannot reconstruct history, but it does tell us about the museum effect, the history of the relationship between the arrangers and their objects, about how the arrangers see and understand the objects they have selected, as well, perhaps, as how they don't see other objects not included, or miss aspects of what they display. As Svetlana Alpers observes, "It is to ourselves, then, that we are representing things in museums" (Alpers 31).

We must shift our perspective to see all they can show us about our past and the challenge of seeing itself. By putting these museums in a series, or a pattern, with other museums, their exhibits juxtaposed to each other, a broader museal perspective—one reminiscent of Foucault's Renaissance episteme—is created. Museums, after all, are one of the systems that ask us to tell stories about the relationships among things, and "the persistence of the museum idea can aid us in not reducing the past to a form of the present and the other to a form of the same."[32] Not all meaning is lost, but the meaning we so often claim to be in search of—the Past, History—is inaccessible except by admittedly incommensurate creative patterning, recombination, an avowed aestheticism. For Sebald, history can only be rendered as art, is only as knowable as the shifting ambiguities of art.

EPILOGUE

ON BEING EMBEDDED: SOME NOTES ON THE ENVIRONMENTAL CURIOSITIES OF AIR TRAVEL

CHRISTOPHER SCHABERG

In some remote corner of the universe, poured out and glittering in innumerable solar systems, there once was a star on which clever animals invented knowledge…
—Friedrich Nietzsche, "On Truth and Lie in an Extra-Moral Sense"

Food Studies

Consider the JetBlue in-flight briefing card from early 2000s:

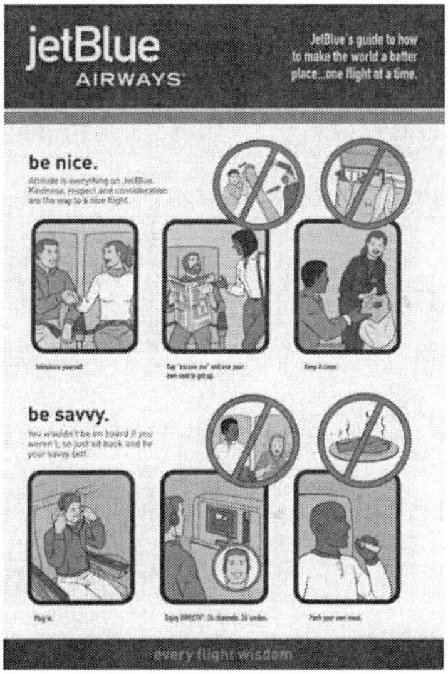

Fig F-1: JetBlue Airways "every flight wisdom," in-flight card. 2003

One instructional no-no depicts a plate with a fish on it; the idea is that your seatmate would be grossed out by the smell—*fish stinks*. This is a reminder that on the plane, passengers ought to be sensitive to the environmental constraints of the space: there is only so much air being circulated (and re-circulated), and a single fish can make the place reek. In this image, JetBlue advocates simple courtesy while traveling. However, the insinuations of this silly semiotic are penetrating. The JetBlue briefing card was one of the most honest and ethical examples in this rather bland genre: instead of showing how passengers should brace for crash landings, JetBlue simply advised passengers to "be nice." It is as if the flight was not just about the miles traveled, but also about humanity, and how we act in the world. In this essay I explore some of the environmental curiosities of air travel. These curiosities are often collected into imagistic trifles, but they usually contain profound implications when considered seriously in terms of what they suggest about how humans imagine themselves *in flight*.

Embedded in the Cabinet

Also in the early 2000s, Hawaiian Airlines advertised their travel services by embedding a single, miniature-scale Boeing 767 airliner in the midst of images of native bird species of the Hawaiian Islands.

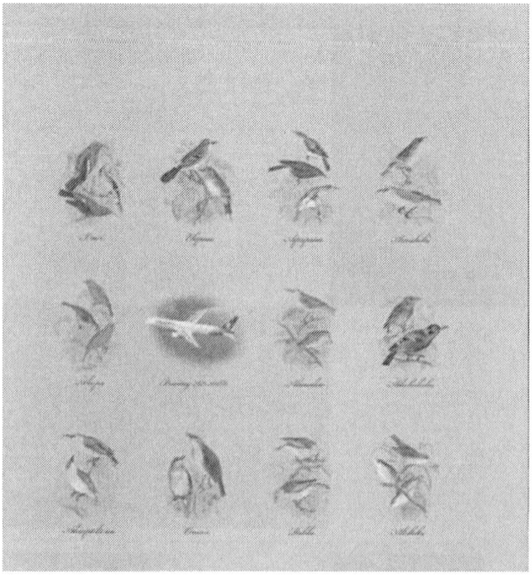

Fig F-2: Hawaiian Airlines advertisement. 2002

This ad campaign, visually striking and aesthetically pleasing, places the commercial airliner in a curio cabinet of sorts: outside the aviary, we are called on to be spontaneous naturalists, to view a series of specimens in their 'natural' elements. The birds are in appropriate foliage, and the plane is cruising at upwards of 25,000 feet. From above this grid, at a safe distance from birds and planes, we are interpellated[1] as consumers to *choose* a product: Fly Hawaiian Airlines.

Where are we, as human beings, in this ad? In many places at once: We are, as readers, above the page, looking at a grid of birds with a discontiguous aircraft stuck in, at an oblique angle. We are poised as if outside nature, in that Enlightenment modality of the detached, scientific observer. This means two things: one position has us *near ground*, seeing the birds dance on tree limbs, perhaps through binoculars, on a plane parallel to the earth. The other position has us looking down at the airliner *from above*—we are in tracking mode, spying on the plane from a satellite viewpoint. Finally, we are embedded in the cabinet: we are *in* that jet plane, or at least we are to imagine ourselves in the plane, reposed in reclined seats, sipping cold Cokes while cruising toward a sublime vacation land. All these choices of subject position are made available to us in this Hawaiian Airlines ad, or rather, we are asked to occupy all these subject positions at once: this is the excitement of the curio cabinet, the feeling of getting to have everything within, from without. The painterly image of the plane, surrounded by Audubon-esque illustrated birds, says more about the reality of our situation—the dark side of being embedded in a real environment where birds exist alongside planes.

Bird Strikes

The Hawaiian Airlines ad turns out to have been eerily anticipatory of the seemingly recent spike in bird strikes, that phenomenon that we would come to know so well through Captain Sully's disabled Airbus 320 (U.S. Airways flight 1547) that managed to land safely in the Hudson River in January 2009, after an unfortunate run-in with a flock of Canada Geese. In turn, the "Miracle on the Hudson," as it came to be called, seemed to reaffirm some of the more standard diagrams on emergency briefing cards: the photos of the passengers exiting the plane were all too reminiscent of the instructions for how to do so:

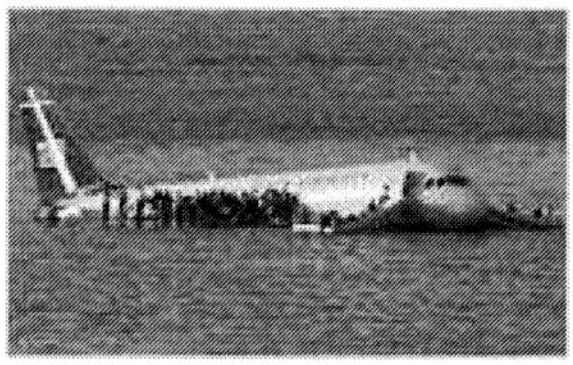

Fig F-3: US Airways Flight #1549. January 15, 2009

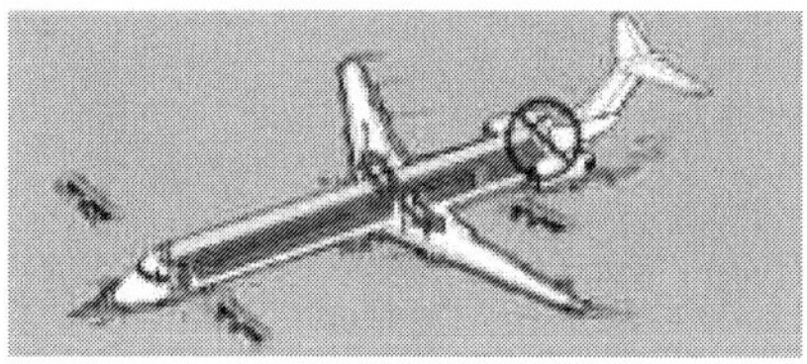

Fig F-4: Alaska Airlines MD80,
Aircraft Safety Information card. 2001

Unlike the Hawaiian schematic, U.S. Airways flight 1547 seemed to suggest that being embedded in birdlife is not the ideal state for airplanes, not to mention the humans in the airplanes. After the passengers were rescued from the sinking plane, many commented on the frigidness of the Hudson River; it was as if their encounter with the birds had caused them to *really* experience the elements. Imagine that: River water in January is cold! Here, the contents of the cabinet got too close for comfort: the plane flew into a V-formation of migrating birds, and the outside permeated the inside—first as the stench of roasted geese filled the cabin, and then as the climate controlled airliner was inundated with the cold flow of river water and sank to the bottom of the Hudson. Indeed, around air travel our tidy structures of curiosities can quickly collapse: a smelly tuna sandwich can break the allegedly inalienable rule of private space, and geese that go through a turbine fan can be more sinking—and demand as much storytelling—as a dead albatross.[2]

Choose a Seat

In the aftermath of U.S. Airways flight 1547, stories of bird strikes flooded the news. The sensational topic was gradually seen to be banal, as a simple Google image search will reflect:

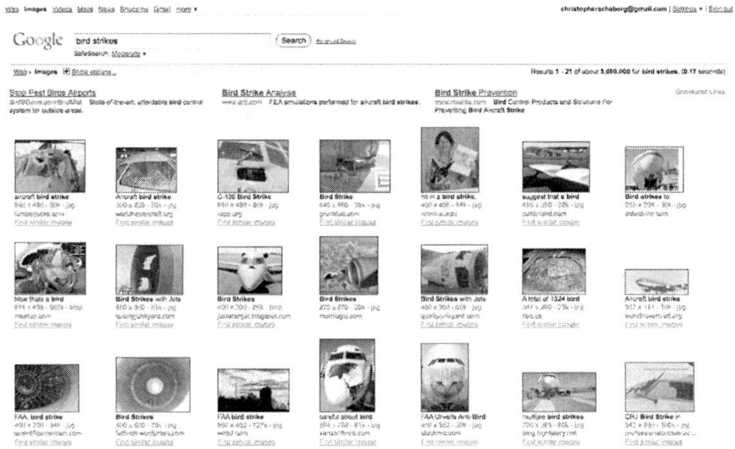

Fig F-5: "Bird strikes," Google image search. April 18, 2010

Notice how this grid resembles the Hawaiian Airlines ad: it presents many different scales and perspectives, and posits us on the outside, looking in, prompting us to select an image. The position of the bird fancier is related to the position of the modern computer user, and thus also to the position of the modern air traveler selecting a seat. On most airline websites, one can view the seat map for each flight, and choose a seat: are you a first class passenger? Economy class? Or do you prefer the emergency exit row?

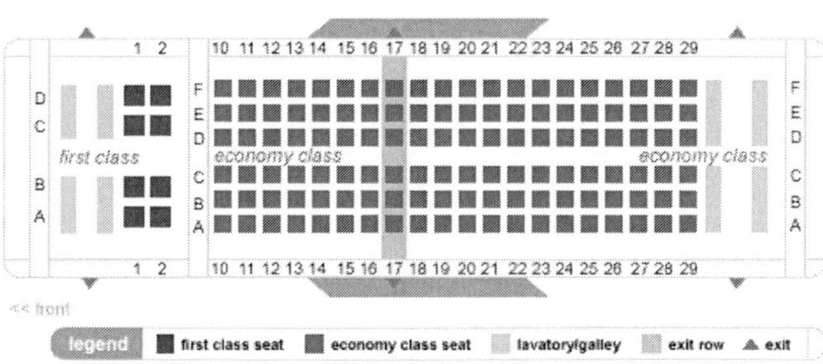

Fig F-6: Seat Map, Delta Airlines. 2010

Like an aircraft seat map, the Google image search allows us to choose our bird strike—and in each case, each episode has its contact narrative, gory remains, and an unsettling sense of environmental inevitability. Read enough stories of bird strikes, and one gradually realizes that there is no empirical way to avoid bird strikes, aside from emptying the sky of birds—a Sisyphean task that we may very well have already started to work on. To some, this might not sound like a bad option; to others, it reeks of ecological ignorance and ecosystem imbalance. In fact, if this dilemma sounds familiar, it may be because many of us witnessed it in 3D on the movie screen, taking place on a moon called Pandora.

The Empire Strikes; Birds Strike Back

In James Cameron's 2009 blockbuster film *Avatar*, an exploitative, proto-American corporation is colonizing the native people (the Navi) who live on the moon Pandora in the year 2145. The Navi are required to relocate, and their sacred tree is violently toppled[3] in order to allow the mining company access to a very valuable resource known as "unobtanium." In this over-determined environmental allegory, the Navi pray to their parallel world, and they are pleasantly rewarded with a form of vicious yet utterly 'natural' retribution aimed at the earthlings. In the penultimate battle of the movie, the heavily military-aided company encroaches on one of the sacred, 'wild' spaces of the moon, fully armed with not-so-futuristic helicopters and bombers. At this point, the Navi are trembling with fear, and unsure whether or not their prayers to the organic network have been heard. All of a sudden, the flying reptiles that we have become familiar with over the course of the film swoop in, autonomously yet collective, and debilitate the armed aircraft by hurling themselves into the turbofans and disrupting the flying surfaces.

In other words, *bird strikes* cause the earthlings to quit their mission, and the moon Pandora is restored to its state of nature: an enlightened, conscious balance of species who live symbiotically, in peace. In the end, the remaining humans are seen boarding their spacecraft, grumpily headed home to their own wasted planet.

Avatar serves as a polemic against environmental injustice; but where does this film leave human beings? Quite literally: *up in the air.*[4] In *Avatar* humans are neither consciously nor conscientiously embedded in an environment—they are left in outer space. Humans are kept out of the species matrix, or seen to be an almost purely parasitic species, a para-species worth keeping at bay. We must say *almost* because the main character played by Sam Worthington in fact ends up converting to the mindset—indeed to the *bios*—of the native people. In a weird way, then, the film functions as another sort of curio cabinet: the lesson is that by looking in at a variety of lifestyle choices, one can *choose* to be embedded, or not. As if humans are *ever* outside of "the mesh."[5]

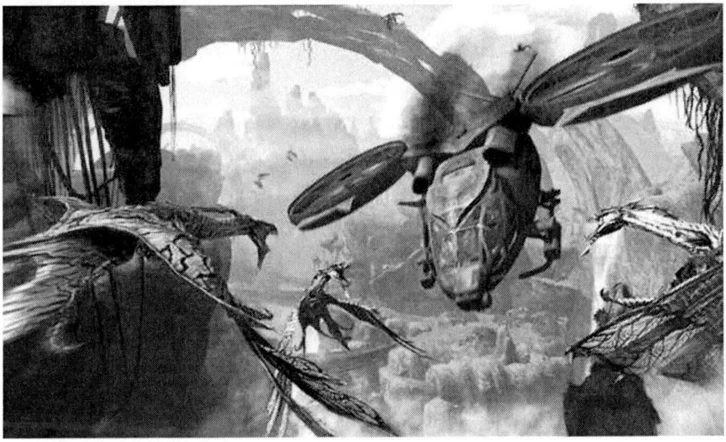

Fig F-7: James Cameron's *Avatar*. 20th Century Fox, 2009

Embedded, Everyday

"Turtles Invade Runway"—This was a dramatic headline in July 2009, when one afternoon 78 diamondback terrapin turtles crawled from the brackish water of Jamaica Bay and onto the tarmac at New York's JFK airport.[6] Flights were consequently delayed for several hours, as ground crews herded the turtles and removed them from the runways and taxiways. It was a rare but not unprecedented incident, as it turned out that Jamaica Bay is a rich breeding ground for this kind of turtle, and the mass movement from water to land is a normal part of the ecosystem. But the humans in this ecosystem did not like being reminded of their embeddedness: the turtles were removed,[7] and planes soon took to the sky again. In a way, it was as if the fantastic scene in *Avatar* had already occurred, in mundane everyday life—but in this case, the humans simply brushed the animals aside and went about their business. Whereas *Avatar* distinguishes rigorously between the moon Pandora (including its native people and animals) and the Other species (the humans), the JFK turtle takeover blurred such boundaries between the so-called natural realm and human culture.

One view of this incident might emphasize the starkness of human control, exercised bluntly and swiftly against the discrete 'natural' world.

From the standpoint of *Avatar*, this would have looked like a tragic win for human culture. But another perspective would show this as evidence that humans have their own organic logic of force and dissemination. From this perspective, the "turtles on the runway" incident at JFK serves as a more helpful "environmental" tale than *Avatar*, as it demonstrates the inescapable embeddedness of humans in the ecological mesh—even as humans (falsely) assert their independence from the ecosystem. Whatever we (decide to) do, we nevertheless act as an elaborate species-function in an intricate mix, and thus the JFK airport delay should remind us of our complex place in the world: we are always interacting with other creatures, things that do *not* fit in a grid, and even when in flight, we are flying through a biosphere—*itself in flight*—that is indifferent to our manic schedules. Those turtles might very well come back to haunt us.

The volcanic cloud of April 2010 that issued forth from Iceland and wafted over Europe marked the most recent curiosity that thrusts us at once in and out of the cabinet, via flight. First, the ash cloud is a news item: people are stranded at airports, flights are cancelled—it is the story of the hour. We are the figures on the shelves of the cabinet, in a predicament. Second, the ash cloud hovers as an "airborne toxic event"[8] that is as ominous as it is ephemeral, as encompassing as it is invisible. In short, it *is* everyday life—it is the space around us, the feelings of distance and proximity that make us anxious, expectant, eager, and uncertain. There is no cabinet—the more you look for it, the more it disappears. This is telling in the way that the ash cloud was compared obliquely to an indisputably human constructed event: as the *New York Times* put it, it was the worst disruption of air travel *since 9/11*. And as one stranded passenger, a Hong Kong businessman, put it succinctly: "It's a natural issue. Never complain. You can't change this."[9]

Being embedded is not a choice, but it does require choices. We may not be able to change the outcome of a volcanic event—but what can we change? We sometimes seem to forget that humans invented our means of flight. Humans also invented the idea of 'environment.' These are things we can change. Taken seriously, environment is not just that thing we fly through—it is what we eat, what we breathe, and what grounds us, too. In a sense, *we* are environment. This is what the birds and turtles show us, and Hawaiian Airlines, too.

Environment means being embedded, everyday—and it is no more and no less than the experience of *time*.[10] The curiosities of air travel might teach us that environment is less about *space*, and more about *time*. Time is what we try to save when we fly. But there's no receptacle for time saved, no cabinet for captured time. This is an uncanny awareness:

you can't get out of time (while alive), and you can't save it. Perhaps instead of bumper stickers that say SAVE THE EARTH, we should wear T-Shirts that say DON'T SAVE TIME. Being embedded in time is not an option—there is no getting away from it, no place "out there" where time can be held in reserve. Our everyday habits are inextricably environmental, but in more of a *temporal* than an exclusively spatial way. Time is the cabinet we cannot escape, and yet it is difficult to ever see this framework, "poured out and glittering" though it is. Glimpses arrive in the form of "ordinary affects."[11] Thus, alongside planes and birds, bumper stickers and T-shirts are two more timely objects in this curious cabinet known as everyday life.

NOTES

Introduction

[1] Michel Foucault. "Of Other Spaces." *Diacritics* 16. 1 (Spring 1986): 22-27; 26.
[2] Stephen Greenblatt. *Marvelous Possessions.* (Chicago: University of Chicago, 1992).
[3] Walter Benjamin. "Unpacking My Library." *Illuminations.* Trans. Harry Zohn. Ed. Hannah Arendt. (New York: Schocken Books, 1968) 59-67; 60.
[4] Susan A. Crane. "Curious Cabinets and Imaginary Museums." *Museums and Memory.* Ed. Crane (Stanford: Stanford University Press, 2000) 60-90; 64.
[5] Greenblatt 24.
[6] "Of Other Spaces" was originally one of a series of many tape-recorded, public lectures that Michel Foucault gave at the Collège de France. This particular lecture was given in March 1967. Shortly after Foucault's death in 1984, "Of Other Spaces" appeared in the public domain as part of museum exhibition dedicated to Foucault in Berlin. With its release into the public domain—via a museum display no less—and its subsequent reprints and translations, this pivotal article can be encountered as a collected curiosity in and of itself.
[7] Foucault 26.
[8] Ibid. 22.
[9] Greenblatt 19 and qtd, 81.
[10] *Primi Decem Anni: Jubilee Catalogue.* The Museum of Jurassic Technology. (West Covina, CA: Society for the Diffusion of Useful Information Press, 2002); 14.
[11] Ibid. 14-15.
[12] Tumlir, Jan. "The Museum Museum." Interview with David Wilson. Issue 38. March/April 1988. http://www.frieze.com/issue/article/the_museusm_museum
[13] Ibid.
[14] Greenblatt 21.
[15] *Jubilee Catalogue* 11.
[16] Greenblatt 74.
[17] James Clifford. "On Collecting Art and Culture." *The Predicament of Culture: Twentieth-Century Ethnography, Literature, and Art.* (Harvard: Harvard University Press, 1988) 215-251; 229.
[18] See Svetlana Alpers, "The Museum as a Way of Seeing." *Exhibiting Cultures: The Poetics and Politics of Museum Display.* Eds. Ivan Karp and Steven D. Lavine. (Washington: Smithsonian Institution Press, 1991); Mieke Bal, "Telling Objects: A Narrative Perspective on Collecting." *Cultures of Collecting.* Eds. John Elsner and Roger Cardinal. (Cambridge: Harvard University Press, 1994); 97-115; Tim Barringer, "The South Kensington Museum and the colonial project." Eds.

Barringer and Tom Flynn, *Colonialism and the Object: Empire, Material Culture and the Museum.* (London: Routledge, 1998); 11-27. Bennett, Tony. *The Birth of the Museum: History, Theory, Politics.* (London: Routledge, 1995); Eilean Hooper-Greenhill, *Museums and the Shaping of Knowledge.* (London: Routledge, 1992); Susan Stewart, *On Longing: Narratives of the Miniature, the Gigantic, the Souvenir, the Collection.* (Durham: Duke University Press, 1993); David K. Van Keuren, "Museums and Ideology: Augustus Pitt-Rivers, Anthropological Museums, and Social Change in Later Victorian Britain." *Victorian Studies* 28.1 (Autumn 1984); 171-189; Peter Vergo, ed., *The New Museology.* (London: Reaktion Books, 1989).

[19] Kenneth Hudson. "Arrangement and Communication." *A Social History of Museums*. (Atlantic Highlands, New Jersey: Humanities Press, 1975); 88.

[20] *Jubilee Catalogue* 16.

[21] Benjamin 61.

[22] See for example Thomas H. Davenport and John C. Beck, *The Attention Economy: Understanding the New Currency of Business* (Cambridge: Harvard Business Press, 2002).

Chapter One

[1] http://grandeexhibitions.com/CreatorsProducers.php

[2] http://davincithegenius.com

[3] RYP Australia Major Projects, *Da Vinci: An Exhibition of Genius* (Brighton, Victoria, Australia: RYP Australia Pty Ltd, 2007); 3. (Note: RYP Australia Major Projects, in partnership with The Anthropos Association, has since been renamed Grande Exhibitions, when it expanded the company's operating footprint from Melbourne, Australia into Rome, Italy.)

[4] Ibid, 3. (emphasis mine)

[5] http://grandeexhibitions.com/index.php

[6] Robert Zwijnenberg, *The Writing_and Drawings of Leonardo da Vinci: Order and Chaos in Early Modern Thought.* Caroline van Eck, trans. (Cambridge, New York: Cambridge University Press, 1999); 7.

[7] Ibid, 100.

[8] "Anatomical Study of the Muscles of the Leg, c. 1490," Royal Library, Windsor Castle: *The Drawings of Leonardo da Vinci in the Collection of Her Majesty the Queen at Windsor Castle*, ed. K. Clark/C. Pedretti, 3 v, London 1968-1969 (first published 1935) .

[9] Walter Benjamin, "The Work of Art in the Age of Mechanical Reproduction," *Illuminations*. Harry Zohn, trans. (New York: Schocken Books Inc., 1955).

[10] http://grandeexhibitions.com/VG.php

[11] http://grandeexhibitions.com/DesignProduction.php

[12] John Berger, *Ways of Seeing* (Great Britain: British Broadcasting Coroporation and Penguin Books, 1972); 7-34.

[13] Jacques Derrida, *The Truth in Painting* (Chicago: The University of Chicago Press, 1987), 12.

[14] http://grandeexhibitions.com/index.php

[15] Ibid.
[16] Maddalena Dalla Mura , "Re : Focus Design Display Design in Museums: Towards an Integrative Approach: The Potential of Science and Technology Museums," *Journal of Design History* (Oxford University Press on behalf of Design History Society, 22:3 (Sept. 2009); 259-270.

Chapter Two

My gratitude to Mary Baine Campbell, Thomas King, and Ryan Howlett for reading and responding to drafts of this article with astute and generous suggestions for its improvement.
[1] Neil Kenny, *The Uses of Curiosity in Early Modern France and Germany* (Oxford: Oxford UP, 2004); 4.
[2] Marjorie Swann, *Curiosities and Texts: The Culture of Collecting in Early Modern England* (Philadelphia: Penn UP, 2001); 26.
[3] Stephen Orgel, *The Illusion of Power: Political Theater in the English Renaissance* (Berkeley: California UP, 1975); Christopher Pye, *The Regal Phantasm: Shakespeare and the Politics of Spectacle* (New York: Routledge, 1990).
[4] See Barabara Benedict, *Curiosity: A Cultural History of Early Modern Inquiry* (Chicago: Chicago UP, 2001). The two landmark studies that trace these shifts are Lorraine Daston and Katherine Park, *Wonders and the Order of Nature 1140-1750* (New York: Zone Books, 1998) and Mary Baine Campbell, *Wonder and Science: Imagining Worlds in Early Modern Europe* (Ithaca: Cornell UP, 1999).
[5] In addition to major contributions of the past decade and a half (Kenny, Daston and Park, Findlen, Benedict, and Campbell) the past several years have witnessed an outpouring of interest in the discourses of wonder and curiosity attendant to the cabinet of curiosity. A few key titles pertaining specifically to early modern curiosity and collection are: R.J.W. Evans and Alexander Marr, *Curiosity and Wonder from the Renaissance to the Enlightenment* (Aldershot: Ashgate, 2006); Patrick Mauries, *Cabinets of Curiosities* (London: Thames and Hudson, 2002); Ken Arnold, *Cabinets for the Curious: Looking Back at Early English Museums* (Aldershot: Ashgate, 2006); and Arthur MacGregor, *Curiosity and Enlightenment: Collectors and Collections from the Sixteenth to the Nineteenth Century* (New Haven: Yale UP, 2007).
[6] Findlen argues against representations of the cabinet as disordered and chaotic, offering a view instead of the cabinet as a highly deliberate construction of the self. See especially, chapter 7, "Inventing the Collector" in *Possessing Nature: Museums, Collecting, and Scientific Culture in Early Modern Italy* (Berkeley: California UP, 1994).
[7] On the structures of desire associated with the gape, the look and the gaze, see chapter 4, "The Eye's Castration, the Subject's Plenitude" in Thomas King, *The Gendering of Men, 1600-1750*. Vol.1, *The English Phallus* (Madison: Wisconsin UP, 2004).
[8] Stephen Greenblatt, *Marvelous Possessions: The Wonder of the New World* (Chicago: Chicago UP, 1991); 135.

[9] Ibid. 136.
[10] Karen Kupperman, *Indians and English: Facing off in Early America* (Ithaca: Cornell UP, 2000); 58.
[11] Campbell 261.
[12] On the figure of the book as a means of colonial subordination, and on the relationship between literacy and colonization see Walter D. Mignolo's *The Darker Side of the Renaissance: Literacy, Territoriality and Colonization*, 2nd ed. (Ann Arbor: Michigan UP, 2006).
[13] From the letter announcing the Discovery, or the "First Voyage of Columbus." In *The Four Voyages of Columbus Vol. I*, ed and trans. Cecil Jane (London, 1929); 8.
[14] Thomas Hariot, *The True Pictures and Fashions of the People in that parte of America Now Called Virginia*, trans. Richard Hakluyt, in Theodor de Bry, *America, Part 1* (1590) reprinted with introduction by Paul Hulton, ed. (New York: Dover, 1972); 51. Page references are to the 1972 edition, hereafter cited in text.
[15] For profound reading of Hariot's and his contemporaries' interpretive impasse at the sounds and voices of Native Americans see Bruce R. Smith, "Mouthpieces: Native American Voices in Thomas Harriot's *True and Brief Report of...Virginia*, Gaspar Perez de Villagra's *Historia de la Nuevo Mexico*, and John Smith's *General History of Virginia*," *NLH* 32.3 (2001); 501-517.
[16] Aphra Behn, *Oroonoko, or, The Royal Slave,* ed. Catherine Gallagher (Boston: Bedford/St. Martin's, 2000); 81. Hereafter cited in text.
[17] For a reading of Behn's narrative strategies for enfolding her own complicity in the story through telling stories and diverting the hero, see: Moira Ferguson, "*Oroonoko*: Birth of a Paradigm," *New Literary History* 23.2 (Spring 1992); 348.
[18] Jonathan Goldberg describes how the accusation or 'discovery' of sodomy operates discursively as a signifier of European identification and disidentification with native bodies, beliefs, and practices. *Sodometries* part 3.
[19] Grace Stewart, "A History of the Medicinal Use of Tobacco 1492-1860," *Medical History* 11.3 (July 1967); 228-68.
[20] Mary Baine Campbell, to whom I am indebted for the reminder of the association between tobacco and anesthesia as well as for her observation of the *unheimlich* resemblance between the Empress's fire-stones (which burn so long as they are kept wet) and Oroonoko's persistent smoking throughout his own execution, also notes the sensorial muteness of this scene, remarking in that "Sensation has been evacuated in this passage both from the character who experiences it and the experience of those who observe...No one but the reader feels pain" (*Wonder and Science,* 277).
[21] Vernon Guy Dickson offers a recent reading of the rhetorical claim to 'truth' in *Oroonoko*, noting that the debate over the biographical and historical veracity of events depicted in the novella continues in work by Bernard Dhuicq and Joanna Lipking. See "Truth Wonder and Exemplarity in Aphra Behn's *Oroonoko,*" *Studies in English Literature* 47.3 (2007); 586.

[22] See Cavendish's autobiography appended to her memoirs of her husband's life: *Memoirs of the Duke of Newcastle: To Which is Added the True Relation of My Birth Breeding and Life*, ed. C.H. Firth. (London: Routledge, 1916).
[23] This entanglement at one point includes the author herself paying a visit to the Empress (in spirit form) who commissions her to write the *Blazing World* and with whom she travels home for an immaterial ménage a trois in the body of the real life Duchess's husband.
[24] Charles Darwin, *The Beagle Record,* ed. R.D. Keynes (Cambridge: Cambridge UP, 1979), 96. Cited in Michael Taussig, *Mimesis and Alterity: A Particular History of the Senses* (New York: Routledge, 1993); 76. Hereafter cited in text.
[25] Taussig's analogy postulates a parental/infantile relationship between colonizer and colonized (particularly as giver/recipient of language) that is, itself, of note.
[26] Roger Caillois, "Legendary Psychaesthenia," trans. John Shepley, *October* 31 (1984); 25. Hereafter cited in text.

Chapter Three

[1] Giorgio Agamben, "The Cabinet of Wonder." *Man Without Content.* (Stanford: Stanford University Press, 1999); 34.
[2] Agamben 30.
[3] See Jacques Lacan, *Le Séminaire. Livre VIII. Le Transfert, 1960—61*. Jacques-Alain Miller, ed. (Paris: Seuil, 1991); 414.
[4] Agamben, *Man Without Content* 34 (See n1).
[5] Giorgio Agamben, "The Man of of Taste and the Dialectic of the Split," in *The Man Without Content.* (Stanford: Stanford University Press, 1999); 13.
[6] Agamben 34.
[7] Francis Bacon, *The Major Works*. Brian Vickers, ed. (Oxford: Oxford University Press, 1996); 178.
[8] Andrew Marvell, "The Mower Against the Gardens," *Seventeenth-century Poetry and Prose*. Alexander M. Witherspoon and Frank J Warnke, eds. (San Diego: Harcourt Brace Janovich, 1982); 968.
[9] Thomas Moisan, "Herrick, Hollar, and the Tradescants: piecing together a seventeenth-century triptych," *Criticism: a Quarterly for Literature and the Arts.* 43.3 (Summer 2001); 309-324. *Literature Online* Dec. 13, 2007.
[10] Wilma George, "Alive or Dead: Zoological Collections in the Seventeenth Century," in Impey, Oliver and MacGregor, Arthur. *The Origins of Museums: The Cabinet of Curiosities in Sixteenth-and seventeenth- Century Europe* (Oxford: Clarendon, 1985); 185.
[11] Of the many texts written on Tradescant's museum and collecting habits, only Margorie Swann, *Curiosities and Texts: The Culture of Collecting in Early Modern England* (Philadelphia: U of Penn P, 2001); 32. Here she suggests that the younger Tradescant significantly contributed to the museum. Arthur MacGregor, on the other hand, suggests that the bulk of the acquisitions were made by the elder Tradescant. See Arthur MacGregor, ed. *Tradescant's Rarities: Essays on the Foundation of the Ashmolean Museum with a Catalogue of the Surviving Early Collections* (Oxford: Clarendon, 1983); 23. Contrary to both MacGregor and

Swann, Martin Welch suggests that Elias Ashmole is the most important contributor to the museum because of his interest in widening the scope of who could contribute. See Martin Welch, "The Foundation of the Ashmolean Museum," in *Tradescant's Rarities: Essays on the Foundation of the Ashmolean Museum with a Catalogue of the Surviving Early Collections.* Arthur Macgregor, ed. (Oxford: Clarendon, 1983).

[12] MacGregor, *Tradescant's Rarities: Essays on the Foundation of the Ashmolean Museum with a Catalogue of the Surviving Early Collections* 130-134.

[13] Welch, "The Foundation of the Ashmolean Museum" 41 (Note 10).

[14] Oliver Impey and Arthur MacGregor, *The Origins of Museums: The Cabinet of Curiosities in Sixteenth- and Seventeenth-Century Europe.* (Oxford: Clarendon, 1985);150.

[15] Walter Benjamin, "The Paris of the Second Empire," *Charles Beaudelaire: A Lyric Poet in the Era of High Capitalism.* Harry Zohn, trans. (New York: Version, 1983); 54.

[16] Martin Welsh, "The Foundation of the Ashmolean Museum," *Tradescant's Rarities: Essays on the Foundation of the Ashmolean Museum with a Catalogue of the Surviving Early Collections.* Arthur Macgregor, ed. (Oxford: Clarendon, 1983); 63.

[17] Welch, "The Foundation of the Ashmolean Museum" 50-51 (Note 10).

[18] Qtd. in Welch, "The Foundations of the Asholian Museum" 51 (Note 10).

[19] Gilles Deleuze and Felix Guattari, "Introduction: Rhizome," in *A Thousand Plateaus: Capitalism and Schizophrenia.* Brian Massumi, trans. (Minneapolis: U of Minnesota P, 1987); 3-25.

[20] Giorgio Agamben, *The Coming Community.* Michael Hardt, trans. (Minneapolis: University of Minnesota Press, 1993); 43.

Chapter Four

[1] Stephen Greenblatt, "Resonance and Wonder," in *Exhibition Cultures: The Poetics and Politics of Museum Display.* Ed. Ivan Karp and Steven D. Lavine (Washington: Smithsonian Institution Press, 1991); 42.

[2] Walter Benjamin, *The Arcade Project.* Trans. Howard Eiland and Kevin McLaughlin (Cambridge, Mass.: The Belknap Press of Harvard University Press); 211.

[3] Steve Baker, *The Postmodern Animal* (London: Reaktion Books, 2000); 61.

[4] Paula Findlen, *Possessing Nature: Museums, Collecting, and Scientific Culture in Early Modern Italy* (Berkeley: University of California Press, 1996); 56.

[5] The list is aggregated from multiple sources including Marina Belozerskaya, *The Medici Giraffe and Other Tales of Exotic Animals and Power* (New York: Little, Brown and Company, 2006), Oliver Impey and Neil MacGregor, eds., *The Origins of Museums: The Cabinet of Curiosities in Sixteenth- and Seventeenth-Century Europe* (Oxford: Clarendon Press, 1985), Arthur MacGregor, ed., *Sir Hans Sloane: Collector, Scientist, Antiquary, Founding Father of the British Museum* (London: British Museum Press 1994), John Tredescant, *Musæum Tredescantianum or a Collection of Rarities Preserved at South-Lambeth Neer London* (London: 1656).

[6] Krzysztof Pomian, *Collectors and Curiosities: Paris and Venice, 1500-1800*, trans. Elizabeth Wiles-Portier (Cambridge: Polity, 1990).
[7] Svetlana Alpers, "The Museum as a Way of Seeing," in *Exhibition Cultures: The Poetics and Politics of Museum Display*. Eds. Ivan Karp and Steven D. Lavine (Washington: Smithsonian Institution Press, 1991); 26.
[8] Taxidermy got its great leap forward in the mid-eighteenth century with the innovative chemical experiments of Jean-Baptiste Bécoeur, a French pharmacist and naturalist from the town of Metz in north-eastern France. In 1738, Bécoeur began experimenting with 50 different chemicals to determine which were most effective against insects. He tested one chemical on 50 different specimens, leaving the birds exposed. After four years only four specimens were free from insect attacks. He decided to mix these four chemical – ground arsenic, camphor, potassium carbonate, and powdered calcium hydroxide - together with soap in a preparation which has become known as arsenical paste. After years of tests and trials, failures and eventual unparalleled success, Bécoeur was loath to divulge his secret preparation and never published his hard-earned secret. The formula was eventually popularized by a French taxidermist named Louis Dufresne in 1820. See Paul Lawrence Farber, "The Development of Taxidermy and the History of Ornithology," *Isis* 68:4 (1977). Also L. C. Rookmaaker et al., "The Ornithological Cabinet of Jean-Basptiste Bécoeur and the Secret of the Arsenical Soap," *Archives of Natural History* 33:1 (2006).
[9] Karen Wonders, *Habitat Dioramas: Illusions of Wilderness in Museums of Natural History* (Uppsala: 1993); 25.
[10] Qtd. in Karl Schulze-Hagen et al., "Avian Taxidermy in Europe from the Middle Ages to the Renaissance," *Journal für Ornithologie* 144 (2003); 471.
[11] Schulze-Hagen 471.
[12] Farber, 472 n. 8.
[13] Glass jars and cork stoppers or sealed with paper and wax had been used widely from about the mid sixteenth century, but it wasn't until the seventeenth that alcohol become a standard preservative. Petiver's contemporary, Robert Boyle was among the first to widely advocate the use of alcohols for studying nature's intricacies and mysteries. In 1665, Boyle published his formula for embalming chicken foetuses in Spirit of Wine at various embryonic stages. He suggested soaking the foetus – a method which was applicable to the fluid preservation of any creature – in spirits for several days, "the Foetus being remov'd into more pure and well dephlegm'd Spirt of Wine, might no discolour it, but leave it almost limpid, as before it was put in." What caused the alcohol to become "phelgm'd" was protein leaching from specimens which stained the liquid an dark opaque red. See Robert Boyle, "A Way of Preserving Birds Taken out of the Egge, and Other Samll Faetus's; Communicated by Mr. Boyle," *Philosophical Transactions* 1:12 (1666).
[14] James Petiver, "Appendix," in *Musei Petiveriani Centuria Secunda & Tertia Rariora Naturae Continens* (London: 1698).
[15] T. S. Kuckhan, "Four Letters from Mr. T.S. Kuckhan, to the President and Members of the Royal Society, on the Preservation of Dead Birds," *Philosophical Transactions* 60 (1770); 304.

[16] Zacharias Conrad Von Uffenbach, *Oxford in 1710 from the Travels of Zacharias Conrad Von Uffenbach*, ed. W. H. Quarrell and W. J. C. Quarrell (Oxford: Basil Blackwell, 1928); 27.
[17] Quoted in Wonders, 25.
[18] Elias Ashmole, *Elias Ashmole (1617-1692): His Autobiographical and Historical Notes, His Correspondence, and Other Contemporary Sources Relating to His Life and Work* ed. C. H. Josten (Oxford Clarendon Press, 1966); 1823.
[19] David Freedberg, "Ferrari on the Classification of Oranges and Lemons," in *Documentary Culture: Florence and Rome from Grand-Duke Ferdinand I to Pope Allexander VII*, ed. Elizabeth Cropper, Giovanna Perini, and Francesco Solinas (Bologna: Nuovo Alfa Editoriale, 1990); 304-05.
[20] Findlen 38.
[21] Francis Bacon, *The New Organon and Related Writings*, ed. Fulton Anderson (Toronto: The Liberal Arts Press, 1960); 279.
[22] Nehemiah Grew, *Musaeum Regalis Societatis, or, a Catalogue & Description of the Natural and Artificial Rarities Belonging to the Royal Society and Preserved at Gresham Colledge* (London: 1681); "Preface".
[23] Grew "Preface."

Chapter Five

[1] Fielding, The Wesleyan Edition of the Works of Henry Fielding, *Joseph Andrews*, ed. Martin C. Battestin (Middletown, Conn.: Wesleyan University Press, 1967); 187-88.
[2] Beattie, "On Fable and Romance," *Dissertations Moral and Critical* (London, 1783); 509.
[3] *The London Magazine, or, Gentleman's Monthly Intelligencer* (London, 1772); 42:187-188.
[4] *Prudence Triumphing over Vanity and Dissipation; Or the History of the Life, Character and Conduct of Mr. Robert and Mr. Daniel Perreau, and Mrs. Rudd* (London: 1776); 102.
[5] *The Loiterer* (Oxford, 1790), 1:6. Interestingly, this periodical was founded, and most of the issues authored, by Jane Austen's brother James Austen, with occasional assistance from their brother Henry. See Claire Tomalin, *Jane Austen: A Life* (New York: Vintage Books, 1999); 65-67.
[6] I quote from the fourth edition of 1713, the earliest edition available from Eighteenth Century Collections Online that contains the first volume. Robert Mack's otherwise convenient edition from Oxford University Press (1995) does not include the preface or the dedication.
[7] Montagu, *Letters of the Right Honourable Lady M--y W---y M----e: Written, During Her Travels in Europe, Asia and* Africa (London: 1763), 2:160. These letters were written between 1716 and 1718, but only published after Lady Mary's death. They appeared, with a foreword written by Mary Astell in 1724, in 1763. Montagu's reference to "Arabian tales" here is vague enough that I hesitate to state that she referred to the *Arabian Nights' Entertainments* or the French *Les Mille et une Nuits*. It is possible that she, like Pope, had read Pétis de al Croix's text

instead. For a discussion of Lady Mary's *Letters* and their portrayal of the East, see Srinivas Aravamudan, "Lady Mary Wortley Montagu in the Hammam: Masquerade, Womanliness, and Levantinization," *ELH* 62.1 (1995); 69-104 and Arthur J. Weitzman, "Voyeurism and Aesthetics in the Turkish Bath: Lady Mary's School of Female Beauty," *Comparative Literature Studies* 39:4 (2002); 347-359.

[8] Blackwell, *An Enquiry into the Life and Writings of Homer* (London, 1735); 44.

[9] Richardson, *A Dissertation on the Languages, Literature, and Manners of Eastern Nations* (Oxford: 1778); 68. A shorter essay with this same title was originally published with Richardson's *A Grammar of the Arabick Language in which the Rules are Illustrated by the Authorities from the Best Writers* (London, 1776) and then separately in 1777. The 1778 version, however, is greatly expanded and contains the comment on the *Arabian Nights' Entertainments*.

[10] Beattie, "On Fable and Romance," 510.

[11] Charles de Secondat, Baron de Montesquieu, *Persian Letters*, trans. Mr. Ozell (London, 1722); 2:99-103. Note: in modern editions this letter is numbered 102.

[12] Nicolas Boulanger, *The Origin and Progress of Despotism* (Amsterdam, 1764); 1-2.

[13] Interestingly, however, Naji B. Oueijan documents how the eighteenth century saw an increase in more accurate portrayals of the East as trade and travel increased and studies of Eastern cultures and languages were taken up by increasingly scholarly authors, such as Henry Maundrell, Thomas Shaw, and Richard Pococke. See Oueijan, *The Progress of an Image: The East in English Literature*, American University Studies, vol. 181 (New York: Peter Lang, 1996); 37-66.

[14] This view was supported by Galland's false claim to have accurately translated the entire text from an authoritative Arabic manuscript. For an excellent discussion of Galland's distortion of the translation history, see Muhsin Mahdi's *The Thousand and One Nights* (Leiden: E.J. Brill, 1995); 17-49.

[15] Published in *A Compendium of the Most Approved Modern Travels* (Dublin, 1757), 254. This description reappeared in John Barrow's *A New Geographical Dictionary* (London, 1759-60) under the entry for "Aleppo."

[16] *The North British Intelligencer; or, Constitutional Miscellany* (Edinburgh, 1776), 2:200. Pope made a similar complaint about paper money in his *Epistle to Bathurst* (1733).

[17] *A Key to the Parliamentary Debates; Being an Humble Attempt to Render them Intelligible* (London, 1785); 16-17; James Beattie, *An Essay on the Nature and Immutability of Truth; In Opposition to Sophistry and Scepticism* (Edinburgh, 1770); 293; *The Remembrancer, or Impartial Repository of Public Events for the Year 1777* (London, 1778); 26-27.

[18] Brydone, *A Tour Through Sicily and Malta, In a Series of Letters to William Beckford* (London, 1773); 2:126.

[19] *The Ambulator; Or, The Stranger's Companion in a Tour Round London*, 2nd edition (London, 1782); 200.

[20] *The London Magazine, or, Gentleman's Monthly Intelligencer* (London, 1780), 49:59. Note: the title page of this work lists it as Volume XLIX; it appears in ECCO as vol. 50.

[21] John Aikin, *Evenings at Home; or, The Juvenile Budget Opened* (London, 1796); 5:32-33.
[22] Cited in Conant, *The Oriental Tale in England in the Eighteenth Century*, 262-263; Tobias Smollett, *The Expedition of Humphry Clinker*, ed. Thomas R. Preston and O M Brack, Jr (Athens: The University of Georgia Press, 1990); 91.
[23] Miss Bates exclaims, upon entering a ball organized by Mr. Weston, "Oh! Mr. Weston, you must really have had Aladdin's lamp." She later adds "This is meeting quite in fairy-land" (Austen, *Emma*, ed. Alistair M. Duckworth (Boston: Bedford/St. Martin's 2002); 258-9).
[24] Forster, *Index to Book Reviews in England 1749-1774* (Carbondale and Edwardsville: Southern Illinois University Press, 1990); ix; 3.
[25] *The Critical Review, or Annals of Literature* n.s. 27 (1799); 356.
[26] *British Critic* 14 (1799): 90; *Gentleman's Magazine* 69 (1799); 55.
[27] *Monthly Review* n.s. 29 (1799): 474-476. Benjamin Christie Nangle, in his essay on Charles Burney's criticism, offers some insight into the differences between the *Monthly Review's* style of reviewing and that of its competitors (Nangle, "Charles Burney, Critic," in *The Age of Johnson: Essays Presented to Chauncey Brewster Tinker* (New Haven: Yale University Press, 1949); 99-109).
[28] Benedict, "Jane Austen and the Culture of Circulating Libraries," in *Revising Women: Eighteenth-Century "Women's Fiction" and Social Engagement*, ed. Paula R. Backscheider (Baltimore: The Johns Hopkins University Press, 2000); 162.
[29] Gildon, *The New Metamorphosis: Or, Pleasant Transformation of the Golden Ass of Lucius Apuleius of Medaura,* (London, 1724); 1: A4v.
[30] Voltaire, *The General History and State of Europe* (Edinburgh, 1758); 3:5. The earlier London edition of 1754-1757 is, unfortunately, not available on ECCO.
[31] *The Works of M. de Voltaire*, trans. T. Francklin, A New Edition (London, 1780); 19:72.
[32] Beattie, "On Fable and Romance," 510.
[33] Fordyce, *Dialogues Concerning Education* (London, 1745); 1:383-384.
[34] Knox, *Essays Moral and Literary,* A New Edition (London, 1782); 1:314.
[35] Bettelheim, *The Uses of Enchantment: The Meaning and Importance of Fairy Tales* (New York: Alfred A. Knopf, 1976; New York: Vintage Books, 1989); 5.
[36] Hawksworth, *The Adventurer* (London, 1753); 1:22-23.
[37] Hurd, "Letters on Chivalry and Romance," in *Moral and Political Dialogues; with Letters on Chivalry and Romance* (London: 1765); 303-304.
[38] Hole, *Remarks on the Arabian Nights' Entertainments; In Which the Origin of Sindbad's Voyages, and Other Oriental Fictions, Is Particularly Considered* (London, 1797); 3, 31, 43. A reviewer of Hole's work in *The Scientific Magazine and Freemason's Repository* (London, 1797) compliments Hole on his "ingenuity and considerable learning" but concludes that his "very fertile imagination has led him from more profitable studies, to indulge in fanciful conjectures on a point of little importance" (2:334).
[39] Ibid., 2:263-267.
[40] Ibid., 2:264.
[41] Ibid., 2:263.

[42] Aboubakr Chraïbi provides a detailed and illuminating analysis of Galland's method of writing and rewriting Hanna's tales in "Galland's 'Ali Baba' and Other Arabic Versions," *Marvels & Tales* 18:2 (2004); 159-169. For additional literary analyses of the first English translation of the Arabian Nights, see Arthur J. Weitzman, "Scheherazade's Risk: Male Voyeurism and the Female Narrative Gambit," *1650-1850: Ideas, Aesthetics, and Inquiries in the Early Modern Era*, 5(2000); 151-161; Sylvette Larzul, "Further Considerations on Galland's Mille et une Nuits: A Study of the Tales Told by Hanna," *Marvels & Tales* 18.2 (2004); 258-71; and Ros Ballaster, "Narrative Transmigrations: The Oriental Tale and the Novel in Eighteenth-Century Britain," in *A Companion to the Eighteenth-Century English Novel and Culture*, ed. Paula R. Backscheider & Catherine Ingrassia (Oxford: Blackwell, 2009); 75-96.

Chapter Six

[1] James Cook, *The Journals* (New York: Penguin, 2003); 436. All citations to follow from Cook's journal come from this edition.
[2] For a contextual discussion of Cook's refusal to believe in the "fairy tales" of previously found passages between the Pacific and Atlantic Oceans, see Richard Hough, *The Last Voyage of Captain James Cook* (New York: William Morrow & Co., Inc. 1979). Cook's motivation for finding the Northwest Passage was twofold: the love of money and the pride of an explorer. Alongside the £20,000 reward (today worth over half a million dollars), the potential to add even more to the then-held one-eighth of the earth's surface to the control of the British Empire, and the desire to return to the sea, Cook's stubborn dedication to the realities of marine navigation drove him to debunk contemporary myths of polar travel. His failure to locate a navigable Northwest Passage thus became its own accomplishment.
[3] Early maps of the Arctic, from Vitus Bering and others, suggested that Alaska was an island. Not until Cook's failure to find the Northwest Passage were these maps corrected and concretized. More often than not, Cook is noted for his "non-discoveries"; he is what Stephen J. Pyne portrays in *The Ice: A Journey to Antarctica* (Seattle: University of Washington Press, 1988); 75, as "the great practioner of 'negative discovery.'" See also Jeannette Mirsky, *To the Arctic!: The Story of Northern Exploration from Earliest Times to the Present* (New York: Alfred A. Knopf, 1948).
[4] Cook enjoyed fame as a national hero after the publication of his journals from his First Voyage (to Tahiti). He helped to establish what Jen Hill describes as "a powerful national investment in the Arctic as a space of national identity formation and discipline," in *White Horizon: The Arctic in the Nineteenth-Century British Imagination* (Albany: State University of New York Press, 2008); 36.
[5] Barbara Maria Stafford, "The Eighteenth-Century: Toward An Interdisciplinary Model." *The Art Bulletin*, 70:1 (March 1988); 6.
[6] Michel Foucault, "Of Other Spaces," Jay Miskowiec, trans. *Diacritics* 16:1 (Spring 1986); 27.
[7] Foucault 24.
[8] Ibid. 24.

[9] "I try in vain to be persuaded that the pole is the seat of frost and desolation; it ever presents itself to my imagination as the region of beauty and delight. … There—for with your leave, my sister, I will put some trust in preceding navigators—there snow and frost are banished; and, sailing over a calm sea, we may be wafted to a land surpassing in wonders and in beauty every region hitherto discovered on the habitable globe." These are the words of Walton to his sister, Margaret Saville, upon his departure from St. Petersburgh, Dec. 11th, 17—, for his own arctic expedition. As his statements suggest, the polar north was indeed thought to be not only a place of paradise, but one of singular character: "Its productions and features may be without example." It held for Walton the promise of disclosure: the Arctic would reveal "the secret of the magnet" and "satiate [his] ardent curiosity with the sight of a part of the world never before visited." See Mary Shelley, *Frankenstein; or, the Modern Prometheus* (1818). D. L. MacDonald and Kathleen Scherf, eds.; 2nd ed. (Peterborough, Ontario: Broadview Literary Texts, 2004); 49-50. For further discussion of the role of *Frankenstein* in polar studies, see Jessica Richard, "A Paradise of My Own Creation": *Frankenstein* and the Improbable Romance of Polar Exploration. *Nineteenth-Century Studies* 25:4 (2003); 295-314.

[10] During his Second Voyage, on 18 January 1773 (approximately 75 miles away from the Antarctic continent), Cook wrote: "From the masthead I could see nothing to the Southward but Ice, in the Whole extent from East to WSW without the least appearance of any partition, this immence Feild [sic] was composed of different kinds of Ice, such as high Hills or Islands, smaller pieces packed close together and what Greenland men properly call field Ice, a piece of this kind, of such extend [sic] that I could see no end to it" (Cook 249). The travelogue of Cook's Second Voyage details the 60,000 mile expedition that finally disproved the existence of a warm southern continent.

[11] Foucault 24.

[12] Cook 434, 436.

[13] Gananath Obeyesekere, *The Apotheosis of Captain Cook: European Mythmaking in the Pacific* (Princeton: Princeton University Press, 1992); 12.

[14] Cook 540.

[15] Cook often cited the explicit number of canoes with which the *Resolution* interacted—e.g. "thirty-two Canoes" on 29 March 1778; "Six or eight Canoes" on 18 April 1778; "twelve or fourteen Canoes" on 22 April 1778;and "six Canoes" on 5 June 1778—perhaps in an effort to quantify the dramatic interactions between indigneous peoples and European explorers (539, 545, 559).

[16] Foucault 23.

[17] Cook 576.

[18] "The season," wrote Cook, "was now so very far advanced and the time when the frost is expected to set in so near at hand, that I did not think it consistant with prudence to make any farther attempts to find a passage this year in any direction so little was the prospect of succeeding" (Cook 577).

[19] In *Voyages of Delusion: The Quest for the Northwest Passage* (New Haven: Yale University Press, 2002), Glyn Williams describes this as "the contrast

between those effortless voyages of the imagination and the daunting experiences of the eighteenth-century explorers" (xix).

[20] See, for example, Ken McGoogan, *Race to the Polar Sea: The Heroic Adventures of Elisha Kent Kane* (Berkeley: Counterpoint, 2008). While not explicitly about the exploits of James Cook, McGoogan's text provides one of the most recent exhibitions of the sensationalism that consumed arctic exploration in the nineteenth century—after it grew out of the explorations from centuries past.

[21] Foucault 27.

[22] Sarah Moss, *The Frozen Ship: The Histories and Tales of Polar Exploration* (New York: BlueBridge, 2006); 2.

[23] 20 October 1778, Cook to Admirality (qtd. in Williams, 287).

[24] Cook 586.

[25] "Over [Rock Point and Halibut isles] we could see the main land covered with snow; but particularly some hills whose elevated summits were seen towering above the clouds to a most stupendious [sic] height. The most South westerly was discovered to be a Volcano which continually threw out a vast column of black smoke" (Cook 561-562).

[26] "The land near the shoar is low, part clear and part wooded, the clear ground was covered two or three feet thick with Snow, but very little lay in the woods. The trees were all of the Spruce or fir kind and some were tolerable large. The very summits of the neighbouring hills were covered with wood, but those farther inland seemed to be naked rocks burried in snow" (Cook 556).

[27] When the *Resolution* sailed south from Unalaska on 7 November 1778 "in the latitude of 41° 20', longitude 202° E," Cook remarked "a shag, or Cormorant [that] flew several times round the ship: as these birds are seldom, if ever, known to fly far out of sight of land, I judged some was not far distant, we however could see none" (Cook 591). Undoubtedly, this observation both emphasizes Cook's notion of his ship as an echo of Noah's Ark, with the cormorant drawing a parallel to the biblical dove, and anticipates the albatross in "Rime of the Ancient Mariner." This latter parallel is perhaps more apropos to the context of this chapter, given that the albatross appears first, like the dove, a harbinger of relief, but is then quickly transformed into an ominous symbol of suffering. Cook's search for the Northwest Passage can be similarly realized as a consistent flip-flop between potential success and positive failure, temporary relief and permanent suffering. See Eric G. Wilson, *The Spiritual History of Ice: Romanticism, Science, and the Imagination*" (New York: Palgrave Macmillan, 2003); 168-174, for an insightful reading of Coleridge's "Rime," the poles and the impact of Cook's voyages.

[28] Cook 556-557.

[29] Foucault 27.

[30] Ibid. 26.

[31] As is well known, marine expeditions, like the *Resolution*, were almost always outfitted with a coterie of specialists to document and collect specimens from the far north (many of whom were Friends of the Royal Society of London). For a catalogue of the collections from Cook's First and Second Voyages to the South Pacific, see Rüdiger Joppien and Bernard Smith, *The Art of Captain Cook's Voyages*, Vol 1-2 (New Haven: Yale University Press, 1985). Significantly, recent

years have seen a greater focus on the impact of Cook's voyages on visual culture (thereby trading the material objects for aesthetic vistas). See Bernard Smith, *Imagining the Pacific: In the Wake of the Cook Voyages* (New Haven: Yale University Press, 1992) and Russell A. Potter, *Arctic Spectacles: The Frozen North in Visual Culture, 1818-1875* (Seattle: University of Washington Press, 2007).

[32] Vanessa Collingridge, *Captain Cook: A Legacy Under Fire* (Guildford, CT: The Lyons Press, 2002); 319.

[33] Cook 556.

[34] Ibib. 563.

[35] Ibid. 564.

[36] Ibid. 564.

[37] Ibid. 558.

[38] Ibid. 540.

[39] Ibid. 547.

[40] Ibid. 547.

[41] "Heterotopias," writes Foucault, "always presuppose a system of opening and closing that both isolates them and makes them penetrable" (26).

Chapter Seven

[1] See Tom Gunning, "The Cinema of Attractions: Early Film, Its Spectator and the Avant-Garde"; in Early Film ed. Thomas Elsaesser and Adam Barker (British Film Institute, 1989).

[2] See Vanessa Schwartz, "Cinematic Spectatorship before the Apparatus: The Public Taste for Reality in *Fin-de-Siecle* Paris" in *Cinema and the Invention of Modern Life*. Eds. Leo Charney and Vanessa Schwartz (Berkeley: University of California Press, 1995); 297-317.

[3] See Jonathan Crary, *Techniques of the Observer: On Vision and Modernity in the Nineteenth Century* (Cambridge: MIT Press, 1990).

[4] Richard W. Burkhardt, "Ethology, Natural History, the Life Sciences, and the Problem of Place," *Journal of the History of Biology* 32 (1999); 491.

[5] Ibid. 493.

[6] Ibid. 492.

[7] It seems that the projected images were traced from the original photography, thus precluding it from actual cinematography. Nevertheless, the indexical tie obtains in this display of animal movement. See Gordon Hendricks *Eadweard Muybridge: The Father of the Motion Picture* (New York: Grossman Publishers, 1975); 114-115.

[8] For a list of zoos and their dates throughout the world see the appendix in Vernon Kisling, *Zoo and Aquarium History: Ancient Animal Collections to Zoological Gardens* (New York: CRC Press, 2001); 369-390.

[9] See Gordon Hendricks' chapter "Occident in Motion" in Hendricks, *Eadweard Muybridge,* 97-129.

[10] See John Edwards, *London Zoo from Old Photographs 1852-1914,* 1996. The first photographs of several species of animals, including a tiger, a hippopotamus, and a giraffe, occur in the London Zoo after the society's decision to hire

photographer, Count de Montizon in 1852. Here two spaces of animal observation overlap, wherein both apparatuses of operation perform the "holding still" for the archiving function of the other.

[11] Etienne Jules Marey, *Animal Mechanism: A Treatise on Terrestrial and Aerial Locomotion* (London: Henry S. King & Co., 1874); 1.

[12] Charles Sanders Peirce (Harvard Lectures on Pragmatism, CP 5.73, 1903).

[13] It is worth noting here a piece of Muybridge's biography which perhaps doesn't determine the nature of his self-imaging, but suggests, at least, that his step in front of his cameras is an attempt to escape and counter normative modes of meaning making. Eadweard Muybridge was not born "Eadweard Muybridge." In the span of his life, he had as many as seven different names. Born Edward James Muggeridge, he changes not only his surname from Muggeridge to Muggridge to Muybridge but his first name from Edward to Eadweard. When he travels to Central America he begins referring to himself, apparently without explanation, as Eduardo Santiago Muybridge. At times he refers to himself as EJM jr, even though his father's name was John and upon taking up photography as a profession, signs his photographs as Helios, the Greek sun god, who, it is worth noting, at times stands in for Apollo. Rather than read this as a concerted effort to fashion himself into a public figure of note—though surely it was—we might read it more literally. Muybridge's repeated self naming amplifies the arbitrariness of language in contrast to an Adamic naming, wherein the animal is the word and the word is the animal, and yet suggests a longing for just that, a name that captures him. While Muybridge no doubt delighted in refashioning himself, his continual search for a name not only destabilizes human language by foregrounding its arbitrary nature, it suggests an unflappable desire to rebind the signifier and the signified. Thus, as Muybridge invents a supplement to human vision, steps into a position that he himself marked as animal, and escapes the arbitrariness of signification by imaging his animal body, we might think of this as fully in line with his search for a name for himself. See Hendricks, *Eadweard Muybridge* (1975) for a full account of his name changes.

[14] John Berger, *About Looking* (New York: Vintage, 1980); 21.

[15] Akira Mizuta Lippit, *The Electric Animal: Toward a Rhetoric of Wildlife* (Minneapolis: University of Minnesota Press, 2000); 2-3.

[16] Jonathan Crary, *Suspensions of Perception: Attention Spectacle and Modern Culture* (Cambridge: MIT Press, 2001); 147.

[17] Think of "neo-time" which appeared to slow down time as the camera arced around Keanu Reeves's character in *The Matrix.*

[18] See Hendricks, *Eadweard Muybridge*; 63-77.

[19] Gunning "Tracing the Individual Body" in *Cinema and the Invention of Modern Life.* eds. Leo Charney and Vanessa Schwartz, (Berkeley: University of California Press, 1995); 18.

[20] Ibid. 19.

[21] Ibid. 32.

[22] Ibid. 24. The camera thus reveals not only animality but criminality as well. The implication that something is caged here should not go unnoted. Indeed, that the camera and other observational structures replaced the need to mark the body with

the pervasive observation of it, is precisely the turn from monarchic structures of control to disciplinarism and the emergence of panopticism that Foucault argues for in *Discipline and Punish*. The famous panopticon designed by Jeremy Bentham allowed for the control of its inmates by structuring the very threat of observation. Bentham's stated inspiration for that design was the Royal Menagerie at Versailles, which was laid out such that one could observe all of the animals in the collection from a single vantage point.

Chapter Eight

[1] André du Bouchet, "Hercules Segers", in *L'Incohérence* (Paris: Hachette, 1979), not paginated. All translations are my own. Given the way du Bouchet places his words on the page, it is difficult to accurately and unobtrusively cite him. In order to make my own text more uniform, I have not reproduced his spacing when I quote in my text or in the notes, but have tried to recreate the gaps between words when I have block-cited larger passages.
[2] Both published by Hachette in 1979.
[3] André du Bouchet, *Qui n'est pas tourné vers nous* (Paris: Mercure de France, 1972).
[4] "treat a subject, of thought, unique". Stéphane Mallarmé, epigraph to *Divagations* (1897), in vol. 2 of *Œuvres complètes*, ed. Bertrand Marchal (Paris: Gallimard, Bibliothèque de la Pléiade, 2003); 82.
[5] If only immediately biographically. Born in 1924, fleeing to the United States in 1941 where he finished his education first at Amherst and then at Harvard, du Bouchet returned to France at the end of the 40s where he became friendly with many poets, most importantly Pierre Reverdy and Francis Ponge, as well as with philosophers and art theorists and artists, such as Georges Duthuit, Henri Maldiney and Pierre Tal Coat. At this point, as well as writing poems, du Bouchet wrote articles on other poets and on painting. In 1966, along with poets Yves Bonnefoy, Jacques Dupin, Louis-René des Forêts and critic Gaëton Picon, he co-founded the revue *L'Éphémère*, which published poems, translations, texts on art and on poetry, as well as ethnographic and philosophical texts. The last issue was published in 1973. *L'Incohérence* collects many texts first published in the revue, albeit frequently reworked to a degree that nearly effaces their origin. Du Bouchet continued to publish poetry, prose on painting, on poetry, and on translation, often mixing them together in a single volume, up until his death in 2001. For more biographical details, see the "notes biographiques" at the end of Clément Layet, *André du Bouchet* (Paris: Seghers, Poètes d'aujourd'hui, 2002); 239-243.
[6] André du Bouchet, *L'emportement du muet* (Paris: Mercure de France, 2000).
[7] If not addressing a unique subject of thought. When asked by Alain Veinstein in a November 2000 interview why he chose a phrase from an earlier book, *Carnet 2* (Saint-Clément-la-Rivière: Fata Morgana, 1998), du Bouchet responded: "j'avais réuni ces textes et je cherchais un titre dont aucun n'était satisfaisant. Et un jour, en effet, ouvrant ce carnet, ce *Carnet 2*, je suis tombé sur ces mots qui étaient des mots qui ne se voulaient nullement destinés à composer un titre, mais ça m'a semblé rendre compte un peu de ce qui était tenté dans ces différentes réflexions."

["I had brought together these texts and I was looking for a title of which none was satisfying. And one day, in fact, opening this carnet, this *Carnet 2*, I stumbled on these words which were words that were not at all destined to compose a title, but that seemed to me to account a little for what was attempted in these different reflections."]

[8] "there is perhaps in *Incoherence* a contradiction found in the title itself. At bottom, it is a book that, in a certain fashion, appears to me very constructed all the while escaping the order of succession. The book is not paginated. A text leads to another, a page is read in regard to another, yet one could begin the book in the middle or read it backwards in all senses." "André du Bouchet, Poète de l'abrupt", interview with Monique Petillon, dated May 4, 1979. In Monique Petillon, *À mi-voix: Entretiens et portraits 1976-2006* (Tours: Farrago, 2006); 22.

[9] For example, in the text on May 1968, du Bouchet quotes the text on Pasternak he has just translated; the text on Seghers opens with an epigraph by Dutch lay mystic Hadewijch where she invokes the limits of language and of her native Flemish in particular, and in the margins of his text du Bouchet places in their original Flemish the titles of Seghers' engravings addressed by the text, as well as reflections on language and translation, many of which will be picked up in the translation section or in some of the other metapoetic texts.

[10] "a book as I do not like them, scattered and devoid of architecture".

[11] "Un tas de gravats déversés au hasard; le plus bel ordre du monde." ["a pile of rubble randomly heaped; the most beautiful order of the world."] Heraclites, *Les fragments d'Héraclite*, trans. Roger Munier (Saint-Clément-la-Rivière: Fata Morgana, 1991); 75.

[12] André du Bouchet, *Poèmes et Proses* (Paris: Mercure de France, 1995).

[13] Giorgio Agamben, *The Man Without Content* (Stanford: Stanford University Press, 1999); 30.

[14] "language—content, already, of the poem underway: at the start, the content was not language. but that which overflows language, as soon as it has taken the figure of a poem, is then discovered under-pinning, and the poem at last—itself a content in turn." André du Bouchet, ... *désaccordée comme par de la neige* (Paris: Mercure de France, 1989); 63.

[15] As he explicitly states a few pages earlier: "en regard de lui-même le langage dès lors placé—et, à vue de ce qui se localise hors de la langue, comme dédoublé pour un contenu dont le réceptacle ne sera pas langue exclusivement, mais elle-même, la langue, part déjà de son propre contenant—le nôtre aujourd'hui—qui l'absorbera […]."... *désaccordée comme par de la neige*, 59. ["in regard of itself language at that moment placed—and, in view of that which is localized outside of language, like split in two for a content of which the receptacle will not exclusively be language, but itself, language, part already of its own container—ours, today—which will absorb it".]

[16] "… the incoherence/ of the parts of water."

[17] "knots in the current". *peinture* (Saint-Clément-la-Rivière: Fata Morgana, 1983); 118.

[18] In resonance with the epigraph, let us not forget the famous fragment: "Pour ceux qui entrent dans les mêmes fleuves, autres et autres sur eux roulent les eaux."

["For those who enter in the same rivers, other and other over them roll the waters."] Trans. Munier 17.

[19] "INCOHERENCE. s. f. Quality of that which is incoherent. *The incoherence of the parts of water. The incoherence of ideas.*" *Dictionnaires d'autrefois*, The ARTFL Project, The University of Chicago. General site: <http://portail.atilf.fr/dictionnaires/index.htm>; the entry for "incoherence": <http://portail.atilf.fr/cgi-bin/dico1look.pl?strippedhw=incoherence>.

[20] "broken and undivided like the pebble (pebble named Sainte-Victoire, or in the air mountain no less deprived of a name than on the ground the pebble)." André du Bouchet, "peinture", in *L'Incohérence*, not paginated.

[21] Another echo, after Agamben, of the *Wunderkammer*: "[…] the individual objects seem to find their meaning only side by side with the others, between the walls of a room in which the scholar could measure at every moment the boundaries of the universe" (30).

[22] "Individual. Undivided." In *L'Incohérence*, not paginated.

[23] "be it about works by Tal Coat or by Seghers, or pages written by Pasternak, Hölderlin or Hopkins, these are works which exist completely independently. I take them under my care with all the attention I have, but in this attention they are also lost." Petillon 23.

[24] "If I want to speak of a work or translate a text, it is because its life incites me to a displacement. It's a feeling I often have in a painting exhibition. If a picture strongly touches me, it incites me more so to take my distance quickly in order to pursue, outside, what the picture was able to awaken in me. It is a wakeful connection: I go further away, in order to verify." Petillon 23. I have explored this turn away in much more detail in my unpublished dissertation, "Aversion: André du Bouchet on Painting" (Ph.D. diss., New York University, 2003).

[25] "La couleur", in *L'Incohérence*, not paginated.

[26] If not liberated by the turn. This singularity of purpose which seems to ignore the work, whether we think of it remembered in the turn away or, as du Bouchet says to Petillon, lost in and by his attention, undoes the static frontality of looking, and thereby frees painting from its phenomenal role as a flat surface repeating the equally flat and vertical surface of the wall. The frontal relationship, then, even in the pause before one turns away, supports—like the canvas the paint, like the wall the painting—a sudden opening out of space, and this opening out allows poet and paintings each "to go—like color—one's way". Thus the interval contained between viewer and painting becomes a container in turn. For the frontal relationship as spatial dilation, see *peinture*, 21: "impossible de ne pas penser, devant une peinture, que […] elle-même ne sera qu'un point, « pas grand chose », parmi ce monde que des murs auxquels elle aura été rapportée, elle fait en avant d'elle valoir momentanément en tant qu'espace—élargi ou vacant. […]" ["impossible to not think, in front of a painting, that […] itself will only be a point, 'nothing much', among this world that from the walls to which the painting will have been brought back, it makes out in front of itself worth as space—enlarged or vacant […]"]

[27] "Far from painting, and up to losing sight of it—if what I see has struck me."

[28] If writing isn't already such a proximal distance: "un mot après l'autre—degrés de l'éloignement qui rapprochera. la proximité, elle, intraitable toujours." ["one word after the other—degrees of distancing that will bring closer together. Proximity, itself, always untreatable."] André du Bouchet, "notes sur la traduction", in *Ici en deux* (Paris: Mercure de France, 1986), not paginated.
[29] "up to what limit can one pulverize the text, stretch the thread which binds the words", du Bouchet admits that, "strictly, if one were to give in to the work of critical reflection, a lacunae-free thought could be reconstituted. But this reconstitution, I must say, would not really interest me. What appears more interesting to me is the sentiment of a movement which does not minimize forgetting, which does not smooth over the contradictions, the incoherencies, which does not cut us off from the irreducible instant." Petillon 24.
[30] Such a gap, in many ways, is language, is what language does: "chose imprononçable. mot incarné." ["unpronounceable thing. incarnated word."] André du Bouchet, *aujourd'hui c'est* (Saint-Clément-la-Rivière: Fata Morgana, 1994), 17. Many critics have noted this element of du Bouchet's work. The philosopher Henri Maldiney, for example, opens an article by placing the poet between two realities: "Il y a celle à laquelle la parole dit quand la langue parle et il y a celle à laquelle nous nous heurtons dans l'expérience sensible et dans notre commerce avec les autres." ["There is that [reality] that speech says when language speaks and that one against which we collide in our sensuous experience and in our commerce with others."] Henri Maldiney, "Naissance de la parole dans la poésie d'André du Bouchet", in *Saluer André du Bouchet* (Paris: William Blake & Co., 2004); 45. Antoine Emaz, trying to situate himself and his own work vis-à-vis du Bouchet, admits that "[o]n ne peut réduire du Bouchet à une sorte de post-Mallarmé ; pareillement, même si c'est mon accès privilégié à l'œuvre, on ne peut la réduire à une pure et simple confrontation physique au dehors." ["one cannot reduce du Bouchet to a sort of post-Mallarmé; equally, even if it is my privileged access to his work, one cannot reduce it to a pure and simple confrontation with the outside." Antoine Emaz, *André du Bouchet, « debout sur le vent »* (Paris: Jean-Michel Place, 2003); 6. Gilles Quinsat notes a similar confrontation with the "dehors" in "Parler depuis un autre lieu", in *Autour d'André du Bouchet (actes du colloque des 8, 9, 10 décembre, 1983)*, ed. Michel Collot (Paris: Presses de l'École Normale Supérieure, 1983). See also Jean-Michel Reynard, *L'Interdit de langue : solitudes d'André du Bouchet* (Paris: Fourbis, 1994).
[31] "is like bleached by the rapidity with which it takes distance on the circumstance which gave it seeming justification. So distant that it appears cleaned of the past, that one finds it in front of self as not having happened, its point of origin letting itself be localized only in the instant, and in an instant which deprives it, blow by blow, of the significations to which one was able to subject it." In *L'Incohérence*, not paginated.
[32] Such subjection runs both ways for du Bouchet, since normative language also subjects us to a certain kind of signification, as he points out in "… sur un coin éclaté": "… je n'existe pas moins, lorsque j'ai cessé d'être assujetti, nonobstant ce que peut affirmer la langue, et ce que d'elle-même, dans sa servilité, toujours elle a voulu dire…". ["… I do not exist any less, when I have ceased to be subjected,

notwithstanding what language can affirm, and what of itself, in its servility, always it had wanted to say…"] In *L'Incohérence*, not paginated. In italics and reduced font as part of a "parallel" text running intermittently throughout both the margins.

[33] "to the side, suddenly, of signification". In *L'Incohérence*, not paginated.

[34] "the present: a separation." *peinture*, 20. This separation is already echoed in the margins of "… sur un coin éclaté": "… mais être—ici—fend." ["… but to be—here—splits."] In *L'Incohérence*, not paginated.

[35] "far from being a grandiose and difficult aberration, André du Bouchet's poetry updates, at each step, a universal situation inscribed in the most ancient roots of language". See note 36 for bibliographic information.

[36] Henri Maldiney, "Les « blancs » d'André du Bouchet", *L'Ire des vents*, « Espaces offerts à André du Bouchet », no. 6-8 (1983); 205-6.

[37] See note 34 above. Or as du Bouchet will more directly put it in "Cendre tirant sur le bleu" (1986), "à l'occasion—sur le trajet du soleil—les *ici* sont des *maintenant*." ["on the occasion—following the sun's trajectory—the *here*s are *nows*."] In *L'emportement du muet* 43.

[38] "memory is only the consciousness of the present". *peinture* 28.

[39] "Gangue: m e who can say it—say me—only in bursting it: me"; "there I am, I am not there…". Both texts in *L'Incohérence*, not paginated.

[40] "Cold thought (I remember the heat) cold thought is here constrained to pass through the paths of language which isn't its own. Moreover, there are no paths, no language". In *L'Incohérence*, not paginated.

[41] "the dose of a material conductor of the fore-felt perception—to communicate without the perception being lost, or that it is not the only thing lost—quickly mixed with what will have been perceived". *peinture*, 141. Therefore no different from paint as it is applied to canvas. This is perhaps one reason nearly half of *L'Incohérence* and more than half of all of du Bouchet's writing turns towards and away from painting.

[42] "… the articulation of a thought, where it engages, again appears buried, like taken back into its gangue, inapt, again, to indicate…/ I recognize, I do not know." In *L'Incohérence*. Italicized in the original.

[43] As du Bouchet states explicitly in "Essor" (1988), a text also addressing Tal Coat: "sur le point d'être nommé, ce qu'on voit ayant pris de court, l'omission du nom—fraîcheur reconduite—peut, sans faire défaut, de nouveau s'inscrire dans le temps de la nomination." ["on the point of being named, what one sees having taken by surprise, the omission of the name—freshness accompanied—can, without lacking, be inscribed again in the time of naming."] In *L'emportement du muet* 71.

[44] Echoing Maldiney's observation that "[i]t is the dimensional structure of presence to have to rejoin itself, itself *and* its world […]."

[45] "The movement: by poem which sends back to a thought — and the thought, to what will remain unthought." *peinture* 125.

[46] Something du Bouchet notes in his first carnet: "le langage a cela de merveilleux que chaque fois il donne à pressentir ce qui lui a échappé". ["language is marvelous in that each time it allows one to have the presentiment of what has

escaped it"]. André du Bouchet, *Carnet* (Saint-Clément-la-Rivière: Fata Morgana, 1994); 29. The entry is dated June 1952.

[47] "the gaze's incessant successive back-and-forth, one line finished, to the next, in order to begin again". Stéphane Mallarmé, "Quant au livre" (1897), in ed. Marchal 226.

[48] "there, I have—marking the page, wanted to halt. like, further away, on the edge of the fraction, to pin down the sense. But it cannot be pinned down." "notes sur la traduction", in *Ici en deux*, not paginated.

[49] If not in our attention "getting it wrong", as he indicates a page later: "vivant, le contre-sens procuré sur un excès, aussitôt, de l'attention. jusqu'à l'inattention, qui emporte—et jusqu'à ces choses—être et mots et choses." ["living, the mistranslation procured from an excess, suddenly, of attention. up to the inattention which carries away—and up to these things—being and words and things."]

[50] "starting point". Attending a 1983 academic conference on his work, du Bouchet was asked, in the discussion following Gilles Quinsat's paper, "s'il se reconnaît lui-même dans ces exégèses, ou se découvre en partie à travers ce qui a été dit." ["if he recognizes himself in these exegeses or discovers himself in part through what has been said."] The poet responded: "Je découvre beaucoup de choses dans ce qui a été dit, mais je ne peux m'exprimer que dans ce que j'ai écrit. Je suis très sensible à la façon dont nombre d'interventions ont pris appui sur le point de départ que je propose. Je ne propose que des points de départ, qu'il revient à chacun de prendre sur soi." ["I discover many things in what has been said, but I can only express myself in what I have written. I am very sensitive to the way in which a number of the speakers have gained footing in the starting point that I propose. I only propose starting points, and it is up to each person to take them on themselves."] In the discussion section following Gilles Quinsat, "Parler depuis un autre lieu", in ed. Collot 65.

[51] "… reader himself on his way is only a bookmark… […]" In *L'Incohérence*, not paginated.

[52] Georges Poulet describes how a book "should" disappear: "Where is the book I held in my hands? It is still there, and at the same time it is there no longer, it is nowhere. That object wholly object, that thing made of paper, as there are things made of metal or porcelain, that object is no more, or at least it is as if it no longer existed as long as I read the book. For the book is no longer a material reality. It has become a series of words, of images, of ideas which in their turn begin to exist. And where is this new existence? Surely not in the paper object. Nor, surely, in external space. There is only one place left for this new existence: my innermost self." Georges Poulet, "Criticism and the Experience of Interiority" (1972), in *Reader-Response Criticism: From Formalism to Post-Structuralism*, ed. Jane Tompkins (Baltimore: The Johns Hopkins University Press, 1980); 42.

[53] "mais chaque fois la jubilation d'être—la parole qui n'aura pas été prononcé, exultante, comportant elle aussi sa place—en avant des mots brièvement." ["but each time the jubilation of being—the word which will not have been pronounced, exultant, having also its place—briefly out in front of words."] "notes sur la traduction", in *Ici en deux*, not paginated.

[54] "Hercules Segers", in *L'Incohérence*, not paginated. See translation after the epigraph above.
[55] the "singular existence [...] of the word which detaches itself when, our attention brought to bear on it, one stops longer on the word than its use warrants". "Homère", in *matière de l'interlocuteur* (Saint-Clément-la-Rivière: Fata Morgana, 1992); 11.
[56] The text is in italics in the original. I have done my best to reproduce du Bouchet's spacing, although have reduced the space between text-blocks. To save space, I will "condense" the spacing by translating in a more linear fashion, marking breaks between text blocks with a back-slash. "... from one letter to another, *yes* and *no*.../ (to interletter.../ *yes* and *no* that the eye apprehends across the alignment which constitutes itself, letter aired against letter, into a word.../ *yes* the *null* is displaced without any indication of movement. A source is not a sign.../ ... *null* is a source.../ (sign—no more than by the middle of a horizontal word, letter succeeding aligned letter, that one which will articulate it upright.../ What he has right under his eyes, being there, will escape the spectator of the written word, but he feels, leafing through the poorly cooled volume, also the lack—like in front of him his hand.../ (from one word to the other, like each time it is possible, before making it to the other, to become lost.../ *yes* and *no*: joining link.../ ... here I lose, having remained on its intonation, the word which follows.../ ... lost, it is here."
[57] "Tu remarquas, on n'écrit pas, lumineusement, sur champ obscur, l'alphabet des astres, seul, ainsi s'indique, ébauché ou interrompu ; l'homme poursuit noir sur blanc." ["You remarked, one does not write, luminously, on a dark field, the starry alphabet, alone, thus is indicated, sketched out or interrupted; man pursues black on white."] Stéphane Mallarmé, "Quant au livre", in ed. Marchal 215.
[58] As du Bouchet explicitly says in *peinture*: "je ne suis pas assuré de ma place sur le papier." ["I am not assured of my place on the paper."] 133.
[59] See the list of critics in note 30 above. To that list, I'd like to add Pierre Chappuis, *André du Bouchet* (Paris: Seghers, Poètes d'aujourd'hui, 1979); many of the articles in ed. Collot and in *L'ire des vents*, not directly referred to above; Serge Champeau, *Ontologie et Poésie, trois études sur les limites du langage* (Paris: Vrin, 1995); and my "In Mallarmé's Harness? André du Bouchet and Stéphane Mallarmé," *French Forum* 32, nos. 1-2 (2007); 117-135.
[60] "the mute". "The mute—resource of the word.../ ... before the letter, like at the very level of the mute.../ for the hand which removes or whittles down, freshness from before the letter... [...]"
[61] "speech:/ The support carries away.../ the air/ interrupted/ calls.../ ... the air, the same as the paper, representation of the air, before carrying it away, will cross through the words which are placed there.../ terraces—squared out representation of the paper (the air, I don't send it to anything, leave it, voiceless, to its rustlings—thus like myself, carrier sometimes—without a word—of speech.../ [...]/ ... without a word burns as well as burns under the words the paper..."
[62] I have tried to be as accurate as possible, especially for the marginal text-blocks, but I was not able to reproduce the spacing exactly. The "main" text: "(words or men obliterated, when their inhuman support, having come to light, finishes

again—words or men—its coming through.../ ... and the word in its voice—like I go beyond—more quickly still: speech.../ ... and mixed together... words and men, by instants mixed together—mute—with the inhuman support raised up when day breaks (I have slept in the mass of the mountains—at waking like undone—having had footing, rest..." The "marginal" text: "... facing is on the other side.../ ... interstice of this whiteness through the middle of signs which are inscribed there, untouched, then interposing itself, like on the cold pane breath or a cloud... mute, the opaque on which I write, transpierces..."

63 "... the inhuman widens: as unequal as between words or hands the paper... through their middle, as well, this paper—or, higher up, the rock, when it pushes through, mixed in with the remains of the stone walls encircling the slopes of the Auch..."

64 "thing among things". The phrase "chose parmi les choses", taken from philosopher Maurice Merleau-Ponty, appears frequently in du Bouchet's later writing. See the end of "Tübingen, le 22 mai 1986", in ... *désaccordée comme par de la neige*, and his homage to Henri Maldiney, "pourquoi si calmes", in *pourquoi si calmes* (Saint-Clément-la-Rivière: Fata Morgana, 1996).

65 "the power of the figuration of the paper". The whole text block is worth citing: "la puissance de figuration du support, comme en soi ciel tour à tour et terre, est illimitée. la puissance de la figuration du papier." ["the power of figuration of the support, like in itself sky and earth alternating, is unlimited. the power of the figuration of the paper."] André du Bouchet, "aveuglément, peinture", in *Une tache* (Saint-Clément-la-Rivière: Fata Morgana, 1988), not paginated.

66 "there, what I have wanted to stay, the paper, better than me—and before me, illuminates it." "aveuglément, peinture", not paginated. Gilles Quinsat also notes the mobility of what he calls du Bouchet's "pivot-words": "[...] les mots « air », « figure », « espace », « fond », « support », sont pour du Bouchet des mots-pivots, sans aucun doute. Mais ils sont aussi les plus libres qui soient : au lieu de se fixer en eux le sens vient s'y épuiser, leur donnant fonction d'interstice ou d'ajour à partir desquels pourra s'actualiser le débordement de la parole par le dehors." ["[...] the words 'air', 'figure', 'space', 'back/bottom', 'support', are for du Bouchet pivot-words, without any doubt. But they are also the most free that are: instead of being fixed in them, sense comes to be exhausted, giving them an interstitial or breaching function from which the flooding of speech by the outside can be actualized."] "Parler depuis un autre lieu", in ed. Collot 57.

67 As du Bouchet notes in his third carnet: "la langue—d'être ce qu'elle est, au contraire, ne doit pas servir, et jamais, sinon à *rien*, n'aura servi". ["language—to be what it is, on the contrary, must not serve, and never, if not for *nothing*, will have served".] *annotations sur l'espace non datées (carnet 3)* (Saint-Clément-la-Rivière: Fata Morgana, 2000); 55.

68 "... there this void is necessary... and, through the middle of ventilated signs in which, a moment, the figure of a word, will be constituted, like with a squeaking sound a cleared place... the void... freshness which disperses the signs...". "Hercules Segers", in *L'Incohérence*, not paginated.

69 The motif of the face/gaze I can never see is frequent in *L'Incohérence* and in du Bouchet's work more generally. See, for instance, "sous le linteau en forme de

joug": "[…] que le pourtour de la face, qui circonscrit, soustrait à nos yeux, fasse irruption jusqu'au centre… […]" ["[…] that the complete way around the face, which circumscribes, subtracted from our eyes, bursts in all the way to the center… […]"] In *L'Incohérence*, not paginated.
[70] "there I am, I am not there" since "not being assured of my place here as on the paper, I have interrupted myself in order to begin". The first citation is from "Hercules Segers", *L'Incohérence*, not paginated; the second is from *peinture* 135.

Chapter Nine

[1] W. G. Sebald. *Rings of Saturn*. (New York: New Directions Books, 1998).
[2] Paul Valéry, "The Problem of Museums," *The Collected Works of Paul Valéry. Volume 12*. Ed. Jackson Matthews (New York: Pantheon Books, 1960); 203-05.
[3] David Kaufmann described *The Rings of Saturn* as a "morose *Wunderkammer*," though he does not elaborate on the analogy ("Angels Visit the Scene of Disgrace: Melancholy and Trauma from Sebald to Benjamin and Back." *Cultural Critique* 70 (Fall 2008): 96).
[4] Patrick Mauriès, *Cabinet of Curiosities* (London: Thames & Hudson, Ltd. 2002); 25, 34, 43.
[5] Lessons such as those offered by *memento mori*, however satirical or absurd they may now seem, certainly appear to be the aim of many present-day cabinets—both works of art such as those of Elizabeth McGrath (see *Everything That Creeps: The Art of Elizabeth McGrath* (San Francisco: Last Gasp, 2005)) and David Wilson's Museum of Jurassic Technology in Culver City, California.
[6] In the growing field of museology, or museum studies, there is an increasing amount of discussion about the way that museums "discipline" (in the Foucauldian sense) the visitor's experience, both in terms of directing where the visitor walks, in what order and which narratives the visitor is able to (allowed to) create given the physical discipline of the walking and the way in which the objects have been pre-arranged in exhibits. A good example of this discipline is the recent exhibit at the Chicago Art Institute (Summer 2004) on the development of Seurat's famous painting, *La grande jatte*. In addition to the now ubiquitous availability of a recorded guide to the exhibit which directs you to certain objects in a particular order, emphasizing some, skipping others, this exhibit was ordered in the following way: First, there were rooms with paintings contemporary with pre-*jatte* Seurat, then Seurat's studies for *La grande jatte*—these in particular order—beginning with the *jatte* itself, then the people, then the lady's monkey (who appears in the foreground of the finished painting). All of these lead the visitor to the center of the exhibit, the painting itself. There was one final room after the painting with other works of art which the exhibit claimed had been inspired or influenced by *La grande jatte*. (Finally, and predictably, one was dumped out into the special Seurat exhibit-only gift shop, which had been installed on the second floor of the Institute.) The argument for this kind of order has been usefully critiqued by Tony Bennett in his 1988 essay "The Exhibitionary Complex," which suggests that the museum is 'exhibitionary' rather than 'disciplinary,' opening bodies and objects up to new kinds of display and different routes for power.

[7] Literary uses of the metaphor of the museum are not new. In this, *The Rings of Saturn* places itself in a series of texts that have explicitly concerned themselves with museums or collections—J.K. Huysmans's *Against Nature* (1884), Oscar Wilde's *The Picture of Dorian Gray* (1891), William Morris's *News from Nowhere* (1891), H.G. Wells's *The Time Machine* (1895), Henry James's *The Spoils of Poynton* (1897), John Galsworthy's *The Man of Property* (1906), Jorge Luis Borges's "The Library of Babel" (1960, trans.), and Bruce Chatwin's *Utz* (1988), to name but a few.
[8] Barbara J. Black, *On Exhibit: Victorians and Their Museums* (Charlottesville: University Press of Virginia, 2000); 176. Museums and museum-like institutions were particularly important to Victorians as Black and others, including Germain Bazin in *The Museum Age*, have argued, at least in part because of their increasing numbers and accessibility.
[9] See, for example, Section VI of *Grasping the World: The Idea of the Museum.* Eds. Preziosi and Farago (Hants: Ashgate, 2003). Almost any contemporary collection on anthropological or national museums airs this skepticism or, more recently, accepts it as a given. *New Museology* (ed. Peter Vergo, 1989); *Museums and the Shaping of Knowledge* (Hooper-Greenhill, 1992); *Colonialism and the Object: Empire, Material Culture and the Museum* (Ed. Tim Barringer and Tom Flynn, 1998); *Museum Frictions: Public Cultures/Global Tranformations* (Ed. Ivan Karp, Corinne A. Katz, Lynn Szwaja, and Tomás Ybarra-Frausto, 2006).
[10] I have come across this term elsewhere (Barbara J. Black's *On Exhibit* and Svetlana Alpers' "The Museum as a Way of Seeing," *Exhibiting Cultures: The Poetics and Politics of Museum Display*. Ed. Ivan Karp and Steven D. Lavine. (Washington: Smithsonian Institution Press, 1991), but not in any defined or rigorous use. Alpers first defines it thus: "The museum effect—turning all objects into works of art" (26), and then refines it to "the tendency to isolate something from its world, to offer it up for attentive looking and thus to transform it into art like our own....The museum effect, I want to argue, is a way of seeing." (27) I agree that the museum effect is "a way of seeing," but I argue here that it is more nuanced than "objectifying" things as works of art in a museum, as with Valéry's complaint that all "things end up on the wall or in a glass case" (205). The museum effect is one that depends on the relationship of objects to each other, as in a museum exhibit, as well as their relationship to us (or ours to them), that relationship offering a particular narrative. Furthermore, that "effect" is one that should give us pause, one that we should not accept as "natural," "true," or "authentic."
[11] Critics have complained that Sebald's distinctive, peripatetic links are "fundamentally unimportant and, like punctuation, a mere matter of convention" (Fin Keegan, qtd. in *Understanding W. G. Sebald*, Mark R. McCulloh (Columbia: University of South Carolina Press, 2003); 15). Rather than being 'unimportant,' the links seem to be the heart of the matter. Amir Eshel has argued that "The unique significance of Sebald's prose lies in its formal characteristics, not just in the scope of its thematic and semantic domains." The importance of form for Sebald is perhaps nowhere clearer than in *The Rings of Saturn*, where the connections that he draws between different representations of destruction form the

pattern that emerges, a pattern that gives the individual objects in the novel a larger context through which to understand their meaning. What Eshel claims for *Austerlitz* is true of all Sebald's novels: it "demands a wide-ranging attention to all details, to the development of continuing associative chains… Reading…involves a constant return to other parts of the plot" ("Against the Power of Time: The Poetics of Suspension in W.G. Sebald's *Austerlitz*." *New German Critique: An Interdisciplinary Journal of German Studies* 88 (Winter 2003): 92). The chains in *The Rings of Saturn* are unusual in narrative specifically in that they are not based on plot or on the development of character, nor do they adhere to a particular theme except in the broadest of ways. But these links are the heart of the novel in that one cannot offer a reading of its themes without an explanation of the novel's structure; far from being random, these links are how Sebald creates a new pattern in which we can begin to see both our habits of perception and what they hide from us.

[12] It is important to note that the German-language editions of Sebald's novels are different from the English-language ones in the use of photographs and reproductions. They are frequently placed differently, often to create irony in relation to the German text, and some items are not reproduced at all in the English versions (though this is not one of those cases). There are also important discrepancies between the different language editions in that the photographs in the German editions are frequently captioned, as Noam Elcott has pointed out in his 2004 essay, "Tattered Snapshots and Castaway Tongues: An Essay at Layout and Translation with W.G. Sebald," *The Germanic Review* 79. 3 (Summer 2004); 203-23. See his footnote 9.

[13] Schama explains: "Had the painting been a faithful representation of the dissection, the Kid would have been a mess: the stomach cavity opened and the intestines drawn and displayed long before Tulp got anywhere near the muscles and tendons" (*Rembrandt's Eyes*. (New York: Alfred A. Knopf, 1999); 352).

[14] Schama offers a more art historical version of this explanation for starting with the hand: "Instead Tulp had selected that element of the anatomy which most spoke to his association with predecessors like Adriaen van den Spieghel and perhaps Vesalius, and more particularly to the capacity which was the most emphatic sign of God's providential ingenuity in differentiating man from beast: dexterity….In fact, Tulp is seen at the precise moment of demonstrating two of the unique attributes of man: utterance and prehensile flexibility. With his right hand he is lifting and separating the flexor muscles (both carpal and digital), while with his left hand he is actually demonstrating precisely the action enabled by the relevant muscles and tendons [pointing]" (352). Vesalius was the author of *De Humani Corporis Fabrica Libri Septem*, the frontispiece of which showed Vesalius dissecting a forearm, and which Schama claims might have been Rembrandt's model for Kindt's forearm in *The Anatomy Lesson* (342).

[15] Sebald returns to this aspect of Rembrandt's painting in his essay on Peter Weiss: "A striking feature of another work of art on an anatomical subject, the famous picture painted by Rembrandt von Rijn early in the bourgeois era, is the way in which none of the surgeons present at Dr. Nicholas Tulp's demonstration is looking at the body of the poor thief Aris Kindt of Leyden, here shown under the

knife; instead all eyes are bent on the open textbook of anatomy, lest they be overwhelmed by the fascination of the business. Rembrandt's picture of the dissection of a hanged body in the interests of higher ideals is an unsettling comment on the particular kind of knowledge to which we owe progress" ("The Remorse of the Heart: On Memory and Cruelty in the Work of Peter Weiss," *On the Natural History of Destruction.* Trans. Anthea Bell (New York: Random House, 2003); 178).

[16] Sebald elaborates on this in Part VIII: "It was Cornelis de Jong who drew my attention to the fact that many important museums, such as the Mauritshuis in The Hague or the Tate Gallery in London, were originally endowed by the sugar dynasties....The capital amassed in the eighteenth and nineteenth centuries through various forms of slave economy is still in circulation, said de Jong, still bearing interest, increasing many times over and continually burgeoning anew. One of the most tried and tested ways of legitimizing this kind of money has always been patronage of the arts, the purchase and exhibiting of paintings and sculptures" (194).

[17] See Schama's *Rembrandt's Eyes*: "As the earliest commentators on the painting like Joshua Reynolds recognized, Rembrandt went to extraordinary lengths to fix the precise tone and bluish pallor of dead flesh, using a finely adjusted tint of lead white mixed with lampblack, red and yellow ochres, and a trace of vermilion—in effect another of his virtuoso demonstrations of *stofuitdrukking*, the *stof* in this case being the cadaver's waxy skin. Earlier anatomies like Aert Pietersz.'s 1603 painting, or Michiel and Pieter van Mierevelt's Delft anatomy of 1617, had hardly bothered to register in color the startling difference between the rosy complexions of the living breathing surgeons, working in midwinter, and the stony object on which they were performing. They also observed the usual decorum by partly or wholly masking the face, lower trunk, and legs. The body was thus properly reduced to its role as the *subiectum anatomicum*, no longer a human but rather an arrangement of organs conveniently awaiting the anatomist's instructive hand. But Rembrandt, who was almost certainly present at Dr. Tulp's anatomy on January 12, 1632, does something quite shocking. Instead of concealing the cadaver's face, he fully reveals it, shadowing the eyes....In fact, he devotes almost as much detailed attention to the dead man's head as to the paying customers, tucking it between two of them as though it were very much part of the company. As a result, despite the pallor of the cadaver, he manages to rehumanize, rather than dehumanize, that body, forcing the beholder into an uncomfortable kinship with the dead as well as with the living" (351).

[18] W. G. Sebald. *On the Natural History of Destruction* (New York: Modern Library, 2004); 26.

[19]Michel Foucault, *The Order of Things* (New York: Vintage Books, 1994); 17.

[20] Wilde, "The Soul of Man Under Socialism." *The Critic as Artist*. Ed. Richard Ellmann (Chicago: University of Chicago Press, 1982); 284.

[21] Eilean Hooper-Greenhill's book Museums and the Shaping of Knowledge (London: Routledge, 1992) is particularly helpful in shedding light on the antiquated way of seeing Sebald finds efficacious in exploring the ethics of perception. Using Foucault's epistemological history in The Order of Things,

Hooper-Greenhill offers a history of arrangement in museum exhibits from the Renaissance to the present. Her broader point, that collections of things which seem to us now to be without logic or order in fact subscribe to other notions of logic and order, is perhaps best demonstrated through her discussion of Rudolf II's Kunstkammer. According to Hooper-Greenhill, Rudolf's Kunstkammer, "long regarded as a joke which expressed the disorder and confusion both of Rudolf and his collections," is made meaningful again by understanding Foucault's Renaissance episteme: "In outlining the system of resemblances and the play of sympathies, and in underlining the importance of the unity of the world, an insight is offered into a totally different form of organisation of the world that is extremely difficult to grasp from the standpoint of the late twentieth century" (131).

[22] Cf. Hayden White's "Introduction" to *Metahistory: The Historical Imagination in Nineteenth-Century Europe* (Baltimore: Johns Hopkins University Press, 1973), and "The Value of Narrativity in the Representation of Reality," *Critical Inquiry* (7:1 1980 Autumn, 5-27).

[23] As Arthur Williams has noted, "Sebald's works, especially *The Emigrants* and *The Rings of Saturn*, are rich in references to perspective and such optical aids as glasses, microscopes, reversed telescopes, watchmakers' eye-glasses. His first-person narrators often overfly areas or stand on high vantage points, sometimes in dreams, affording them and the reader a bird's eye view of the world, revealing its past and hinting at its future" ("W.G. Sebald: A Holistic Approach to Borders, Texts and Perspectives." *German-Language Literature Today? International and Popular?* Eds. Williams, Stuart Parkes, Julian Preece. (Oxford: Peter Lang, 2000); n4).

[24] Museum studies offers a reminder, then, for readers as well as museums-goers: "[Museums] implicitly pose the question—what has been left out, what is outside the frame or still in storage down in the basement, or, for that matter, what was never thought important enough to collect in the first place?" (Preziosi and Farago, eds. "General Introduction: What are museums *for*?" *Grasping the World*; 4)

[25] Ibid. 94. See also Jonathan Loesberg's recent *A Return to Aesthetics: Autonomy, Indifference, and Postmodernism* (2005) for a discussion of aesthetics as a history of perception rather than of art objects or their emotional/moral effects.

[26] Sebald addresses this in *ONHD*'s chapter on Alfred Andersch, "Between the Devil and the Deep Blue Sea." In the chapter, "a compromised moral position" refers to Andersch's literal betrayal of his Jewish wife by abandoning her to certain death. That Andersch was an "inner emigrant," a dissenter who claimed to stay in Germany as a "witness," suggests that perhaps Sebald's definition of a morally compromised position allows for metaphysical betrayals as well as literal ones.

[27] Michael Hamburger "Translator's Note." *Unrecounted: 33 poems by W.G. Sebald, 33 lithographs by Jan Peter Tripp* (New York: New Directions, 2004); 8. Hamburger continues: "it did not matter at all whether or not his account of [something] accorded with [the "facts" about it]. …Sebald's versions of it will have been and what is significant in the contradiction is Sebald's reinterpretation" (ibid).

[28] Sebald, W.G. "An Attempt at Restitution." Trans. Anthea Bell. *The New Yorker* 80.4 (20 & 27 Dec 2004): 110-114; 114.

[29] We will perhaps not be surprised to discover that Sebald's narrator also shares Browne's interest in silkworms: "Those strange and mysticall transmigrations that I have observed in Silkewormes, turn'd my Philosophy into Divinity. There is in these workes of nature, which seeme to puzzle reason, something Divine, and hath more in it than the eye of a common spectator doth discover" (110). Beginning with the narrator's question—"what does [that piece of silk] mean?"—through the last pages of the novel, where silk is connected in various ways to suffering and torture—the persecuted French Huguenot weavers, victims of the Amritsar massacre and the effort of the Nazi regime to use silk worms and silk cultivation as an "object lesson for the classroom" in breeding and "retrogressive mutations" (294)—silk recurs throughout the novel, making an appearance in each of its "places," every chapter, every country, every era. Sebald recounts how even before the Industrial Age "at least in some places…a great number of people…spent their lives with their wretched bodies strapped to looms made of wooden frames and rails, hung with weights and reminiscent of instruments of torture or cages" (282). Weaving is torturous cultural production, like writing which likewise attempts to keep hold of the right thread.

[30] The beginning of the novel resembles the beginning of a case of melancholia, when, as Freud says, "the inhibition of the melancholic seems puzzling to us because we cannot see what it is that absorbs him so entirely." Freud's description of melancholy eerily echoes the plotting and patterning of Sebald's book: "first one, then another memory is activated and…the laments which are perpetually the same and wearisome in their monotony nevertheless each time take their rise in some different unconscious source. If the object had not this great significance, strengthened by a thousand links, to the ego, the loss of it would be no meet cause for either mourning or melancholia" ("On Mourning and Melancholia" *General Psychological Theory* (New York: Collier Books, 1963); 177). By establishing an identification of the ego with what has been abandoned or lost, the melancholic feels that the loss—whatever it may be—is in him (rather than an outside object lost), and that it is the world that is over-full, as it were. This corresponds nicely to the sense of the world as a museum in which the narrator is a stranger. Yet even the melancholic himself, Freud argues, "cannot consciously perceive what it is that he has lost. He knows whom he has lost but not what it is he has lost in them" (166). The melancholic, Freud claims, "has a keener eye for the truth than others who are not melancholic" (167), for it is the melancholic who suspects that "the truth lies elsewhere, away from it all, somewhere as yet undiscovered" (*Austerlitz* Trans. Anthea Bell (New York: The Modern Library, 2001); 71-72).

[31] *Iliad*, XXIII, 254. See Martin Corless-Smith's "That purple piece of silk between Sebald and Browne, or how we spin our literary shrouds." *Denver Quarterly* 40:1 (2005); 27-39.

[32] Preziosi and Farago 8.

Epilogue

[1] In "Ideological State Apparatuses," Louis Althusser writes that ideology hails 'you' as a subject who can be called into being separately from others, at a

moment's notice. Another way to read this is that ideology keeps people on edge about being embedded, as if the State can wrest one 'out' of the world at any time.

[2] Consider Samuel Taylor Coleridge's "Rime of the Ancient Mariner," a poem about a person doomed to tell his tale of spontaneous violence committed against birdlife.

[3] In a sort of perverse wish image reproduction of the fall of the Twin Towers, the Navi people run in fear as the tree collapses on top of them, fire and smoke swirling around.

[4] Walter Kirn's novel of this title is an astute meditation on the human ecology of flight.

[5] See Timothy Morton, *The Ecological Thought* (Cambridge: Harvard University Press, 2010).

[6] http://www.aolnews.com/story/turtles-invade-runway/562870 (viewed May 3 2010).

[7] The reports were sketchy about what this 'removal' actually meant—if it meant put on land somewhere else, or exterminated en masse.

[8] See Don DeLillo, *White Noise* (New York: Penguin, 1985).

[9] *The New York Times*, April 17 2010, "Air Travel Crisis Deepens as Europe Fears Wider Impact."

[10] This idea is echoed in Don DeLillo's novel *Point Omega*: "It's all embedded, the hours and minutes, words and numbers everywhere … train stations, bus routes, taxi meters, surveillance cameras. It's all about time, dimwit time, inferior time, people checking watched and other devices, other reminders. This is time draining out of our lives. Cities were built to measure time, to remove time from nature. There's an endless counting down…" (New York: Picador, 2010); 44-45.

[11] See Kathleen Stewart, *Ordinary Affects* (Durham: Duke University Press, 2007).

CONTRIBUTORS

Amy Johnson earned her PhD in English Literature from the University of Wisconsin-Madison and is currently teaching at the University of Louisiana-Monroe. "Anatomy of an Exhibition" draws on a chapter from her thesis, "Artificial Order: Ethical Aestheticism in 20th-century Literature and Contemporary Narrative." Her research interests include genre study in film and literature, narrative objects, and zombies.

Amanda Kenny earned her PhD in English Literature from the University of Wisconsin-Madison and is currently a Lecturer in Professional Communications at the Wisconsin School of Business at the University of Wisconsin-Madison. Her research interests include the Arabian Nights in eighteenth-century Britain, the history of the novel, and narrative theory, as well as how businesses are using social networking sites to communicate (effectively or otherwise) with consumers.

Jan Olesen is a Contract Instructor at Trent University in Peterborough, Ontario. He is working on the connection between collection, history and science, and has a forthcoming article on Nehemiah Grew's *Musaeum Royalis*.

Rachel Poliquin is currently working with all things taxidermy. Her forthcoming book, *Taxidermy and Longing*, is a cultural and poetic exploration of taxidermy from early cabinets of curiosity to contemporary animal art. She maintains the taxidermy blog www.ravishingbeasts.com, curated the exhibition *Ravishing Beasts: The Strangely Alluring World of Taxidermy* at the Museum of Vancouver, and designed the vertebrate exhibits at the Beaty Biodiversity Museum at the University of British Columbia in Vancouver, Canada.

William Nolan's research follows the shifting roles of animals in screen media. His current project investigates the peculiar abundance of animals in not only the emergence of the cinematic apparatus and the proto-cinematic technologies, but also the practices of collection and display so central to nineteenth century culture in the West. He is currently an

Assistant Professor in the Honors College at the University of Alabama at Tuscaloosa.

Christopher Schaberg is Assistant Professor of English at Loyola University New Orleans. Concerning the topic of air travel, Schaberg has published an article entitled "Bird Citing: On the Aesthetics and Techno-Poetics of Flight" in the multidisciplinary journal *Nebula*, and an essay "Terminal Immaterial: The Uncertain Subject of the Hardy Boys Airport Mysteries" in the edited volume *The Boy Detectives* (Ed. Michael Cornelius). Schaberg's forthcoming book on the subject of flight is entitled *Airport Reading*.

Janelle A. Schwartz is Assistant Professor of English and Environmental Studies at Loyola University New Orleans. Her current research is in the history of science and Romantic literature, specifically on the relationship between aesthetics and entomological studies. Her forthcoming book is entitled *Worm Work: Eighteenth-Century Natural History and Romantic Aesthetic Frontiers*, and will be published by the University of Minnesota Press in 2011.

Nhora Lucía Serrano is Assistant Professor of Comparative Literature at California State University, Long Beach. Her research interests include travel narratives, Visual Studies, and Medieval Studies. She is completing a book manuscript on visual images from illuminated manuscripts to graphic narratives.

Stephanie Shirilan is Assistant Professor of Seventeenth-Century British Literature and Culture at Syracuse University, where she teaches courses on early modern prose and drama. Her broad research interests are in the history and representation of bodies, minds, and the contact between them in early modern literatures, especially of travel and discovery, science and medicine. She is completing a book manuscript on the poetics of pleasure and mimetic sympathy in Robert Burton's *The Anatomy of Melancholy*.

Michael Sohn is a Full Time Instructor, Mentor and Faculty Development coordinator in the English Department at Long Island University in Brooklyn, New York. He received his PhD in French from NYU, where he specialized in contemporary French poetry and French poets' writing on the visual arts. He recently published "In Mallarmé's Harness? André du Bouchet and Stéphane Mallarmé" (*French Forum* 32, nos. 1-2, 2007).

INDEX